THE PRESIDENT'S SPEECH

THE PRESIDENT'S SPEECH

The Stories behind the Most
Memorable Presidential Addresses

C. Edwin Vilade

LYONS PRESS
An imprint of Globe Pequot Press
Guilford, Connecticut

Lyons Press is an imprint of Globe Pequot Press.

Text by C. Edwin Vilade
Designed by Sunita Gahir

Library of Congress Cataloging-in-Publication Data is available on file.

ISBN 978-0-7627-7981-9

1 2 3 4 5 6 7 8 9 10

Printed and bound in China

Contents

Contents

Introduction

When Abraham Lincoln rose to address the assembled crowd after taking the oath of office as president, he began by stating that he was doing so in compliance with "a custom as old as the government itself." He was correct. Over more than two centuries since the election of George Washington, presidents have addressed the American people thousands, if not tens of thousands of times. Although they direct their words to the audiences seated and standing in front of them, all presidents have been aware that their words would eventually reach to the furthest corners of the ever-expanding country. Direct communication between the chief executive and the citizenry is a bedrock tradition in America, and a hallmark of democracy.

The first presidential address was delivered by George Washington at his inauguration on April 30, 1789. In the flowery style of the day, he said almost nothing but took more than 1,400 words to say it. He simply invoked the blessings of God and indicated his willingness to work with the Congress. But in delivery of an inaugural address, as in so many other matters during his two terms in office, he established a precedent that has endured to this day.

If George Washington confined himself to ambiguous niceties during his first speech as president, his final one was much more substantive. He established another tradition—the presidential farewell address. That tradition has not always been followed in the centuries since. Some unsuccessful presidents have slunk out of town without a word, while others—most tragically those such as Abraham Lincoln and John F. Kennedy—have been denied the opportunity. The most memorable farewell since Washington was delivered by a president not known for his eloquence, Dwight D. Eisenhower.

In his farewell, Washington spoke at length of his hopes for the future of the country, and issued warnings that have remained influential in shaping the policies of the US government ever since. In the intervening two centuries,

▲ **President Theodore Roosevelt forcefully speaking to a crowd.**

other presidents have spoken enduring words that have influenced the course of the country. One of the purposes of this volume is to examine those important speeches, the issues and situations that prompted them, the ways in which they changed between concept and delivery, and their impacts.

In his farewell, Washington also established another practice that has been followed ever since, at first quietly and later openly: he had help in composing the address. James Madison and Alexander Hamilton, among the most prominent of the Founding Fathers, were also arguably the first presidential speechwriters. Each submitted a draft of Washington's farewell, and some of the language of each was used.

Neither, of course, claimed public credit for his contribution. Scholars have had to comb through the correspondence and the papers of all three and their contemporaries to determine the process of development of the speech. During the eighteenth and nineteenth centuries, as indeed since the days of Greece and Rome, public men were presumed to have composed their own speeches. A man who could not write and deliver a stirring address was at a great disadvantage in pursuing a political career.

Many of the Founding Fathers of the United States were somewhat flawed in this regard. Thomas Jefferson and Madison were superb writers, for example, but were somewhat lacking on the platform. Jefferson clearly wrote his own inaugural address—it ranks among the very best—but did not like to speak in public. He established the practice, which endured for more than one hundred years, of delivering the State of the Union message to the Congress in writing, rather than orally.

James Monroe, on the other hand, has been judged by history as something of an intellectual lightweight. Questions have persisted as to whether he, or his secretary of state and successor John Quincy Adams, actually wrote what has become known as the Monroe Doctrine. Adams clearly contributed, but Monroe scholars are adamant about his primary authorship.

Even presidents who are demonstrably eloquent have turned to others for help and advice. Lincoln, undoubtedly the most elegant and poetic writer ever to occupy the office, sought assistance from William Seward, his new secretary of state and former political rival, in composing his first Inaugural Address.

Woodrow Wilson was also in the first rank of presidential writers and speakers. Nevertheless he had the help of no fewer than 150 scholars in composing his famous Fourteen Points for settlement of World War I.

The pretense of presidential self-authorship began to crumble after Wilson. Warren G. Harding, who followed Wilson, hired an old newsman named Judson Welliver as a congressional liaison. Welliver's role gradually evolved toward writing speeches before Harding died in office. Welliver was retained by Calvin Coolidge when the latter assumed the presidency.

Coolidge, a matter-of-fact New Englander, saw no point in disguising the nature of Welliver's duties, giving him the title of "literary clerk." Welliver has thus been dubbed the first White House speechwriter.

Every president since has employed speechwriters more or less openly. Franklin Delano Roosevelt numbered two Pulitzer Prize winners among his many speechwriters. There is evidence, however, that Roosevelt contributed many first-rate phrases to his memorable speeches. One small example, contained in this book, is his alteration of "a day that will live in history" to "a day that will live in infamy" in his December 7, 1941, speech.

The proliferation of White House speechwriters has led to a proliferation of speech drafts. Harry S. Truman's and Dwight D. Eisenhower's most notable speeches, included in this volume, went through many drafts, and the development process is of interest. John F. Kennedy's almost symbiotic relationship with his principal speechwriter, Ted Sorensen, was an exception to the rule of multiple authorship and review of speeches. The quality showed.

The trend toward institutionalization of the White House speechwriting process has continued in recent decades. Speechwriters are given assignments, produce drafts, and they are then subjected to a process called "staffing," wherein the drafts are sent around to literally dozens of White House and Cabinet department experts. Each of these experts marks up the draft and the speechwriters incorporate the changes into the next draft to be circulated.

Sometimes the changes conflict, leading to battles over turf and policy. Most frequently, the changes made by policy wonks to the nicely turned phrases of the speechwriters leads to a flat and sometimes disorganized final product. The drafts of each speech by recent presidents, preserved in their presidential libraries, fill cartons and boxes.

Most recent presidential addresses have been mediocre, homogenized statements bearing the fingerprints and sometimes footprints of government officials. Memorable recent addresses, such as the ones included in this volume, are ever more rare exceptions to the rule. The author has endeavored to reflect in the speeches selected both the exceptional circumstances that have led to addresses and the impediments to the production of more of them.

◀ President Ronald Reagan delivering a speech to the nation from the Oval Office at the White House.

President George Washington

"
I hold the maxim no less applicable to public than to private affairs, that honesty is always the best policy.
"

Many leaders cement their reputations by the way they leave public life. Some leave in disgrace, while others overstay their welcome and are finally pushed off into retirement.

George Washington, however, only enhanced his enormous popularity by leaving while he was still wanted and needed by his country. He further augmented his legacy by delivering a farewell address in 1796 that has come to be acknowledged as one of the great pronouncements ever issued (and the best advice ever offered) by a president.

Washington was revered as a national hero and as the father of his country from the first moments of its existence. He could have ruled the United States as a dictator or a king. But fortunately for the country, he wasn't so inclined. He never particularly wanted even to be president. He only took office after being persuaded that he was the only man who could unite all factions and shades of opinion, and guide the fledgling republic through its dangerous formative years.

Once convinced to become the nation's first chief executive, Washington made it clear that he intended to limit his service to one term. But in 1792, men like Thomas Jefferson, James Madison, and Alexander Hamilton prevailed on him to serve again. It is interesting that these Founding Fathers combined to convince Washington to accept another term, since one of his reasons for serving four more years was that Hamilton and Jefferson in particular were already hardening the political

▲ The inauguration of George Washington as the first President of the United States, at the Federal Hall in New York City on April 30, 1789.

differences that led them to form the country's first political parties, the Federalist (Hamilton) and Democratic-Republican (Jefferson and Madison). Washington hated the idea of political factions, and thought he could delay or blunt the formation of parties by serving another term.

Quality of Character

In his eight years in office, Washington took many actions and set many precedents that have helped to preserve and strengthen the country over more than two centuries. His chief impact, though, was through the quality of his character. His modesty, sense of duty, and dedication to the principles of democracy put a stamp on the office of president that defines it to this day.

Washington could have been president for life, and the pressure on him to accept a third term was intense. But this time, he resisted. As his second term drew to a close, Washington planned a farewell address to take his leave of the people and explain to them why he would not run again.

In fact, Washington had been working on the farewell speech for more than four years. In 1792, near the end of his first term, Washington was determined to retire and confided his decision to Madison—author of the Constitution and a fine writer. Washington wrote a letter to Madison containing ideas for his farewell address, but left much of the responsibility for its content to him. Madison prepared a draft of the address but, by the time he completed it, Washington had already been induced to accept a second term and the project was shelved.

▲ A 1792 letter from James Madison in which he recounts a conversation with Washington regarding Washington's desire to step down as President after one term.

with respect to his farewell Address, to the authorship of which, it seems, there are conflicting claims, I can state to you some facts. he had determined to decline a reelection at the end of his first term, and so far determined that he had requested mr Madison to prepare for him something valedictory to be addressed to his constituents on his retirement. this was done: but he was finally persuaded to acquiesce in a second election, to which no one more strenuously pressed him than myself, from a conviction of the importance of strengthening, by longer habit, the respect necessary for that office, which the weight of his character only could effect. when, at the end of his second term, his Valedictory came out, mr Madi= son recognised in it several passages of his draught, several others we were both satisfied were from the pen of Hamilton, and others from that of the President himself. these he probably put into the hands of Hamilton to form into a whole, and hence it may all appear in Hamilton's handwriting, as if it were all of his composition.

I have stated above that the original objects of the Federalists were
1. to warp our government more to the form and principles of monarchy &
2 to weaken the barriers of the state governments as co-ordinate powers.
in the first they have been so completely foiled, by the universal spirit of the nation, that they have abandoned the enterprise, shrunk from the odium of

40070

▲ An extract from a letter written by Jefferson in 1823 within which he discusses the authorship of Washington's farewell address.

New Ideas

The draft did not just sit and gather dust. During his second term, letters were exchanged between Washington, Jefferson, Hamilton, Madison, and other leaders discussing the state of the country and its direction. These letters and many other debates, discussions, and developments helped to shape and advance the ideas contained in the second version of the address, when Washington revisited the idea toward the end of his second term.

This time, Washington turned to Hamilton for help in drafting the address. Hamilton had been a close confidant of Washington's since his service as the general's aide de camp during the Revolution. As Washington's secretary of the treasury and chief financial advisor, Hamilton frequently drafted important communications for the president.

Washington began the redrafting process by transmitting to Hamilton a version of Madison's 1792 version, which he had heavily edited and amended. Washington made it clear in letters to Hamilton that Madison's version, and Washington's own revisions of it, would form the core of the 1796 document. He did this in part to make it clear to Madison and Jefferson, who were growing ever more hostile to Hamilton, that he valued Madison's work and the ideas he had contributed. He wanted to make it equally clear that Hamilton was not injecting his own political views—which diverged sharply from those of Madison and Jefferson—into the address, but was simply expanding Washington's ideas in the same way Madison had earlier.

Consultation Breeds Quality

Turning first to Madison, then to Hamilton—with contributions from Jefferson and others—was not unusual for Washington. He was not a natural writer or speaker, and his method of making decisions was to solicit ideas, sort them, and make the final edits himself. It was natural for him to consult with the finest minds in government in the preparation of such a significant address.

▲ **The first page of Madison's 1792 draft of a farewell address for Washington.**

Authorship of the farewell speech became an issue later, after Washington's death, when he had become almost godlike to the American people, and his words carried Olympian weight.

If the farewell address did not originate with Washington, but came from Hamilton and others, should it be given the importance due the great man himself? Along with these lingering doubts came some disillusionment over the notion that Washington even had to resort to others to frame his ideas. Delegating speech-writing is common, even unquestioned today, with presidents employing battalions of writers. But two centuries ago a public man was expected to write and deliver his own orations.

As late as the 1820s, the surviving Founding Fathers—chiefly Madison and Jefferson—argued that the original idea for the address came from Washington, and while he hadn't authored every word, he had certainly shaped, edited, and approved the address. The controversy persisted for decades before Washington's authorship eventually became accepted, when the address entered the ranks of the most important pronouncements of the founding period of the United States.

Published But Never Spoken

Washington never spoke the words of the address. It was published in David Claypoole's *American Daily Advertiser* on September 19, 1796, under the title "The Address of General Washington To The People of The United States on his declining of the Presidency of the United States".

It was widely reprinted in newspapers across the country and in pamphlets. Only much later was it to be known as the Farewell Address, called that because it was Washington's valedictory after forty-five years of public service.

Personal References

In Madison's version the address began with Washington telling the people that he wouldn't run again because the country no longer needed him. With great humility he stated that he had never believed that he was qualified to be president, and

that any success he had had in office was the result of the support of the people. It is doubtful Washington actually believed he was unqualified and deficient—self-deprecation was common—even expected. But it is worth noting that Washington says little in the speech about his own actions and experiences as president.

The final address was a major departure from Washington's own first draft. In that draft, Washington complains about the attacks, criticisms, and insults directed at him by his opponents in Congress. He goes on at length about the hardships he endured to serve his country, and repeatedly proclaims how he never enriched himself while in public service. According to letters exchanged during the drafting of the address, Hamilton convinced Washington to take the high road, and to keep the personal references to a minimum.

After explaining why he no longer needed to be president, Washington devoted the bulk of the address to advice that sounds like the words of a leader. He starts out, interestingly, with a ringing call for a strong union. Some mention of this is made in Madison's draft, but Hamilton expands and emphasizes it, and its very place at the beginning of the speech underscores its importance. Clearly, it is meant to argue against the sectionalism favored by Jefferson and Madison, which they formalized in their party. In later decades and lesser hands, this sectionalism hardened into the states' rights position that led to the Civil War.

A Union Both Large and Strong

It's easy to imagine a young Abraham Lincoln reading Washington's words, and developing his own strong commitment to the union. The Hamilton version argues that a strong union is better able to resist foreign attacks than the individual states would be, and that such a union would not need the "overgrown military establishment" that would be required if each state had to form its own military.

Of equal interest is Washington's warning—a warning mostly forgotten today—to question the motives of any leader who said that the nation could eventually be too large to govern as a republic, and should be carved into smaller republics. This warning could well have helped to forestall the many moves by adventurers—such as Aaron Burr—to carve out their own empires on the frontier. It also undoubtedly influenced the idea of "Manifest Destiny" in the first decades of the nineteenth century that eventually extended US territory "from sea to shining sea."

Washington went on to explain his strong support for the new Constitution and said that citizens should be able to alter government to serve their needs, but only through amending the Constitution, and then only sparingly. He warned against those who would amend the Constitution in order to weaken the government. He also warned against weakening the system of checks and balances in the Constitution, to prevent one branch of government from becoming more powerful than the others.

Dangers of Political Parties

Politics, especially party politics, also rose into Washington's sights. Because Hamilton had formed the Federalist Party and Madison and Jefferson retaliated with the Democratic-Republican Party—all three were presumably in favor of party politics— it's logical to assume that these warnings were Washington's idea. "The alternate domination of one faction over another, sharpened by the spirit of revenge . . . in different ages and countries . . . has perpetrated the most horrid enormities," he wrote.

In worrying about party politics, Washington was concerned about the hostility of one faction toward another, but also about their foreign alliances. As he wrote, the Democratic-Republicans were advocating an alliance with France, while the Federalists favored England. Washington was emphatic that the country should engage in no permanent foreign alliances, because it would lead to involvement in foreign wars, and also make the country susceptible to foreign influence in its own affairs. The United States is remote from Europe, and should remain neutral, he said. Again, the thoughts clearly originated with Washington.

Religion, Morality, Education, and a Lesson for Today's Politicians

Washington strongly supported religion and morality. These not only promoted public happiness, but also political prosperity. A man cannot be a patriot without being moral, and morality springs from religion, he wrote. He also briefly endorsed the importance of education. In his original discussions with Hamilton, Washington indicated that he wanted to speak at length about education, and to call for the establishment of a national university. Hamilton failed to carry out Washington's instruction, and Washington himself added the brief reference to education in the final document—at the last minute.

Washington's address is now universally acknowledged as one of the most important documents in American history. It helped frame political debate for decades (even centuries) on many of the existing and emerging issues faced by a nation trying to find its way in the world.

Cautions against political divisiveness could be taken to heart by modern politicians, along with Washington's warnings about excessive debt, and the importance of balancing the budget. These cautions might—and should—cause politicians who hear Washington's address read every year in the Senate on his birthday to squirm in their seats.

Farewell Address to the American People

Published September 19, 1796, in David Claypoole's *American Daily Advertiser* originally under the title "The Address of General Washington to the People of The United States on his declining of the Presidency of the United States"

Friends and Fellow Citizens:

The period for a new election of a citizen to administer the executive government of the United States being not far distant, and the time actually arrived when your thoughts must be employed in designating the person who is to be clothed with that important trust, it appears to me proper, especially as it may conduce to a more distinct expression of the public voice, that I should now apprise you of the resolution I have formed, to decline being considered among the number of those out of whom a choice is to be made.

I beg you, at the same time, to do me the justice to be assured that this resolution has not been taken without a strict regard to all the considerations appertaining to the relation which binds a dutiful citizen to his country; and that in withdrawing the tender of service, which silence in my situation might imply, I am influenced by no diminution of zeal for your future

▶ The first page of Washington's first draft for an address, enclosed in his letter of May 15, 1796, to Hamilton.

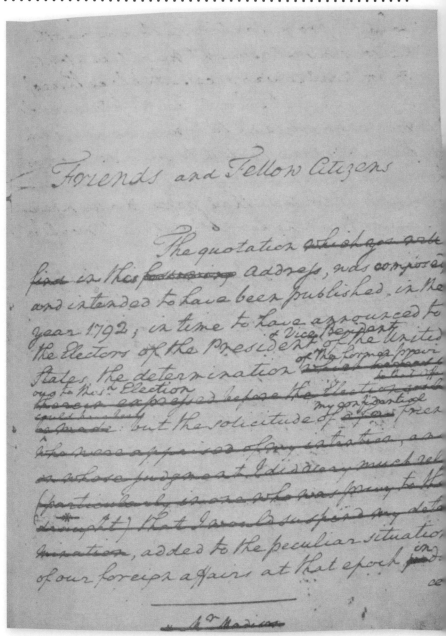

interest, no deficiency of grateful respect for your past kindness, but am supported by a full conviction that the step is compatible with both.

The acceptance of, and continuance hitherto in, the office to which your suffrages have twice called me have been a uniform sacrifice of inclination to the opinion of duty and to a deference for what appeared to be your desire. I constantly hoped that it would have been much earlier in my

power, consistently with motives which I was not at liberty to disregard, to return to that retirement from which I had been reluctantly drawn. The strength of my inclination to do this, previous to the last election, had even led to the preparation of an address to declare it to you; but mature reflection on the then perplexed and critical posture of our affairs with foreign nations, and the unanimous advice of persons entitled to my confidence, impelled me to abandon the idea.

I rejoice that the state of your concerns, external as well as internal, no longer renders the pursuit of inclination incompatible with the sentiment of duty or propriety, and am persuaded, whatever partiality may be retained for my services, that, in the present circumstances of our country, you will not disapprove my determination to retire.

The impressions with which I first undertook the arduous trust were explained on the proper occasion. In the discharge of this trust, I will only say that I have, with good intentions, contributed towards the organization and administration of the government the best exertions of which a very fallible judgment was capable. Not unconscious in the outset of the inferiority of my qualifications, experience in my own eyes, perhaps still more in the eyes of others, has strengthened the motives to diffidence of myself; and every day the increasing weight of years admonishes me more and more that the shade of

◀ The first page of Washington's final draft of the address.

The fifth page of Washington's final draft of the speech, with amendments in the margins.

acknowledgment of that debt of gratitude which I owe to my beloved country for the many honors it has conferred upon me; still more for the steadfast confidence with which it has supported me; and for the opportunities I have thence enjoyed of manifesting my inviolable attachment, by services faithful and persevering, though in usefulness unequal to my zeal. If benefits have resulted to our country from these services, let it always be remembered to your praise, and as an instructive example in our annals, that under circumstances in which the passions, agitated in every direction, were liable to mislead, amidst appearances sometimes dubious, vicissitudes of fortune often discouraging, in situations in which not unfrequently want of success has countenanced the spirit of criticism, the constancy of your support was the essential prop of the efforts, and a guarantee of the plans by which they were effected. Profoundly penetrated with this idea, I shall carry it with me to my grave, as a strong incitement to unceasing vows that heaven may continue to you the choicest tokens of its beneficence; that your union and brotherly affection may be perpetual; that the free Constitution, which is the work of your hands, may be sacredly maintained; that its administration in every department may be stamped with wisdom and virtue; that, in fine, the happiness of the people of these States, under the auspices of liberty, may be made complete by so careful a preservation and so prudent a use of this blessing as will acquire to them the glory of recommending it to the applause, the affection, and adoption of every nation which is yet a stranger to it.

retirement is as necessary to me as it will be welcome. Satisfied that if any circumstances have given peculiar value to my services, they were temporary, I have the consolation to believe that, while choice and prudence invite me to quit the political scene, patriotism does not forbid it.

In looking forward to the moment which is intended to terminate the career of my public life, my feelings do not permit me to suspend the deep

Here, perhaps, I ought to stop. But a solicitude for your welfare, which cannot end but with my life, and the apprehension of danger, natural to that solicitude, urge me, on an occasion like the present, to offer to your solemn contemplation, and to recommend to your frequent review, some sentiments which are the result of much reflection, of no inconsiderable observation, and which appear to me all-important to the permanency of your felicity as a people. These will be offered to you with the more freedom, as you can only see in them the disinterested warnings of a parting friend, who can possibly have no personal motive to bias his counsel. Nor can I forget, as an encouragement to it, your indulgent reception of my sentiments on a former and not dissimilar occasion.

Interwoven as is the love of liberty with every ligament of your hearts, no recommendation of mine is necessary to fortify or confirm the attachment.

The unity of government which constitutes you one people is also now dear to you. It is justly so, for it is a main pillar in the edifice of your real independence, the support of your tranquility at home, your peace abroad; of your safety; of your prosperity; of that very liberty which you so highly prize. But as it is easy to foresee that, from different causes and from different quarters, much pains will be taken, many artifices employed to weaken in your minds the conviction of this truth; as this is the point in your political fortress against which the batteries of internal and external enemies will be most constantly and actively (though often covertly and insidiously) directed, it is of infinite moment that you should properly estimate the immense value of your national union to your collective and individual happiness; that you should cherish a cordial, habitual, and immovable attachment to it; accustoming yourselves to think and speak of it as of the palladium of your political safety and prosperity; watching for its preservation with jealous anxiety; discountenancing whatever may suggest even

a suspicion that it can in any event be abandoned; and indignantly frowning upon the first dawning of every attempt to alienate any portion of our country from the rest, or to enfeeble the sacred ties which now link together the various parts.

For this you have every inducement of sympathy and interest. Citizens, by birth or choice, of a common country, that country has a right to concentrate your affections. The name of American, which belongs to you in your national capacity, must always exalt the just pride of patriotism more than any appellation derived from local discriminations. With slight shades of difference, you have the same religion, manners, habits, and political principles. You have in a common cause fought and triumphed together; the independence and liberty you possess are the work of joint counsels, and joint efforts of common dangers, sufferings, and successes.

But these considerations, however powerfully they address themselves to your sensibility, are greatly outweighed by those which apply more immediately to your interest. Here every portion of our country finds the most commanding motives for carefully guarding and preserving the union of the whole.

The North, in an unrestrained intercourse with the South, protected by the equal laws of a common government, finds in the productions of the latter great additional resources of maritime and commercial enterprise and precious materials of manufacturing industry. The South, in the same intercourse, benefiting by the agency of the North, sees its agriculture grow and its commerce expand. Turning partly into its own channels the seamen of the North, it finds its particular navigation invigorated; and, while it contributes, in different ways, to nourish and increase the general mass of the national navigation, it looks forward to the protection of a maritime strength, to which itself is unequally adapted. The East, in a like intercourse with the West, already finds, and in the

▲ A hand tinted engraving of George Washington, based on an original portrait by Gilbert Stuart.

resource, proportionably greater security from external danger, a less frequent interruption of their peace by foreign nations; and, what is of inestimable value, they must derive from union an exemption from those broils and wars between themselves, which so frequently afflict neighboring countries not tied together by the same governments, which their own rival ships alone would be sufficient to produce, but which opposite foreign alliances, attachments, and intrigues would stimulate and embitter. Hence, likewise, they will avoid the necessity of those overgrown military establishments which, under any form of government, are inauspicious to liberty, and which are to be regarded as particularly hostile to republican liberty. In this sense it is that your union ought to be considered as a main prop of your liberty, and that the love of the one ought to endear to you the preservation of the other.

These considerations speak a persuasive language to every reflecting and virtuous mind, and exhibit the continuance of the Union as a primary object of patriotic desire. Is there a doubt whether a common government can embrace so large a sphere? Let experience solve it. To listen to mere speculation in such a case were criminal. We are authorized to hope that a proper organization of the whole with the auxiliary agency of governments for the respective subdivisions, will afford a happy issue to the experiment. It is well worth a fair and full experiment. With such powerful and obvious motives to union, affecting all parts of our country, while experience shall not have demonstrated its impracticability, there will always be reason to distrust the patriotism of those who in any quarter may endeavor to weaken its bands.

In contemplating the causes which may disturb our Union, it occurs as matter of serious concern that any ground should have been furnished for characterizing parties by geographical discriminations, Northern

progressive improvement of interior communications by land and water, will more and more find a valuable vent for the commodities which it brings from abroad, or manufactures at home. The West derives from the East supplies requisite to its growth and comfort, and, what is perhaps of still greater consequence, it must of necessity owe the secure enjoyment of indispensable outlets for its own productions to the weight, influence, and the future maritime strength of the Atlantic side of the Union, directed by an indissoluble community of interest as one nation. Any other tenure by which the West can hold this essential advantage, whether derived from its own separate strength, or from an apostate and unnatural connection with any foreign power, must be intrinsically precarious.

While, then, every part of our country thus feels an immediate and particular interest in union, all the parts combined cannot fail to find in the united mass of means and efforts greater strength, greater and Southern, Atlantic and Western; whence designing men may endeavor to excite a belief that there is a real difference of local interests and views. One of the expedients of party to acquire influence within particular districts is to misrepresent the opinions and aims of other districts. You cannot shield yourselves too much against the jealousies and heartburnings which spring from these misrepresentations; they tend to render alien to each other those who ought to be bound together by fraternal affection. The inhabitants of our Western country have lately had a useful lesson on this head; they have seen, in the negotiation by the Executive, and in the unanimous ratification by the Senate, of the treaty with Spain, and in the universal satisfaction at that event, throughout the United States, a decisive proof how unfounded were the suspicions propagated among them of a policy in the General Government and in the Atlantic States unfriendly to their interests in regard to the Mississippi; they have been witnesses to the formation of two treaties, that with Great Britain, and that with Spain, which secure to them everything they could desire, in respect to our foreign relations, towards confirming their prosperity. Will it not be their wisdom to rely for the preservation of these advantages on the Union by which they were procured? Will they not henceforth be deaf to those advisers, if such there are, who would sever them from their brethren and connect them with aliens?

To the efficacy and permanency of your Union, a government for the whole is indispensable. No alliance, however strict, between the parts can be an adequate substitute; they must inevitably experience the infractions and interruptions which all alliances in all times have experienced. Sensible of this momentous truth, you have improved upon your first essay, by the adoption of a constitution of government better calculated than your former for an intimate union, and for the efficacious management of your common concerns. This government, the offspring of our own choice, uninfluenced and

◄ The thirteenth page of Washington's final draft of his Farewell Address.

unawed, adopted upon full investigation and mature deliberation, completely free in its principles, in the distribution of its powers, uniting security with energy, and containing within itself a provision for its own amendment, has a just claim to your confidence and your support. Respect for its authority, compliance with its laws, acquiescence in its measures, are duties enjoined by the fundamental maxims of true liberty. The basis of our political systems is the right of the people to make and to alter their constitutions of government. But the Constitution which at any time exists, till changed by an explicit and authentic act of the whole people, is sacredly obligatory upon all. The very idea of the power and the right of the people to establish government presupposes the duty of every individual to obey the established government.

All obstructions to the execution of the laws, all combinations and associations, under whatever plausible character, with the real design to direct, control, counteract, or awe the regular deliberation and action of the constituted authorities, are destructive of this fundamental principle, and of fatal tendency. They serve to organize faction, to give it an artificial and extraordinary force; to put, in the place of the delegated will of the nation the will of a party, often a small but artful and enterprising minority of the community; and, according to the alternate triumphs of different parties, to make the public administration the mirror of the ill-concerted and incongruous projects of faction, rather than the organ of consistent and wholesome plans digested by common counsels and modified by mutual interests.

However combinations or associations of the above description may now and then answer popular ends, they are likely, in the course of time and things, to become potent engines, by which cunning, ambitious, and unprincipled men will be enabled to subvert the power of the people and to usurp

▲ A portrait of Alexander Hamilton.

for themselves the reins of government, destroying afterwards the very engines which have lifted them to unjust dominion.

Towards the preservation of your government, and the permanency of your present happy state, it is requisite, not only that you steadily discountenance irregular oppositions to its acknowledged authority, but also that you resist with care the spirit of innovation upon its principles, however specious the pretexts. One method of assault may be to effect, in the forms of the Constitution, alterations which will impair the energy of the system, and thus to undermine what cannot be directly overthrown. In all the changes to which you may be invited, remember that time and habit are at least as necessary to fix the true character of governments as of other human institutions; that experience is the surest standard by which to test the real tendency of the existing constitution of a country; that facility in changes, upon the credit of mere hypothesis and opinion, exposes to perpetual change, from the endless variety of hypothesis and opinion; and remember, especially, that for the efficient management of your common interests, in a country so extensive as ours, a government of as much vigor as is consistent with the perfect security of liberty is indispensable. Liberty itself will find in such a government, with powers properly distributed and adjusted, its surest guardian. It is, indeed, little else than a name, where the government is too feeble to withstand the enterprises of faction, to confine each member of the society within the limits prescribed by the laws, and to maintain all in the secure and tranquil enjoyment of the rights of person and property.

I have already intimated to you the danger of parties in the State, with particular reference to the founding of them on geographical discriminations. Let me now take a more comprehensive view, and warn you in the most solemn manner against the baneful effects of the spirit of party generally.

This spirit, unfortunately, is inseparable from our nature, having its root in the strongest passions of the human mind. It exists under different shapes in all governments, more or less stifled, controlled, or repressed; but, in those of the popular form, it is seen in its greatest rankness, and is truly their worst enemy.

The alternate domination of one faction over another, sharpened by the spirit of revenge, natural to party dissension, which in different ages and countries has perpetrated the most horrid enormities, is itself a frightful despotism. But this leads at length to a more formal and permanent despotism. The disorders and miseries which result gradually incline the minds of men to seek security and repose in the absolute power of an individual; and sooner or later the chief of some prevailing faction, more able or more fortunate than his competitors, turns this disposition to the purposes of his own elevation, on the ruins of public liberty.

Without looking forward to an extremity of this kind (which nevertheless ought not to be entirely out of sight), the common and continual mischiefs of the spirit of party are sufficient to make it the interest and duty of a wise people to discourage and restrain it.

It serves always to distract the public councils and enfeeble the public administration. It agitates the community with ill-founded jealousies and false alarms, kindles the animosity of one part against another, foments occasionally riot and insurrection. It opens the door to foreign influence and corruption, which finds a facilitated access to the government itself through the channels of party passions. Thus the policy and the will of one country are subjected to the policy and will of another.

There is an opinion that parties in free countries are useful checks upon the administration of the government and serve to keep alive the spirit of liberty. This within certain limits is probably true; and in governments of a monarchical cast, patriotism may look with indulgence, if not with favor, upon the spirit of party. But in those of the popular character, in governments purely elective, it is a spirit not to be encouraged. From their natural tendency, it is certain there will always be enough of that spirit for every salutary purpose. And there being constant danger of excess, the effort ought to be by force of public opinion, to mitigate and assuage it. A fire not to be quenched, it demands a uniform vigilance to prevent its bursting into a flame, lest, instead of warming, it should consume.

It is important, likewise, that the habits of thinking in a free country should inspire caution in those entrusted with its administration, to confine themselves within their respective constitutional spheres, avoiding in the exercise of the powers of one department to encroach upon another. The spirit of encroachment tends to consolidate the powers of all the departments in one, and thus to create, whatever the form of government, a real despotism. A just estimate of that love of power, and proneness to abuse it, which predominates in the human heart, is sufficient to satisfy us of the truth of this position. The necessity of reciprocal checks in the exercise of political power, by dividing and distributing it into different depositaries, and constituting each the guardian of the public weal against invasions by the others, has been evinced by experiments ancient and modern; some of them in our country and under our own eyes. To preserve them must be as necessary as to institute them. If, in the opinion of the people, the distribution or modification of the constitutional powers be in any particular wrong, let it be corrected by an amendment in the way which the Constitution designates. But let there be no change by usurpation; for though this, in one instance, may be the instrument of good, it is the customary weapon by which free governments are destroyed. The precedent must always greatly overbalance in permanent evil any partial or transient benefit, which the use can at any time yield.

Of all the dispositions and habits which lead to political prosperity, religion and morality are indispensable supports. In vain would that man claim the tribute of patriotism, who should labor to subvert these great pillars of human happiness, these firmest props of the duties of men and citizens. The mere politician, equally with the pious man, ought to respect and to cherish them. A volume could not trace all their connections with private and public felicity. Let it simply be asked: Where is the security for property, for reputation, for life, if the sense of religious obligation desert the oaths which are the instruments of investigation in courts of justice ? And let us with caution indulge the supposition that morality can be maintained without religion. Whatever may be conceded to the influence of refined education on minds of peculiar structure, reason and experience both forbid us to expect that national morality can prevail in exclusion of religious principle.

It is substantially true that virtue or morality is a necessary spring of popular government. The rule, indeed, extends with more or less force to every species of free government. Who that is a sincere friend to it can look with indifference upon attempts to shake the foundation of the fabric?

Promote then, as an object of primary importance, institutions for the general diffusion of knowledge. In proportion as the structure of a government gives force to public opinion, it is essential that public opinion should be enlightened.

As a very important source of strength and security, cherish public credit. One method of preserving it is to use it as sparingly as possible, avoiding occasions of expense by cultivating peace, but remembering also that timely disbursements to prepare for danger frequently prevent much greater disbursements to repel it, avoiding likewise the accumulation of debt, not only by shunning occasions of expense, but by vigorous exertion in time of peace to discharge the debts which unavoidable wars may have occasioned, not ungenerously throwing upon posterity the burden which we ourselves ought to bear. The execution of these maxims belongs to your representatives, but it is necessary that public opinion should co-operate. To facilitate to them the performance of their duty, it is essential that you should practically bear in mind that towards the payment of debts there must be revenue; that to have revenue there must be taxes; that no taxes can be devised which are not more or less inconvenient and unpleasant; that the intrinsic embarrassment, inseparable from the selection of the proper objects (which is always a choice of difficulties), ought to be a decisive motive for a candid construction of the conduct of the government in making it, and for a spirit of acquiescence in the measures for obtaining revenue, which the public exigencies may at any time dictate.

Observe good faith and justice towards all nations; cultivate peace and harmony with all. Religion and morality enjoin this conduct; and can it be, that good policy does not equally enjoin it - It will be worthy of a free, enlightened, and at no distant period, a great nation, to give to mankind the magnanimous and too novel example of a people always guided by an exalted justice and benevolence. Who can doubt that, in the course of time and things, the fruits of such a plan would richly repay any temporary advantages which might be lost by a steady adherence to it ? Can it be that Providence has not connected the permanent felicity of a nation with its virtue ? The experiment, at least, is recommended by every sentiment which ennobles human nature. Alas! is it rendered impossible by its vices?

In the execution of such a plan, nothing is more essential than that permanent, inveterate antipathies against particular nations, and passionate attachments for others, should be excluded; and that, in place of them, just and amicable feelings towards all should be cultivated. The nation which indulges towards another a habitual hatred or a habitual fondness is in some degree a slave. It is a slave to its animosity or to its affection, either of which is sufficient to lead it astray from its duty and its interest. Antipathy in one nation against another disposes each more readily to offer insult and injury, to lay hold of slight causes of umbrage, and to be haughty and intractable, when accidental or trifling occasions of dispute occur. Hence, frequent collisions, obstinate, envenomed, and bloody contests. The nation, prompted by ill-will and resentment, sometimes impels to war the government, contrary to the best calculations of policy. The government sometimes participates in the national propensity, and adopts through passion what reason would reject; at other times it makes the animosity

▲ A portrait of James Madison, author of the first draft of Washington's farewell address.

of the nation subservient to projects of hostility instigated by pride, ambition, and other sinister and pernicious motives. The peace often, sometimes perhaps the liberty, of nations, has been the victim.

So likewise, a passionate attachment of one nation for another produces a variety of evils. Sympathy for the favorite nation, facilitating the illusion of an imaginary common interest in cases where no real common interest exists, and infusing into one the enmities of the other, betrays the former into a participation in the quarrels and wars of the latter without adequate inducement or justification. It leads also to concessions to the favorite nation of privileges denied to others which is apt doubly to injure the nation making the concessions; by unnecessarily parting with what ought to have been retained, and by exciting jealousy, ill-will, and a disposition to retaliate, in the parties from whom equal privileges

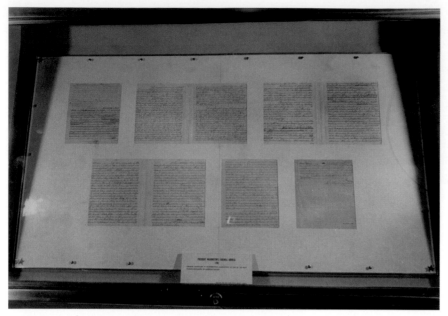

Washington's final manuscript of his Farewell Address on display in the Freedom Train, a special exhibit train that toured the United States between 1947 and 1949 displaying famous documents.

republican government. But that jealousy to be useful must be impartial; else it becomes the instrument of the very influence to be avoided, instead of a defense against it. Excessive partiality for one foreign nation and excessive dislike of another cause those whom they actuate to see danger only on one side, and serve to veil and even second the arts of influence on the other. Real patriots who may resist the intrigues of the favorite are liable to become suspected and odious, while its tools and dupes usurp the applause and confidence of the people, to surrender their interests.

The great rule of conduct for us in regard to foreign nations is in extending our commercial relations, to have with them as little political connection as possible. So far as we have already formed engagements, let them be fulfilled with perfect good faith. Here let us stop. Europe has a set of primary interests which to us have none; or a very remote relation. Hence she must be engaged in frequent controversies, the causes of which are essentially foreign to our concerns. Hence, therefore, it must be unwise in us to implicate ourselves by artificial ties in the ordinary vicissitudes of her politics, or the ordinary combinations and collisions of her friendships or enmities.

Our detached and distant situation invites and enables us to pursue a different course. If we remain

are withheld. And it gives to ambitious, corrupted, or deluded citizens (who devote themselves to the favorite nation), facility to betray or sacrifice the interests of their own country, without odium, sometimes even with popularity; gilding, with the appearances of a virtuous sense of obligation, a commendable deference for public opinion, or a laudable zeal for public good, the base or foolish compliances of ambition, corruption, or infatuation.

As avenues to foreign influence in innumerable ways, such attachments are particularly alarming to the truly enlightened and independent patriot. How many opportunities do they afford to tamper with domestic factions, to practice the arts of seduction, to mislead public opinion, to influence or awe the public councils. Such an attachment of a small or weak towards a great and powerful nation dooms the former to be the satellite of the latter.

Against the insidious wiles of foreign influence (I conjure you to believe me, fellow-citizens) the jealousy of a free people ought to be constantly awake, since history and experience prove that foreign influence is one of the most baneful foes of one people under an efficient government. the period is not far off when we may defy material injury from external annoyance; when we may take such an attitude as will cause the neutrality we may at any time resolve upon to be scrupulously respected; when belligerent nations, under the impossibility of making acquisitions upon us, will not lightly hazard the giving us provocation; when we may choose peace or war, as our interest, guided by justice, shall counsel.

Why forego the advantages of so peculiar a situation? Why quit our own to stand upon foreign ground? Why, by interweaving our destiny with that of any part of Europe, entangle our peace and prosperity in the toils of European ambition, rivalship, interest, humor or caprice?

It is our true policy to steer clear of permanent alliances with any portion of the foreign world; so far, I mean, as we are now at liberty to do it; for let me not be understood as capable of patronizing infidelity to existing engagements. I hold the maxim no less applicable to public than to private affairs, that honesty is always the best policy. I repeat it, therefore, let those engagements be observed in their genuine sense. But, in my opinion, it is unnecessary and would be unwise to extend them.

Taking care always to keep ourselves by suitable establishments on a respectable defensive posture, we may safely trust to temporary alliances for extraordinary emergencies.

Harmony, liberal intercourse with all nations, are recommended by policy, humanity, and interest. But even our commercial policy should hold an equal and impartial hand; neither seeking nor granting exclusive favors or preferences; consulting the natural course of things; diffusing and diversifying by gentle means the streams of commerce, but forcing nothing; establishing (with powers so disposed, in order to give trade a stable course, to define the rights of our merchants, and to enable the government to support them) conventional rules of intercourse, the best that present circumstances and mutual opinion will permit, but temporary, and liable to be from time to time abandoned or varied, as experience and circumstances shall dictate; constantly keeping in view that it is folly in one nation to look for disinterested favors from another; that it must pay with a portion of its independence for whatever it may accept under that character; that, by such acceptance, it may place itself in the condition of having given equivalents for nominal favors, and yet of being reproached with ingratitude for not giving more. There can be no greater error than to expect or calculate upon real favors from nation to nation. It is an illusion, which experience must cure, which a just pride ought to discard.

In offering to you, my countrymen, these counsels of an old and affectionate friend, I dare not hope

▲ A painting by Constantino Brumidi of George Washington in consultation with Thomas Jefferson and Alexander Hamilton.

To the People

ON HIS DECLINING

OF

UNITED

Friends and Fellow-Citizens,

THE period for the new election of a citizen to administer the Executive Government of the United States being not far distant, and the time actually arrived when your thoughts must be employed in designating the person who is to be clothed with that important trust, it appears to me proper, especially as it may conduce to a more distinct expression of the public voice, that I should now apprize you of the resolution I have formed, to decline being considered among the number of those out of whom a choice is to be made.

I beg you, at the same time, to do me the justice to be assured, that this resolution has not been taken without a strict regard to all the considerations appertaining to the relation which binds a dutiful citizen to his country; and that, in withdrawing the tender of service which silence in my situation might imply, I am influenced by no diminution of zeal for your future interest; no deficiency of grateful respect for your past kindness; but am supported by a full conviction that the step is compatible with both.

The acceptance of, and continuance hitherto in the office to which your suffrages have twice called me, have been a uniform sacrifice of inclination to the opinion of duty, and to a deference for what appeared to be your desire. I constantly hoped that it would have been much earlier in my power, consistently with motives which I was not at liberty to disregard, to return to that retirement from which I had been reluctantly drawn. The strength of my inclination to do this, previous to the last election, had even led to the preparation of an address to declare it to you; but mature reflection on the then perplexed and critical posture of our affairs with foreign nations, and the unanimous advice of persons entitled to my confidence, impelled me to abandon the idea.

I rejoice that the state of your concerns, external as well as internal, no longer renders the pursuit of inclination incompatible with the sentiment of duty or propriety; and am persuaded, whatever partiality may be retained for my services, that, in the present circumstances of our country, you will not disapprove my determination to retire.

The impressions with which I first undertook the arduous trust were explained on the proper occasion. In the discharge of this trust I will only say, that I have, with good intentions, contributed towards the organization and administration of the government the best exertions of which a very fallible judgment was capable. Not unconscious, in the outset, of the inferiority of my qualifications, experience in my own eyes, perhaps still more in the eyes of others, has strengthened the motives to diffidence of myself; and every day the increasing weight of years admonishes me more and more that the shade of retirement is as necessary to me as it will be welcome. Satisfied, that if any circumstances have given peculiar value to my services, they were temporary, I have the consolation to believe, that while choice and prudence invite me to quit the political scene, patriotism does not forbid it.

In looking forward to the moment which is intended to terminate the career of my public life, my feelings do not permit me to suspend the deep acknowledgment of that debt of gratitude which I owe to my beloved country for the many honours it has conferred on me; still more for the stedfast confidence with which it has supported me; and for the opportunities I have thence enjoyed of manifesting my inviolable attachment by services faithful and persevering, though in usefulness unequal to my zeal.

If benefits have resulted to our country from these services, let it always be remembered to your praise, and as an

they will make the strong and lasting impression I could wish; that they will control the usual current of the passions, or prevent our nation from running the course which has hitherto marked the destiny of nations. But, if I may even flatter myself that they may be productive of some partial benefit, some occasional good; that they may now and then recur to moderate the fury of party spirit, to warn against the mischiefs of foreign intrigue, to guard against the impostures of pretended patriotism; this hope will be a full recompense for the solicitude for your welfare, by which they have been dictated.

How far in the discharge of my official duties I have been guided by the principles which have been delineated, the public records and other evidences of my conduct must witness to you and to the world. To myself, the assurance of my own conscience is, that I have at least believed myself to be guided by them.

In relation to the still subsisting war in Europe, my proclamation of the twenty-second of April, 1793, is the index of my plan. Sanctioned by your approving voice, and by that of your representatives in both houses of Congress, the spirit of that measure has continually

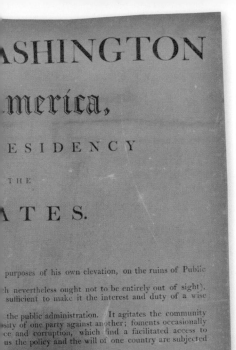

ASHINGTON

merica,

ESIDENCY

THE

ATES.

purposes of his own elevation, on the ruins of Public

h nevertheless ought not to be entirely out of sight),
sufficient to make it the interest and duty of a wise

the public administration. It agitates the community
sity of one party against another; foments occasionally
ce and corruption, which find a facilitated access to
us the policy and the will of one country are subjected

hecks upon the administration of the government, and
in limits, is probably true; and in governments of a
t with favour, upon the spirit of party: but, in those of
irit not to be encouraged. From their natural tendency
ry salutary purpose. And there being constant danger
o mitigate and assuage it. A fire not to be quenched,
lame, lest, instead of warming, it should consume.
e country should inspire caution in those entrusted with
constitutional spheres, avoiding in the exercise of the
irit of encroachment tends to consolidate the powers of
orm of government, a real despotism. A just estimate
ominates in the human heart, is sufficient to satisfy us of
ks in the exercise of political power, by dividing and
h the guardian of the public weal against invasions by
ern; some of them in our own country, and under our
ate them. If, in the opinion of the people, the distri-
particular wrong, let it be corrected by an amendment
be no change by usurpation; for though this, in one
weapon by which free governments are destroyed. The
, any partial or transient benefit which the use can at

osperity, Religion and Morality are indispensable sup-
sm who should labour to subvert these great pillars of
d citizens.—The mere politician, equally with the pious

The top of a 1796 broadside printing of "The Address of General Washington To The People of The United States on his declining of the Presidency of the United States."

governed me, uninfluenced by any attempts to deter or divert me from it.

After deliberate examination, with the aid of the best lights I could obtain, I was well satisfied that our country, under all the circumstances of the case, had a right to take, and was bound in duty and interest to take, a neutral position. Having taken it, I determined, as far as should depend upon me, to maintain it, with moderation, perseverance, and firmness.

The considerations which respect the right to hold this conduct, it is not necessary on this occasion to detail. I will only observe that, according to my understanding of the matter, that right, so far from being denied by any of the belligerent powers, has been virtually admitted by all.

The duty of holding a neutral conduct may be inferred, without anything more, from the obligation which justice and humanity impose on every nation, in cases in which it is free to act, to maintain inviolate the relations of peace and amity towards other nations.

The inducements of interest for observing that conduct will best be referred to your own reflections and experience. With me a predominant motive has been to endeavor to gain time to our country to settle and mature its yet recent institutions, and to progress without interruption to that degree of strength and consistency which is necessary to give it, humanly speaking, the command of its own fortunes.

Though, in reviewing the incidents of my administration, I am unconscious of intentional error, I am nevertheless too sensible of my defects not to think it probable that I may have committed many errors. Whatever they may be, I fervently beseech the Almighty to avert or mitigate the evils to which they may tend. I shall also carry with me the hope that my country will never cease to view them with indulgence; and that, after forty five years of my life dedicated to its service with an upright zeal, the faults of incompetent abilities will be consigned to oblivion, as myself must soon be to the mansions of rest.

Relying on its kindness in this as in other things, and actuated by that fervent love towards it, which is so natural to a man who views in it the native soil of himself and his progenitors for several generations, I anticipate with pleasing expectation that retreat in which I promise myself to realize, without alloy, the sweet enjoyment of partaking, in the midst of my fellow-citizens, the benign influence of good laws under a free government, the ever-favorite object of my heart, and the happy reward, as I trust, of our mutual cares, labors, and dangers.

President Thomas Jefferson

We are all republicans: we are all federalists.

On the morning of March 4, 1801,

Thomas Jefferson left the boardinghouse where he was staying and walked to the US Capitol. After being sworn in as president, he walked back to the boardinghouse. In between those strolls, he delivered an inaugural address that laid out his vision of government while helping to heal the ideological and political divisions that threatened the future of the new republic.

On that March day Jefferson made his points both verbally and symbolically. The only pomp and ceremony accompanying the inauguration was a series of sixteen-gun salutes for various dignitaries—Jefferson included. The Senate Chamber where he delivered the address was, according to newspaper accounts, "the largest concourse of citizens ever assembled here."

Accounts from the day say he was dressed "as a plain citizen, without any distinctive badge of office." Unlike his two predecessors (and many of the attendees), he did not wear a ceremonial sword. And by returning to the boardinghouse after the speech, he presented himself as a common man, drawing a distinction between the presidency and the monarchy the country had fought against not so many years earlier.

Healing Political Wounds

Despite his skills as a writer, Jefferson was said to be a poor public speaker. He delivered the address in "so low a tone that few heard it." If the crowd did not hear the words as they were spoken, they soon read them. The address was quickly published by major periodicals throughout the country.

In a time when flowery language was the norm, his words were relatively simple and straightforward, though fraught with greater meaning because of the background against which they were delivered. Jefferson succeeded prickly John Adams, whose four years in office were filled with controversy. Adams fought not only with Jefferson and his Democratic-Republican Party, but also with Alexander Hamilton, founder of Adams's own Federalist Party. Jefferson and Hamilton were the public faces of their parties,

▲ A colorized engraved portrait of Thomas Jefferson during his time as President of the United States.

▲ An extract from a letter James Madison wrote to Jefferson in which he condemns the Alien Act as "a monster that must for ever disgrace its parents."

and developed most of the policies and principles that continue to define the two-party system today. Hamilton believed in a strong central government and was willing to subordinate the interests of the individual. Jefferson favored a much more limited government, whose only purpose was, as he said in drafting the Declaration of Independence, protection of every individual's life, liberty, and pursuit of happiness.

During George Washington's first term, Jefferson was his secretary of state and Hamilton secretary of the treasury. Jefferson opposed Hamilton's financial strategies because he thought they exceeded the powers granted by the Constitution. Both left Washington's Administration focused on developing the differing political philosophies that characterized their parties.

Adams Era Rough for Federalists

The rift between parties widened during the Adams Administration, with some extremists among the Democratic-Republicans calling for secession of their states from the Union. The Federalists brought matters to a head in 1798 with the passage of the Alien and Sedition Acts, clearly aimed at suppressing Democratic-Republican Party opposition and the party's increasingly strident criticism of the Federalists.

One of the acts made it a crime to criticize the federal government. A number of writers of Jefferson's party—but no Federalists—were convicted, fined, and jailed under the laws. The Alien and Sedition Acts were extremely unpopular, and contributed to the decline of the Federalists as a political power.

In the election of 1800, Democratic-Republican candidates defeated the Federalists decisively at all levels, excepting the presidential. The vote for president split between two Democratic-Republicans, Jefferson and the devious Aaron Burr. The election was thrown into the House of Representatives. Hamilton distrusted Burr even more than he disliked Jefferson, so swung his party loyalists behind Jefferson, who was elected by the House vote. Burr, of course, was later to kill Hamilton in a duel and was also tried for treason, but acquitted. Hamilton's judgment in favoring Jefferson was undoubtedly sound.

To his everlasting credit, Jefferson set out in his inaugural address not to gloat over the defeat of the Federalists, or to heighten partisan feelings, but to begin a process of conciliation that he continued throughout his Administration.

Jefferson the Writer: Speed as Well as Skill

Historians believe that Jefferson began drafting his inaugural address after the decisive House vote on February 17 that made him president; he had only two weeks to write the speech, and he did it all alone. His papers do not show that he consulted even his close and valued friend James Madison.

Jefferson, of course, is viewed as perhaps the finest writer among the Founding Fathers—the Declaration of Independence alone is proof of that—but he authored many other phrases that are still quoted today. He needed only three drafts to produce the final speech. Both his first and second drafts contain many crossed-out words and paragraphs, and several pasted-on bits of paper with revisions, but the overall structure and flow of the speech never changed from draft to draft.

The core of Jefferson's speech was what he had earlier called in a letter to his political cohort Elbridge Gerry his "political faith." He laid it out simply and eloquently and without reference to the differences between his positions and those of the

▲ Elbridge Gerry, Founding Father and friend of Thomas Jefferson, who served as fifth Vice President of the United States (1813–1814), under James Madison.

Federalists. The speech contains no controversial language or explanations of Jefferson's political creed, just positive statements of his beliefs.

If anything, the successive drafts of the speech became more conciliatory and more "democratic." Nothing showed that more clearly than the way Jefferson opened the speech. In the first draft, he said he was "called upon by the voice of our country to undertake the duties of it's (sic) first executive magistrate." By the second draft, he had simplified that to "[c]alled upon to undertake the duties of the first Executive office of our country." He held onto those words in the final version.

In the opening, and throughout, Jefferson chooses his words with care and with full knowledge of their effect. This is particularly true in his second paragraph, where he struggled to avoid any language that might raise the ire of the defeated Federalists. He also worked to develop just the right combination of words to characterize the relationship between the will of the majority and the rights of the minority.

Two Lowercase Letters Make All the Difference

Jefferson said the election had been "decided by the voice of the nation." He had moved that phrase down from the beginning of the first paragraph to the second and altered it slightly. Between the first and second drafts, he also elevated the importance of the will of the majority, calling it a "sacred principle," a phrase that does not appear in the original draft.

Undoubtedly the phrase that has received the most attention from historians and scholars over the past two hundred years is the assertion that "we are all republicans, we are all federalists." Jefferson was a linguistic perfectionist, so it seems likely that he made a conscious choice not to capitalize either term. The use of lower case implies that he is talking about the concepts that constitute federalism, or republicanism, rather than the parties that had grown up around those concepts.

This was not the first time Jefferson had paired the two words—the two parties' development was accompanied by extensive philosophical discussions of just what it meant to be either a federalist or a republican. However, in the heated atmosphere and the hardening of positions of the Adams years, "Federalists" of the capitalized variety were accused of wanting an American monarchy and of trampling on the people's rights. Republicans were in turn accused of being radical revolutionaries wanting to emulate the French Revolution.

Jefferson's use of the two words in tandem was a way of signaling his moderate sentiments. Interestingly, in many newspaper reprints of the address, the two words were capitalized, placed in italics, boldfaced, or otherwise printed in a way that emphasized their importance.

Freedom of Political Opinion Equated with Religious Freedom

Next Jefferson equated freedom of political opinion with freedom of religious belief. "If there be any among us who would wish to dissolve this Union, or to change its republican form, let them stand undisturbed as monuments of the safety with which error of opinion may be tolerated."

He then turned to the heart of his speech, his principles, which from the first draft had survived with few changes. He speaks of "peace, commerce, and honest friendship with all nations, entangling alliances with none." Echoing Washington's Farewell Address, Jefferson added "entangling" to his final draft.

Jefferson closed by invoking the image of George Washington, identifying himself with a man who, even before his death during Adams's presidency, had assumed almost godlike stature. The artful closing reminded the audience of Jefferson's long experience in "subordinate offices" and noted that he entered the most difficult of all without "pretensions to that high confidence you reposed in our first and greatest revolutionary character."

By comparing himself unfavorably with Washington, Jefferson managed to remain humble while reminding people of his relationship with a legend and of his own credentials to lead the country.

A Great Success

The speech was an unqualified success. Those in Jefferson's own party of course were pleased at his affirmation of the founding principles of the party. But they also were pleased that he had expressed them moderately enough that they would not alarm or anger the Federalists.

And most Federalists praised the thoughtfulness and prudence of Jefferson's words. Senator James A. Bayard of Delaware wrote to Hamilton that the speech thing dear & valuable to you, it is proper you should understand what I deem the essential principles of our government, & consequently those which ought to shape it's administration. I will compress them within the narrowest compass they will bear, stating the general principle, but not all it's limitations. — Equal & exact justice to all men, of whatever state or persuasion, religious or political: — Peace, commerce & honest friendship with all nations, entangling alliances with none: — the support of the state governments in all their rights, as the most competent administrations for our domestic concerns, & the surest bulwarks against anti-republican tendencies: — the preservation of the General government in it's whole constitutional vigour as the sheet anchor of our peace at home, & safety abroad: — a jealous care of the right of election by the people, a mild and safe corrective of abuses which are lopped by the sword of revolution where peaceable remedies are unprovided: — — absolute acquiescence in the decisions of the majority, the vital principle of republics, from which is no appeal but to force, the vital principle & immediate parent of despotism: — a well disciplined militia, our best reliance in peace & for the first moments of war, till regulars may relieve them; the supremacy of the civil over the military authority: — economy in the Public expence, that labor may be lightly burthened: — the honest paiment of our debts; and sacred preservation of the public faith: — encouragement of agriculture; and of commerce as it's handmaid: — the diffusion of information, & arraignment of all abuses at the bar of the public reason; — freedom of religion; freedom of the press; & freedom of person, under the protection of the Habeas corpus: — and trial by juries, impartially selected. these principles form the bright constellation, which has gone before us, & guided our steps through an age of revolution & reformation. the wisdom of our sages, & blood of our heroes have been devoted to their attainment: they should be the creed of our political faith; the text of civic instruction, the touchstone by which to try the services of those we trust; and should we wander from them in moments of error or of alarm, let us hasten to retrace our steps, & to regain the road which alone leads to Peace, liberty, & safety.

was "in political substance better than we expected; and not answerable to the expectations of the Partizans of the other side." In fact, many Federalists liked the speech better than some of the more hot-blooded members of Jefferson's own party.

Jefferson's entire performance on that Inauguration Day—from the symbolism of walking to the ceremony and dressing plainly to his carefully chosen words—was designed to defuse the contentious atmosphere of the Adams era. Had that hostility and confrontation continued to escalate, the country might have ripped apart along ideological lines sixty years sooner than it did.

The problems and differences remained, but Jefferson's even-handed, judicious inaugural speech kicked off an equally moderate presidency in which all shades of political opinion could find something to like.

First Inaugural Address
March 4, 1801, United States Capitol, Washington, DC

Friends and Fellow Citizens:

Called upon to undertake the duties of the first executive office of our country, I avail myself of the presence of that portion of my fellow-citizens which is here assembled to express my grateful thanks for the favor with which they have been pleased to look toward me, to declare a sincere consciousness that the task is above my talents, and that I approach it with those anxious and awful presentiments which the greatness of the charge and the weakness of my powers so justly inspire. A rising nation, spread over a wide and fruitful land, traversing all the seas with the rich productions of their industry, engaged in commerce with nations who feel power and forget right, advancing rapidly to destinies beyond the reach of mortal eye – when I contemplate these transcendent objects, and see the honor, the happiness, and the hopes of this beloved country committed to the issue and the auspices of this day, I shrink from the contemplation, and humble myself before the magnitude of the undertaking. Utterly, indeed, should I despair did not the presence of many whom I here see remind me that in the other high authorities provided

▲ The first page of Jefferson's reading copy of his first inaugural address, written in his own hand.

by our Constitution I shall find resources of wisdom, of virtue, and of zeal on which to rely under all difficulties. To you, then, gentlemen, who are charged with the sovereign functions of legislation, and to those associated with you, I look with encouragement for that guidance and support which may enable us to steer with safety the vessel in which we are all embarked amidst the conflicting elements of a troubled world.

During the contest of opinion through which we have passed the animation of discussions and of exertions has sometimes worn an aspect which might impose on strangers unused to think freely and to speak and to write what they think; but this being now decided by the voice of the nation, announced according to the rules of the Constitution, all will, of course, arrange themselves under the will of the law, and unite in common efforts for the common good. All, too, will bear in mind this sacred principle, that though the will of the majority is in all cases to prevail, that will to be rightful must be reasonable; that the minority possess their equal rights, which equal law must protect, and to violate would be oppression. Let us, then, fellow-citizens, unite with one heart and one mind. Let us restore to social intercourse that harmony and affection without which liberty and even life itself are but dreary things. And let us reflect that, having banished from our land that religious intolerance under which mankind so long bled and suffered, we have yet gained little if we countenance a political intolerance as despotic, as wicked, and capable of as bitter and bloody persecutions. During the throes and convulsions of the ancient world, during the agonizing spasms of infuriated man, seeking through blood and slaughter his long-lost liberty, it was not wonderful that the agitation of the billows should reach even this distant and peaceful shore; that this should be more felt and feared by some and less by others, and should divide opinions as to measures of safety.

But every difference of opinion is not a difference of principle. We have called by different names brethren of the same principle. We are all republicans, we are all federalists. If there be any among us who would wish to dissolve this Union or to change its republican form, let them stand undisturbed as monuments of the safety with which error of opinion may be tolerated where reason is left free to combat it. I know, indeed, that some honest men fear that a republican government can not be strong, that this Government is not strong enough; but would the honest patriot, in the full tide of successful experiment, abandon a government which has so far kept us free and firm on the theoretic and visionary fear that this Government, the world's best hope, may by possibility want energy to preserve itself? I trust not. I believe this, on the contrary, the strongest Government on earth. I believe it the only one where every man, at the call of the law, would fly to the standard of the law, and would meet invasions of the public order as his own personal concern. Sometimes it is said that man can not be trusted with the government of himself. Can he, then, be trusted with the government of others? Or have we found angels in the forms of kings to govern him? Let history answer this question.

Let us, then, with courage and confidence pursue our own Federal and Republican principles, our attachment to union and representative government. Kindly separated by nature and a wide ocean from the exterminating havoc of one quarter of the globe; too high-minded to endure the degradations of the others; possessing a chosen country, with room enough for our descendants to the thousandth and thousandth generation; entertaining a due sense of our equal right to the use of our own faculties, to the acquisitions

▶ A page from one of Jefferson's drafts of the speech containing the "We are all republicans: we are all federalists" line. Also noticeable on this page are two pasted on sections where Jefferson has re-worked his text.

as bitter & bloody persecutions. during the throes & convulsions of the antient world, during the agonising spasms of infuriated man, seeking thro' blood & slaughter his long-lost liberty, it was not wonderful that the agitation of the billows should reach even this distant & peaceful shore; that this should be more felt & feared by some & less by others; & should divide opinions as to measures of safety. but every difference of opinion, is not a difference of principle. we have called by different names brethren of the same principle. we are all republicans: we are all federalists. if there be any among us who would wish to dissolve this Union, or to change it's republican form, let them stand undisturbed as monuments of the safety with which error of opinion may be tolerated, where reason is left free to combat it. I know indeed that some honest men fear that a republican government cannot be strong; that this government is not strong enough. but would the honest patriot, in the full tide of successful experiment abandon a government which has so far kept us free and firm, on the theoretic & visionary fear, that this government, the world's best hope, may, by possibility, want energy to preserve itself? I trust not. I believe this, on the contrary the strongest government on earth. I believe it the only one where every man, at the call of the law, would fly to the standard of the law, and would meet invasions of the public order as his own personal concern. sometimes it is said that man cannot be trusted with the government of himself. can he then be trusted with the government of others? or have we found angels, in the form of kings, to govern him? Let history answer this question.

Let us then, with courage & confidence, pursue our own federal & republican principles; our attachment to union & representative government. kindly separated by nature & a wide ocean from the exterminating havoc of one quarter of the globe; too high-minded to endure the degradations of the others; professing a chosen country, with room enough for our descendants to the thousandth & thousandth generation, enjoying the most favourable temperatures of climate, entertaining a due sense of our equal right to the use of our own faculties, to the acquisitions of our own industry, to honour & confidence from our fellow citizens, resulting not from birth, but from our actions & their sense of them, enlightened by a benign religion, professed indeed & practised in various forms, yet all of them inculcating Honesty, truth, temperance, gratitude & the love of man, acknoleging and adoring an over ruling providence, which by all it's dispensations proves that it delights in the happiness of man here, & his greater happiness hereafter; with all these blessings, what more is

I repair then, fellow citizens, to the post which you have assigned me.

with experience enough in subordinate stations to know the difficulties of this the greatest of all,

I have learnt to expect that it will rarely fall to the lot of imperfect man

to retire from this station with the reputation & the favor which bring him into it.

without pretensions to that high confidee you reposed in our first & greatest revolution.y chara.

whose pre-eminent services had entitled him to the first place in his country's love,

and had destined for him the fairest page in the volume of faithful history.

I ask so much confidence only as may give firmness & effect to the legal admin of your aff

I shall often go wrong thro' defect of judgment.

when right, I shall often be thought wrong by y se wh.se posit.n w.d n.t command a view of the whole grou

I ask your indulgence for my own errors, which will never be intentional:

& your support ag.nst the errors of others, who may condemn w.t they w.d n.t if seen in all it's par.

the approbation implied by your suffrage, is a great consolation to me for the past;

and my future sollicitude will be, to retain the good opinion of y se who h.ve bestowed it in adva

to conciliate that of others, by doing them all the good in my power;

and to be instrumental to the happiness & freedom of all.

Relying then on the patronage of your good will, I advance with obedience to the work,

ready to retire fr.m it whenev.r you become sensible how m.ch better choices it is in your power to ma

and may that infinite power which rules the destinies of the universe,

lead our councils to what is best, & give y.m a favorable issue for your peace & prosperity.

of our own industry, to honor and confidence from our fellow-citizens, resulting not from birth, but from our actions and their sense of them; enlightened by a benign religion, professed, indeed, and practiced in various forms, yet all of them inculcating honesty, truth, temperance, gratitude, and the love of man; acknowledging and adoring an overruling Providence, which by all its dispensations proves that it delights in the happiness of man here and his greater happiness hereafter – with all these blessings, what more is necessary to make us a happy and a prosperous people? Still one thing more, fellow-citizens – a wise and frugal Government, which shall restrain men from injuring one another, shall leave them otherwise free to regulate their own pursuits of industry and improvement, and shall not take from the mouth of labor the bread it has earned. This is the sum of good government, and this is necessary to close the circle of our felicities.

About to enter, fellow-citizens, on the exercise of duties which comprehend everything dear and valuable to you, it is proper you should understand what I deem the essential principles of our Government, and consequently those which ought to shape its Administration. I will compress them within the narrowest compass they will bear, stating the general principle, but not all its limitations. Equal and exact justice to all men, of whatever state or persuasion, religious or political; peace, commerce, and honest friendship with all nations, entangling alliances with none; the support of the State governments in all their rights, as the most competent administrations for our domestic concerns and the surest bulwarks against antirepublican tendencies; the preservation of the General Government in its whole constitutional vigor, as the sheet anchor of our peace at home and safety abroad; a jealous care of the right of election by the people – a mild and safe corrective of abuses which are lopped by the sword of revolution where peaceable remedies are unprovided; absolute acquiescence in the decisions of the majority, the vital principle of republics, from which is no appeal but to force, the vital principle and immediate parent of despotism; a well-disciplined militia, our best reliance in peace and for the first moments of war till regulars may relieve them; the supremacy of the civil over the military authority; economy in the public expense, that labor may be lightly burthened; the honest payment of our debts and sacred preservation of the public faith; encouragement of agriculture, and of commerce as its handmaid; the diffusion of information and arraignment of all abuses at the bar of the public reason; freedom of religion; freedom of the press, and freedom of person under the protection of the habeas corpus, and trial by juries impartially selected. These principles form the bright constellation which has gone before us and guided our steps through an age of revolution and reformation. The wisdom of our sages and blood of our heroes have been devoted to their attainment. They should be the creed of our political faith, the text of civic instruction, the touchstone by which to try the services of those we trust; and should we wander from them in moments of error or of alarm, let us hasten to retrace our steps and to regain the road which alone leads to peace, liberty, and safety.

I repair, then, fellow-citizens, to the post you have assigned me. With experience enough in subordinate offices to have seen the difficulties of this the greatest of all, I have learnt to expect that it will rarely fall to the lot of imperfect man to retire from this station with the reputation and the favor which bring him into it. Without pretensions to that high confidence you reposed in our first and greatest revolutionary character, whose preeminent services had entitled him to the first place in his country's love and destined for him the fairest page in the volume of faithful history, I ask so much confidence only as may give firmness and effect to the legal administration of your affairs. I shall often go wrong through defect of judgment. When right, I shall often be thought wrong by those whose positions will not command a view of the whole ground. I ask your indulgence for my own errors, which will never be intentional, and your support against the errors of others, who may condemn what they would not if seen in all its parts. The approbation implied by your suffrage is a great consolation to me for the past, and my future solicitude will be to retain the good opinion of those who have bestowed it in advance, to conciliate that of others by doing them all the good in my power, and to be instrumental to the happiness and freedom of all.

Relying, then, on the patronage of your good will, I advance with obedience to the work, ready to retire from it whenever you become sensible how much better choice it is in your power to make. And may that Infinite Power which rules the destinies of the universe lead our councils to what is best, and give them a favorable issue for your peace and prosperity.

President James Monroe

"The American continents, by the free and independent condition which they have assumed and maintain, are henceforth not to be considered as subjects for future colonization by any European powers."

The Monroe Doctrine sent a clear message to the powerful nations of Europe: hands off North and South America. It effectively ended any further attempts at colonization of the New World, has guided American foreign policy for nearly two hundred years, and has been invoked by presidents ranging from James Polk to Ronald Reagan.

The principle of non-interference sounds simple enough, and even straightforward from today's perspective. But that was not so at the time. In 1823, the United States was still a new nation, relatively weak militarily and economically. The doctrine was an attempt to prevent far more powerful European countries from poaching on the emerging nations of South and Central America as they struggled for independence from Spain. The question was, could America back up its words with force, if necessary?

The answer was, probably not. The success of the doctrine depended on a delicate diplomatic balancing act that played off the competing interests of Great Britain, France, and other European powers. It was a successful finesse, but ever since, a basic question has divided historians. Who was responsible for the idea behind the doctrine and the wording of the speech? Was the author President James Monroe or was it his secretary of state and successor as president, John Quincy Adams?

▲ An early nineteenth century portrait of President James Monroe.

One thing is clear. Monroe delivered the message to the Congress on a December day in 1823 and, as president, the decision to include the words of the doctrine in the message was his. In that sense, the Monroe Doctrine is rightly named. But some historians believe Monroe was little more than an amiable dunce rewarded with the presidency for sheer longevity as a Founding Father. They believe Adams was an underappreciated political mastermind and claim that he was, in effect, Monroe's puppeteer, and the policy should have been called "The Adams Doctrine."

The Colonies Fight Back

The ideas behind the Monroe Doctrine date from the United States' earliest days. From its infancy, the new nation sought to chart its own course independent of France or Britain, the two preeminent powers of Europe. George Washington's advice to avoid foreign entanglements and permanent alliances became a cornerstone of US foreign policy. It was an article of faith for Monroe, Washington's last Revolutionary War colleague remaining in public life.

In the aftermath of the Napoleonic Wars, Europe was in greater than usual turmoil, with constantly shifting alliances and power struggles. Russia, Prussia, and Austria came together in what they called "The Holy Alliance," aimed at defending the system of monarchy against the growing trend toward democracy. Their immediate goal, with the backing of France, was reestablishment of the House of Bourbon on the throne of Spain, and reassertion of its control over Spain's New World colonies.

Spain had been weakened during the Napoleonic struggles, and its South American colonies were taking the opportunity to fight for their independence under leaders like Simon Bolivar and Bernardo O'Higgins. These fledgling republics sought US recognition, and perhaps military assistance, in their fight for independence.

The United States was not in a position to go to war. Moreover, neither Monroe nor Adams believed that Spain was strong enough to retake its colonies alone. Both Monroe and Adams were willing to let the colonies fight their own battles, but drew the line at intervention by the Holy Alliance to help Spain.

No Big Surprise: Kings and Queens Prefer Monarchy

Great Britain also was involved. As a monarchy, Britain was drawn to the monarchist philosophy of the Holy Alliance. As "a nation of shopkeepers" (in the words of Napoleon Bonaparte), the British were eyeing the former Spanish colonies as potential new markets for their goods and as sources of raw materials. Another British concern was French involvement in a potential Bourbon restoration in Spain. Britain had blocked the French from colonizing the Americas in the eighteenth century and wanted to keep them out in the nineteenth century too. In the end, anti-French sentiment and the shopkeepers won out, and Britain proposed to the US government that the two nations join in a declaration forbidding future colonization in Latin America.

▲ An engraving depicting George Canning, the British Foreign Secretary who proposed that the US and Britain jointly declare their opposition to European intervention.

Monroe favored the idea and consulted with his predecessors Jefferson and Madison, who also approved. Adams was less enthusiastic. He also was concerned about Russia's attempt to extend its sphere of influence from its colony in Alaska down the Pacific coast toward California, then owned by Mexico. Russia had made some inflammatory comments asserting the superiority of monarchy over democracy as a form of government, and Adams argued that the United States should do everything possible to prevent the monarchists from gaining a foothold in the Americas.

Adams, Monroe, or Doctrine by Committee?

The situation in Europe and its implications for both Latin America and the Pacific coast were the subject of numerous Cabinet meetings in the months before President Monroe's message to the Congress. These are extensively chronicled in Adams's lengthy diaries, which naturally present his role in the most favorable light.

Among them is his argument in a November 7, 1823, meeting against Britain's offer of a joint declaration. "It would be more candid, as well as more dignified," he said, "to avow our principles explicitly to Russia and France, than to come in as a cockboat to the British man-of-war."

Adams eventually won over the president, and the Monroe Doctrine began to take shape. Here historians divide into two camps. Some claim that Monroe was confused and reluctant, failing to understand the implications of the potential statement, while Monroe partisans portray him as a mature, experienced statesman with long experience in international relations and strong convictions dating back to the Revolution about the dangers of European political influence.

The sixty-five-year-old Monroe was certainly experienced. He had fought ably in the Revolution, studied law under Jefferson, served as governor of Virginia and in the US Senate, and was secretary of state under Madison. As Ambassador to France, he helped to negotiate the Louisiana Purchase. He also engaged in diplomatic missions to Great Britain.

There's also no doubt of Adams's capabilities. As the son of John Adams, he had begun his training in diplomacy and affairs of state as a child.

His presidency was perhaps the least successful part of his career. Both before his term in the Oval Office and after, when he returned to the House of Representatives and earned the nickname "Old Man Eloquent," he was consistently effective.

Who actually initiated and framed the Doctrine? Both men did, and Monroe's Cabinet and many others were also involved. Both Monroe and Adams strongly believed in keeping the United States neutral and avoiding involvement in European affairs. It was not much of a stretch for each to come to the conclusion that expansion of Europe's sphere of influence to the Americas would make it difficult to stay neutral and could lead to war.

The Doctrine contained four main points:
• The United States would not interfere in the internal affairs of European powers, or in their wars.
• The United States recognized and would not interfere with existing colonies in the Western Hemisphere.
• The United States considered the Western Hemisphere closed to future colonization by European powers.
• Any attempt by a European power to colonize or control any country in the Western Hemisphere would be viewed as a hostile act against the United States.

Presidential scholars generally agree that the prohibition on European colonization was entirely Adams's work. Both Adams's accounts of the Cabinet proceedings and those of other participants agree that the language of the non-colonization provision was drafted by Adams.

The first two points were simply a restatement of a principle that had guided American foreign policy since Washington's day: the United States

▲ An illustration depicting James Monroe and Robert Livingstone completing negotiations with Comte Talleyrand for the Louisiana purchase.

Monroe's version of the Annual Message to Congress is a significant historical snapshot of the state of the republic. It was a comprehensive laundry list of issues and housekeeping matters under way in the executive branch of government, down to the detail of a $5,000 expenditure for investigating the site of an armory in the West, and compensation for postmasters and other expenses.

His message was also a good deal longer than those of some other presidents. As Monroe said, "I deem it proper to present this view of public affairs in greater detail than might otherwise be necessary . . . The people being with us exclusively the sovereign, it is indispensable that full information be laid before them on all important subjects, to enable them to exercise that high power with complete effect."

would avoid getting involved in European wars or political battles. Monroe and Adams shared this viewpoint throughout their careers.

As to the "hostile act" warning, the United States simply did not have the firepower to back it up. For nearly a century afterwards, the Monroe Doctrine was tacitly enforced by the British fleet, the most powerful naval force in the world. During this time, the United States ignored several minor incursions by the British—such as their occupation of the Falkland Islands in 1833. But British support also enabled several presidents to invoke the Monroe Doctrine successfully to blunt Spanish and French advances in the same period.

Regardless of who wrote the words, it was Monroe who wrote the Message to Congress. Adams had wanted to transmit the statement of US policy to his European counterparts through private diplomatic channels, but Monroe wanted a more formal declaration. Making the doctrine public made not only the Europeans, but the Congress and the American people, aware that the United States was flexing its muscles.

Monroe's Abrupt Transition

After an exhaustive accounting of foreign and domestic issues, and a discussion of the expenditure of $22,700 for the construction of two piers at Cape Henlopen, Delaware, Monroe launched abruptly into the articulation of his four pronouncements—which, by the way, were referred to as The Principles of President Monroe until the 1850s, when they began to be known by their present name. Records do not show whether members of Congress had been briefed in advance that Monroe was about to deliver a diplomatic bombshell, but if they had not, by the time the president finished with Cape Henlopen, they might have been forgiven for filing the document away without finishing it (contrary to some accounts, Monroe delivered the Message in writing rather than as a speech).

Nevertheless, the Monroe Doctrine's significance quickly became apparent. After its initial period of enforcement by the Royal Navy, the United States began to, as Theodore Roosevelt defined it, "speak softly and carry a big stick." Roosevelt's corollary to the Doctrine extended its interpretation to intervention throughout Latin America whenever the United States thought a particular regime was acting against our interests, which effectively made the US armed forces the policemen of the Western Hemisphere. This somewhat imperialistic interpretation, far beyond anything Monroe would have imagined, was deeply resented in Latin America. Imperialism has since been replaced by a less paternalistic relationship with the governments of Central and South America.

The original statement of American belief in independence is still a keystone of American foreign policy, and it assured Monroe a prime place in the country's history.

Seventh Annual Message to Congress
December 2, 1823, delivered in writing rather than as a speech

Fellow Citizens of the Senate and House of Representatives:

Many important subjects will claim your attention during the present session, of which I shall endeavor to give, in aid of your deliberations, a just idea in this communication. I undertake this duty with diffidence, from the vast extent of the interests on which I have to treat and of their great importance to every portion of our Union. I enter on it with zeal from a thorough conviction that there never was a period since the establishment of our Revolution when, regarding the condition of the civilized world and its bearing on us, there was greater necessity for devotion in the public servants to their respective duties, or for virtue, patriotism, and union in our constituents.

Meeting in you a new Congress, I deem it proper to present this view of public affairs in greater detail than might otherwise be necessary. I do it, however, with peculiar satisfaction, from a knowledge that in this respect I shall comply more fully with the sound principles of our Government.

The people being with us exclusively the sovereign, it is indispensable that full information be laid before them on all important subjects, to enable them to exercise that high power with complete effect. If kept in the dark, they must be incompetent to it. We are all liable to error, and those who are engaged in the management of public affairs are more subject to excitement and to be led astray by their particular interests and passions than the great body of our constituents, who, living at home in the pursuit of their ordinary avocations, are calm but deeply interested spectators of events and of the conduct of those who are parties to them.

To the people every department of the Government and every individual in each are responsible, and the more full their information the better they can judge of the wisdom of the policy pursued and of the conduct of each in regard to it. From their dispassionate judgment much aid may always be obtained, while their approbation will form the greatest incentive and most gratifying reward for virtuous actions, and the dread of their censure the best security against the abuse of their confidence. Their interests in all vital questions are the same, and the bond, by sentiment as well as by interest, will be proportionably strengthened as they are better informed of the real state of public affairs, especially in difficult conjunctures. It is by such knowledge that local prejudices and jealousies are surmounted, and that a national policy extending its fostering care and protection to all the great interests of our Union, is formed and steadily adhered to.

A precise knowledge of our relations with foreign powers as respects our negotiations and transactions with each is thought to be particularly necessary. Equally necessary is it that we should for a just estimate of our resources, revenue, and progress in every kind of improvement connected with the national prosperity and public defense. It is by rendering justice to other nations that we may expect it from them. It is by our ability to resent injuries and redress wrongs that we may avoid them.

The commissioners under the 5th article of the treaty of Ghent, having disagreed in their opinions respecting that portion of the boundary between the Territories of the United States and of Great Britain the establishment of which had been submitted to them, have made their respective reports in compliance with that article, that the same might be referred to the decision of a friendly power. It being manifest, however, that it would be difficult, if not impossible, for any power to perform that office without great delay and much inconvenience to itself, a proposal has been made by this Government, and acceded to by that of Great Britain, to endeavor to establish that boundary by amicable negotiation.

It appearing from long experience that no satisfactory arrangement could be formed of the commercial intercourse between the United States and the British colonies in this hemisphere by legislative acts while each party pursued its own course without agreement or concert with the other, a proposal has been made to the British Government to regulate this commerce by treaty, as it has been to arrange in like manner the just claim of the citizens of the United States inhabiting the States and Territories

A nineteenth century portrait of John Quincy Adams.

bordering on the lakes and rivers which empty into the St. Lawrence to the navigation of that river to the ocean. For these and other objects of high importance to the interests of both parties a negotiation has been opened with the British Government which it is hoped will have a satisfactory result.

The commissioners under the 6th and 7th articles of the treaty of Ghent having successfully closed their labors in relation to the 6th, have proceeded to the discharge of those relating to the 7th. Their progress in the extensive survey required for the performance of their duties justifies the presumption that it will be completed in the ensuing year.

The negotiation which had been long depending with the French Government on several important subjects, and particularly for a just indemnity for losses sustained in the late wars by the citizens of the United States under unjustifiable seizures and confiscations of their property, has not as yet had the desired effect. As this claim rests on the same principle with others which have been admitted by the French Government, it is not perceived on what just ground it can be rejected. A minister will be immediately appointed to proceed to France and resume the negotiation on this and other subjects which may arise between the two nations.

At the proposal of the Russian Imperial Government, made through the minister of the Emperor residing here, a full power and instructions have been transmitted to the minister of the United States at St. Petersburg to arrange by amicable negotiation the respective rights and interests of the two nations on the North West coast of this continent. A similar proposal had been made by His Imperial Majesty to the Government of Great Britain, which has likewise been acceded to. The Government of the United States has been desirous by this friendly proceeding of manifesting the great value which they have invariably attached to the friendship of the Emperor and their solicitude to cultivate the best understanding with his Government. In the discussions to which this interest has given rise and in the arrangements by which they may terminate the occasion has been judged proper for asserting, as a principle in which the rights and interests of the United States are involved, that the American continents, by the free and independent condition which they have assumed and maintain, are henceforth not to be considered as subjects for future colonization by any European powers.

Since the close of the last session of Congress the commissioners and arbitrators for ascertaining and determining the amount of indemnification which may be due to citizens of the United States under the decision of His Imperial Majesty the Emperor of Russia, in conformity to the convention concluded at St. Petersburg on July 12, 1822, have assembled in this city, and organized themselves as a board for the performance of the duties assigned to them by that treaty. The commission constituted under the 11th article of the treaty of February 22, 1819, between the United States and Spain is also in session here, and as the term of three years limited by the treaty for the execution of the trust will expire before the period of the next regular meeting of Congress, the attention of the Legislature will be drawn to the measures which may be necessary to accomplish the objects for which the commission was instituted.

In compliance with a resolution of the House of Representatives adopted at their last session, instructions have been given to all the ministers of the United States accredited to the powers of Europe and America to propose the proscription of the African slave trade by classing it under the denomination, and inflicting on its perpetrators the punishment, of piracy. Should this proposal be acceded to, it is not doubted that this odious and criminal practice will be promptly and entirely suppressed. It is earnestly hoped that it will be acceded to, from the firm belief that it is the most effectual expedient that can be adopted for the purpose.

At the commencement of the recent war between France and Spain it was declared by the French Government that it would grant no commissions to privateers, and that neither the commerce of Spain herself nor of neutral nations should be molested by the naval force of France, except in the breach of a lawful blockade. This declaration, which appears to have been faithfully carried into effect, concurring with principles proclaimed and cherished by the United States from the first establishment of their independence, suggested the hope that the time had arrived when the proposal for adopting it as a permanent and invariable rule in all future maritime wars might meet the favorable consideration of the great European powers. Instructions have accordingly been given to our ministers with France, Russia, and Great Britain to make those proposals to their respective Governments, and when the friends of humanity reflect on the essential amelioration to the condition of the human race which would result from the abolition of private war on the sea and on the great facility by which it might be accomplished, requiring only the consent of a few sovereigns, an earnest hope is indulged that these overtures will meet with an attention animated by the spirit in which they were made, and that they will ultimately be successful.

The ministers who were appointed to the Republics of Colombia and Buenos Ayres during the last session of Congress proceeded shortly afterwards to their destinations. Of their arrival there official intelligence has not yet been received. The minister appointed to the Republic of Chile will sail in a few days. An early appointment will also be made to Mexico. A minister has been received from Colombia, and the other Governments have been informed that ministers, or diplomatic agents of inferior grade, would be received from each, accordingly as they might prefer the one or the other.

The minister appointed to Spain proceeded soon after his appointment for Cadiz, the residence of the Sovereign to whom he was accredited. In approaching that port the frigate which conveyed him was warned off by the commander of the French squadron by which it was blockaded and not permitted to enter, although apprised by the captain of the frigate of the public character of the person whom he had on board, the landing of whom was the sole object of his proposed entry. This act, being considered an infringement of the rights of ambassadors and of nations, will form a just cause of complaint to the Government of France against the officer by whom it was committed.

The actual condition of the public finances more than realizes the favorable anticipations that were entertained of it at the opening of the last session of Congress. On the first of January there was a balance in the Treasury of $4,237,427.55. From that time to the 30th of September the receipts amounted to upward of $16.1M, and the expenditures to $11.4M. During the 4th quarter of the year it is estimated that the receipts will at least equal the expenditures, and that there will remain in the Treasury on the first day of January next a surplus of nearly $9M.

On January 1, 1825, a large amount of the war debt and a part of the Revolutionary debt become redeemable. Additional portions of the former will continue to become redeemable annually until the year 1835. It is believed, however, that if the United States remain at peace the whole of that debt may be redeemed by the ordinary revenue of those years during that period under the provision of the act of March 3, 1817, creating the sinking fund, and in that case the only part of the debt that will remain after the year 1835 will be the $7M of 5% stock subscribed to the Bank of the United States, and the 3% Revolutionary debt, amounting to $13,296,099.06, both of which are redeemable at the pleasure of the Government.

The state of the Army in its organization and discipline has been gradually improving for several years, and has now attained a high degree of perfection. The military disbursements have been regularly made and the accounts regularly and promptly rendered for settlement. The supplies of various descriptions have been of good quality, and regularly issued at all of the posts. A system of economy and accountability has been introduced into every branch of the service which admits of little additional improvement. This desirable state has been attained by the act reorganizing the staff of the Army, passed on April 14, 1818.

The moneys appropriated for fortifications have been regularly and economically applied, and all the works advanced as rapidly as the amount appropriated would admit. Three important works will be completed in the course of this year—that is, Fort

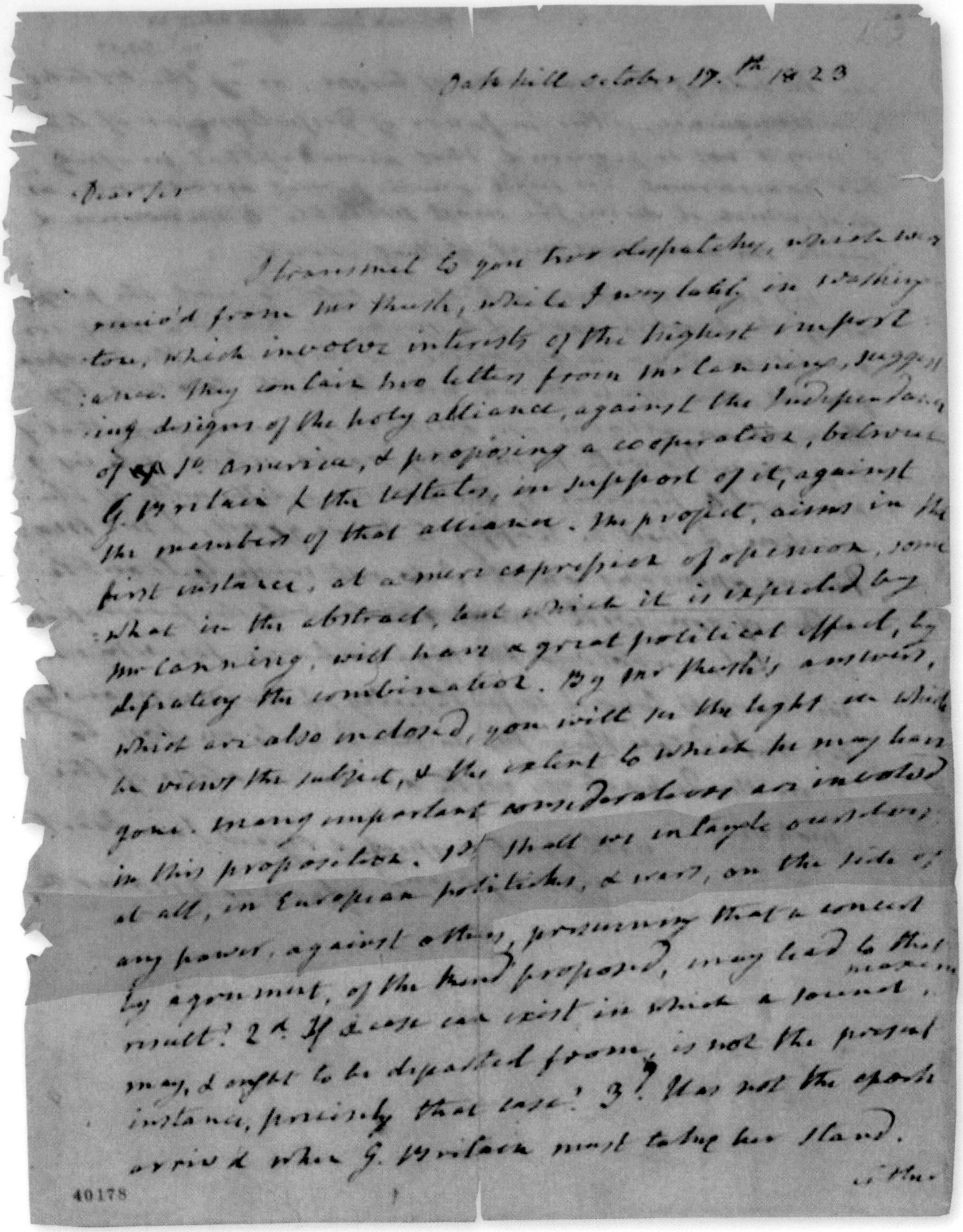

Oak hill October 17th 1823

Dear Sir

I transmit to you two despatches, which were receiv'd from Mr Rush, while I was lately in Washington, which involve interests of the highest importance. They contain two letters from Mr Canning, suggesting designs of the holy alliance, against the Independence of So America, & proposing a cooperation, between G. Britain & the U States, in support of it, against the members of that alliance. The project aims in the first instance, at a mere expression of opinion, somewhat in the abstract, but which it is expected by Mr Canning, will have a great political effect, by defeating the combination. By Mr Rush's answers, which are also enclosed, you will see the light in which he views the subject, & the extent to which he may have gone. Many important considerations are involved in this proposition. 1st Shall we entangle ourselves, at all, in European politicks, & wars, on the side of any power, against others, presuming that a concert by agreement, of the kind proposed, may lead to that result? 2d If a case can exist in which a sound maxim may, & ought to be departed from, is not the present instance, precisely that case? 3d Has not the epoch arrived when G. Britain must take her stand,

either

40178

◀ The first page of a letter that Monroe wrote to Thomas Jefferson on October 17, 1823, seeking advice on foreign policy. The highlighted line reads, "Shall we entangle ourselves at all, in European politicks and wars, on the side of any power against others?"

necessary for its defense.

The Military Academy has attained a degree of perfection in its discipline and instruction equal, as is believed, to any institution of its kind in any country.

The money appropriated for the use of the Ordnance Department has been regularly and economically applied. The fabrication of arms at the national armories and by contract with the Department has been gradually improving in quality and cheapness. It is believed that their quality is now such as to admit of but little improvement.

Washington, Fort Delaware, and the fort at the Rigolets, in Louisiana.

The Board of Engineers and the Topographical Corps have been in constant and active service in surveying the coast and projecting the works

The completion of the fortifications renders it necessary that there should be a suitable appropriation for the purpose of fabricating the cannon and carriages necessary for those works.

Under the appropriation of $5,000 for exploring the Western waters for the location of a site for a Western armory, a commission was constituted, consisting of Colonel McRee, Colonel Lee, and Captain Talcott, who have been engaged in exploring the country. They have not yet reported the result of their labors, but it is believed that they will be prepared to do it at an early part of the session of Congress.

During the month of June last General Ashley and his party, who were trading under a license from the Government, were attacked by the Ricarees while peaceably trading with the Indians at their request. Several of the party were killed and wounded and their property taken or destroyed.

Colonel Leavenworth, who commanded Fort Atkinson, at the Council Bluffs, the most western post, apprehending that the hostile spirit of the Ricarees would extend to other tribes in that quarter, and that thereby the lives of the traders on the Missouri and the peace of the frontier would be endangered, took immediate measures to check the evil.

With a detachment of the regiment stationed at the Bluffs he successfully attacked the Ricaree village, and it is hoped that such an impression has been made on them as well as on the other tribes on the Missouri as will prevent a recurrence of future hostility.

The report of the Secretary of War, which is herewith transmitted, will exhibit in greater detail the condition of the Department in its various branches, and the progress which has been made in its administration during the three first quarters of the year.

I transmit a return of the militia of the several States according to the last reports which have been made by the proper officers in each to the Department of War. by reference to this return it will be seen that it is not complete, although great exertions have been made to make it so. As the defense and even the liberties of the country must depend in times of imminent danger on the militia, it is of the highest importance that it be well organized, armed, and disciplined throughout the Union.

The report of the Secretary of War shews the progress made during the three first quarters of the present year by the application of the fund appropriated for arming the militia. Much difficulty is found in distributing the arms according to the act of Congress providing for it from the failure of the proper departments in many of the States to make regular returns. The act of May 12, 1820 provides that the system of tactics and regulations of the various corps of the Regular Army shall be extended to the militia. This act has been very imperfectly executed from the want of uniformity in the organization of the militia, proceeding from the defects of the system itself, and especially in its application to that main arm of the public defense. It is thought that this important subject in all its branches merits the attention of Congress.

The report of the Secretary of the Navy, which is now communicated, furnishes an account of the administration of that Department for the three first quarters of the present year, with the progress made in augmenting the Navy, and the manner in which the vessels in commission have been employed.

The usual force has been maintained in the Mediterranean Sea, the Pacific Ocean, and along the Atlantic coast, and has afforded the necessary protection to our commerce in those seas.

In the West Indies and the Gulf of Mexico our naval force has been augmented by the addition of several small vessels provided for by the "act authorizing an additional naval force for the suppression of piracy", passed by Congress at their last session.

That armament has been eminently successful in the accomplishment of its object. The piracies by which our commerce in the neighborhood of the island of Cuba had been afflicted have been repressed and the confidence of our merchants in a great measure restored.

The patriotic zeal and enterprise of Commodore Porter, to whom the command of the expedition was confided, has been fully seconded by the officers and men under his command. And in reflecting with high satisfaction on the honorable manner in which they have sustained the reputation of their country and its Navy, the sentiment is alloyed only by a concern that in the fulfillment of that arduous service the diseases incident to the season and to the climate in which it was discharged have deprived the nation of many useful lives, and among them of several officers of great promise.

In the month of August a very malignant fever made its appearance at Thompsons Island, which threatened the destruction of our station there. Many perished, and the commanding officer was severely attacked. Uncertain as to his fate and knowing that most of the medical officers had been rendered incapable of discharging their duties, it was thought expedient to send to that post an officer of rank and experience, with several skilled surgeons, to ascertain the origin of the fever and the probability of its recurrence there in future seasons; to furnish every assistance to those who were suffering, and, if practicable, to avoid the necessity of abandoning so important a station. Commodore Rodgers, with a promptitude which did him honor, cheerfully accepted that trust, and has discharged it in the manner anticipated from his skill and patriotism. Before his arrival Commodore Porter, with the greater part of the squadron, had removed from the island and returned to the United States in consequence of the prevailing sickness. Much useful information has, however, been obtained as to the state of the island and great relief afforded to those who had been necessarily left there.

Although our expedition, cooperating with an invigorated administration of the government of the island of Cuba, and with the corresponding active exertions of a British naval force in the same seas, have almost entirely destroyed the unlicensed piracies from that island, the success of our exertions has not been equally effectual to suppress the same crime, under other pretenses and colors, in the neighboring island of Porto Rico. They have been committed there under the abusive issue of Spanish commissions.

At an early period of the present year remonstrances were made to the governor of that island, by an agent who was sent for the purpose, against those outrages on the peaceful commerce of the United States, of which many had occurred. That officer, professing his own want of authority to make satisfaction for our just complaints, answered only by a reference of them to the Government of Spain. The minister of the United States to that court was specially instructed to urge the necessity of immediate and effectual interposition of that Government, directing restitution and indemnity for wrongs already committed and interdicting the repetition of them. The minister, as has been seen, was debarred access to the Spanish Government, and in the mean time several new cases of flagrant outrage have occurred, and citizens of the United States in the island of Porto Rico have suffered, and others been threatened with assassination for asserting their unquestionable rights even before the lawful tribunals of the country.

The usual orders have been given to all our public ships to seize American vessels in the slave trade and bring them in for adjudication, and I have the gratification to state that not one so employed has been discovered, and there is good reason to believe that our flag is now seldom, if at all, disgraced by that traffic.

It is a source of great satisfaction that we are always enabled to recur to the conduct of our Navy with price and commendation. As a means of national defense it enjoys the public confidence, and is steadily assuming additional importance. It is submitted whether a more efficient and equally economical organization of it might not in several respects be effected. It is supposed that higher grades than now exist by law would be useful. They would afford well-merited rewards to those who have long and faithfully served their country, present the best incentives to good conduct, and the best means of insuring a proper discipline; destroy the inequality in that respect between military and naval services, and relieve our officers from many inconveniences and mortifications

President James Monroe with his Secretary of State John Quincy Adams, Secretary of the Treasury William H Crawford, Attorney General William Wirt, Secretary of War John Caldwell Calhoun, Secretary of the Navy Samuel Southard and Postmaster General John McLean discussing the Monroe Doctrine.

which occur when our vessels meet those of other nations, ours being the only service in which such grades do not exist.

A report of the PostMaster-General, which accompanies this communication, will shew the present state of the Post-Office Department and its general operations for some years past.

There is established by law 88,600 miles of post roads, on which the mail is now transported 85,700 miles, and contracts have been made for its

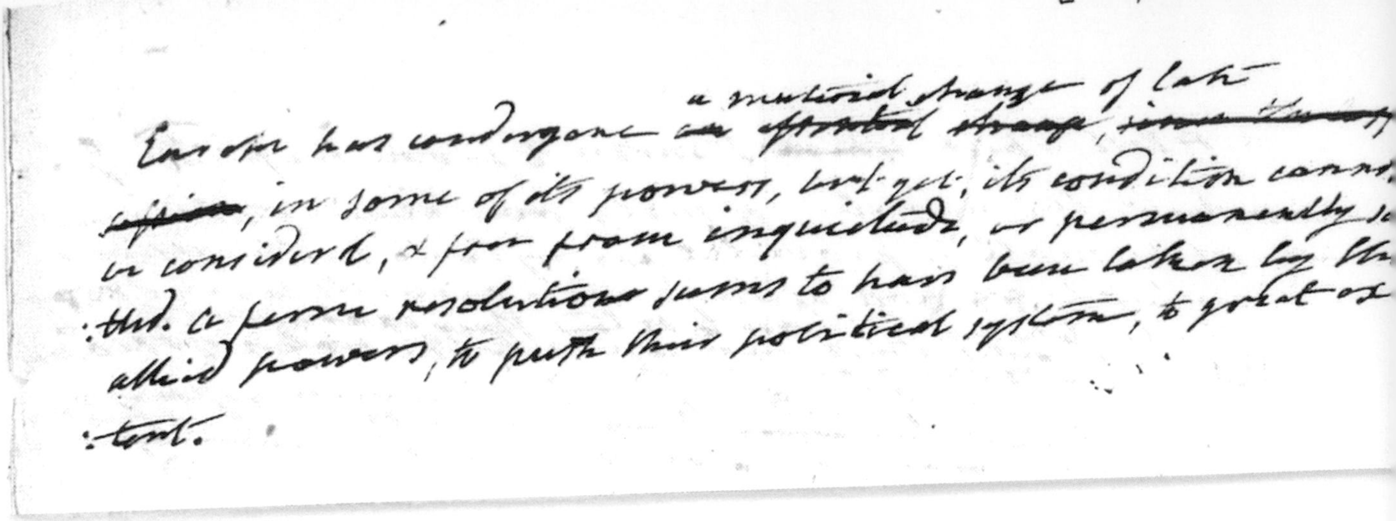

[handwritten fragment of a draft by Monroe, partially legible]

Europe has undergone a material change of late ... in some of its powers, but yet, its condition cannot be considered, ... free from inquietude, or permanently ... that a firm resolution seems to have been taken by the allied powers, to push their political system, to great extent.

transportation on all the established routes, with one or 2 exceptions. There are 5,240 post offices in the Union, and as many post masters. The gross amount of postage which accrued from July 1, 1822 to July 1, 1823 was $1,114,345.12. During the same period the expenditures of the Post-Office Department amounted to $1,169,885.51 and consisted of the following items, viz: Compensation to post masters, $353,995.98; incidental expenses, $30,866.37; transportation of the mail, $784,600.08; payments into the Treasury, $423.08. On the first of July last there was due to the Department from post masters $135,245.28; from late post masters and contractors, $256,749.31; making a total amount of balances due to the Department of $391,994.59. These balances embrace all delinquencies of post masters and contractors which have taken place since the organization of the Department. There was due by the Department to contractors on the first of July last $26,548.64. The transportation of the mail within five years past has been greatly extended, and the expenditures of the Department proportionably increased. Although the postage which has accrued within the last three years has fallen short of the expenditures $262,821.46, it appears that collections have been made from the outstanding balances to meet the principal part of the current demands.

▲▶ Fragments of a draft of the address written by Monroe.

It is estimated that not more than $250,000 of the above balances can be collected, and that a considerable part of this sum can only be realized by a resort to legal process. Some improvements in the receipts for postage is expected. A prompt attention to the collection of moneys received by post masters, it is believed, will enable the Department to continue its operations without aid from the Treasury, unless the expenditures shall be increased by the establishment of new mail routes.

A revision of some parts of the post office law may be necessary; and it is submitted whether it would not be proper to provide for the appointment of post masters, where the compensation exceeds a certain amount, by nomination to the Senate, as other officers of the General Government are appointed.

Having communicated my views to Congress at the commencement of the last session respecting the encouragement which ought to be given to our manufactures and the principle on which it should be founded, I have only to add that those views remain unchanged, and that the present state of those countries with which we have the most immediate political relations and greatest commercial intercourse tends to confirm them. Under this

The sum which was appropriated at the last session for the repair of the Cumberland road, has been applied with good effect to that object. It is understood however, that it was inadequate to its accomplishment. A final report has not yet been rec'd. from the agent who was appointed to superintend it. As soon as it is, it shall be communicated to congress.

Many patriotic & enlightened citizens who have made an object of particular investigation, have suggested an improvement of still greater importance. They are decidedly of opinion, that the waters of the ohio, may be connected together by one continued canal, & at an expense, far short of the importance of the object to be obtained. If this can be accomplished, it is impossible to calculate the beneficial consequences which would result from it. A great portion of the produce of the very fertile country through which it would pass, would find a market through that channel. Troops, might be moved with great facility in war, with cannon, & every kind of munition. In connecting the atlantic with the western country, in a line passing through the seat of the national gov't, it would contribute essentially to strengthen the bond of union itself. Believing as I do, that congress possess the right to appropriate money, for such a national object, the jurisdiction remaining to the states, through which the canal would pass, I submit it to your consideration whether it may not be advisable, to authorize, by an adequate appropriation, the employment of a suitable number of the officers of the corps of engineers, unemployed, to examine the ground, in the next season, impression I recommend a review of the tariff for the purpose of affording such additional protection to those articles which we are prepared to manufacture, or which are more immediately connected with the defense and independence of the country.

The actual state of the public accounts furnishes additional evidence of the efficiency of the present system of accountability in relation to the public expenditure. Of the moneys drawn from the Treasury since March 4, 1817, the sum remaining unaccounted for on the 30th of September last is more than $1.5M less than on the 30th of September preceding; and during the same period a reduction of nearly $1M has been made in the amount of the unsettled accounts for moneys advanced previously to March 4, 1817. It will be obvious that in proportion as the mass of accounts of the latter description is diminished by settlement the difficulty of settling the residue is increased from the consideration that in many instances it can be obtained only by legal process. For more precise details on this subject I refer to a report from the first Comptroller of the Treasury.

The sum which was appropriated at the last session for the repairs of the Cumberland road has been applied with good effect to that object. A final report has not been received from the agent who was appointed to superintend it. As soon as it is received it shall be communicated to Congress.

Many patriotic and enlightened citizens who have made the subject an object of particular investigation have suggested an improvement of still greater importance. They are of the opinion that the waters of the Chesapeake and Ohio may be connected together by one continued canal, and at an expense far short of the value and importance of the object to be obtained. If this could be accomplished it is impossible to calculate the beneficial consequences which would result from it.

A great portion of the produce of the very fertile country through which it would pass would find a market through that channel. Troops might be moved with great facility in war, with cannon and every kind of munition, and in either direction. Connecting the Atlantic with the Western country in a line passing through the seat of the National Government, it would contribute essentially to strengthen the bond of union itself.

Believing as I do that Congress possess the right to appropriate money for such a national object (the jurisdiction remaining to the States through which the canal would pass), I submit it to your consideration whether it may not be advisable to authorize by an adequate appropriation the employment of a suitable number of the officers of the Corps of Engineers to examine the unexplored ground during the next season and to report their opinion thereon. It will likewise be proper to extend their examination to the several routes through which the waters of the Ohio may be connected by canals with those of Lake Erie.

As the Cumberland road will require annual repairs, and Congress have not thought it expedient to recommend to the States an amendment to the Constitution for the purpose of vesting in the United States a power to adopt and execute a system of internal improvement, it is also submitted to your consideration whether it may not be expedient to authorize the Executive to enter into an arrangement with the several States through which the road passes to establish tolls, each within its limits, for the purpose of defraying the expense of future repairs and of providing also by suitable penalties for its protection against future injuries.

The act of Congress of May 7, 1822, appropriated the sum of $22,700 for the purpose of erecting two piers as a shelter for vessels from ice near Cape Henlopen, Delaware Bay. To effect the object of the act the officers of the Board of Engineers, with

Commodore Bainbridge, were directed to prepare plans and estimates of piers sufficient to answer the purpose intended by the act. It appears by their report, which accompanies the documents from the War Department, that the appropriation is not adequate to the purpose intended; and as the piers would be of great service both to the navigation of the Delaware Bay and the protection of vessels on the adjacent parts of the coast, I submit for the consideration of Congress whether additional and sufficient appropriations should not be made.

The Board of Engineers were also directed to examine and survey the entrance of the harbor of the port of Presquille, in PA, in order to make an estimate of the expense of removing the obstructions to the entrance, with a plan of the best mode of effecting the same, under the appropriation for that purpose by act of Congress passed 3rd of March last. The report of the Board accompanies the papers from the War Department, and is submitted for the consideration of Congress.

A strong hope has been long entertained, founded on the heroic struggle of the Greeks, that they would succeed in their contest and resume their equal station among the nations of the earth. It is believed that the whole civilized world take a deep interest in

▼ A fragment of a draft of the address written by Monroe.

their welfare. Although no power has declared in their favor, yet none according to our information, has taken part against them. Their cause and their name have protected them from dangers which might ere this have overwhelmed any other people. The ordinary calculations of interest and of acquisition with a view to aggrandizement, which mingles so much in the transactions of nations, seem to have had no effect in regard to them. From the facts which have come to our knowledge there is good cause to believe that their enemy has lost forever all dominion over them; that Greece will become again an independent nation. That she may obtain that rank is the object of our most ardent wishes.

It was stated at the commencement of the last session that a great effort was then making in Spain and Portugal to improve the condition of the people of those countries, and that it appeared to be conducted with extraordinary moderation. It need scarcely be remarked that the result has been so far very different from what was then anticipated. Of events in that quarter of the globe, with which we have so much intercourse and from which we derive our origin, we have always been anxious and interested spectators.

The citizens of the United States cherish sentiments the most friendly in favor of the liberty and happiness of their fellow men on that side of the Atlantic. In the wars of the European powers in matters relating to themselves we have never taken any part, nor does it comport with our policy so to do.

It is only when our rights are invaded or seriously menaced that we resent injuries or make preparation for our defense. With the movements in this hemisphere we are of necessity more immediately connected, and by causes which must be obvious to all enlightened and impartial observers.

The political system of the allied powers is essentially different in this respect from that of America. This difference proceeds from that which exists in their respective Governments; and to the defense of our own, which has been achieved by the loss of so much blood and treasure, and matured by the wisdom of their most enlightened citizens, and under which we have enjoyed unexampled felicity, this whole nation is devoted.

We owe it, therefore, to candor and to the amicable relations existing between the United States and those powers to declare that we should consider any attempt on their part to extend their system to any portion of this hemisphere as dangerous to our peace and safety. With the existing colonies or dependencies of any European power we have not interfered and shall not interfere, but with the Governments who have declared their independence and maintained it, and whose independence we have, on great consideration and on just principles, acknowledged, we could not view any interposition for the purpose of oppressing them, or controlling in any other manner their destiny, by any European power in any other light than as the manifestation of an unfriendly disposition toward the United States.

In the war between those new Governments and Spain we declared our neutrality at the time of their recognition, and to this we have adhered, and shall continue to adhere, provided no change shall occur which, in the judgment of the competent authorities of this Government, shall make a corresponding change on the part of the United States indispensable to their security.

The late events in Spain and Portugal shew that Europe is still unsettled. Of this important fact no stronger proof can be adduced than that the allied powers should have thought it proper, on any principle satisfactory to themselves, to have interposed by force in the internal concerns of Spain. To what extent such interposition may be carried, on the same principle, is a question in which all independent powers whose governments differ from theirs are interested, even those most remote, and surely none more so than the United States.

Our policy in regard to Europe, which was adopted at an early stage of the wars which have so long agitated that quarter of the globe, nevertheless remains the same, which is, not to interfere in the internal concerns of any of its powers; to consider the government de facto as the legitimate government for us; to cultivate friendly relations with it, and to preserve those relations by a frank, firm, and manly policy, meeting in all instances the just claims of every power, submitting to injuries from none.

But in regard to those continents circumstances are eminently and conspicuously different. It is impossible that the allied powers should extend their political system to any portion of either continent without endangering our peace and happiness; nor can anyone believe that our southern brethren, if left to themselves, would adopt it of their own accord. It is equally impossible, therefore, that we should behold such interposition in any form with indifference. If we look to the comparative strength and resources of Spain and those new Governments, and their distance from each other, it must be obvious that she can never subdue them. It is still the true policy of the United States to leave the parties to themselves, in the hope that other powers will pursue the same course.

If we compare the present condition of our Union with its actual state at the close of our Revolution, the history of the world furnishes no example of a progress in improvement in all the important circumstances which constitute the happiness of a nation which bears any resemblance to it. At the first epoch our population did not exceed 3,000,000. by the last census it amounted to about 10,000,000, and, what is more extraordinary, it is almost altogether native, for the immigration from other countries has been inconsiderable.

At the first epoch half the territory within our acknowledged limits was uninhabited and a wilderness. Since then new territory has been acquired of vast extent, comprising within it many rivers, particularly the Mississippi, the navigation of which to the ocean was of the highest importance to the original States. Over this territory our population has expanded in every direction, and new States have been established almost equal in number to those which formed the first bond of our Union. This expansion of our population and accession of new States to our Union have had the happiest effect on all its highest interests.

That it has eminently augmented our resources and added to our strength and respectability as a power is admitted by all, but it is not in these important circumstances only that this happy effect is felt. It is manifest that by enlarging the basis of our system and increasing the number of States the system itself has been greatly strengthened in both its branches. Consolidation and disunion have thereby been rendered equally impracticable.

Each Government, confiding in its own strength, has less to apprehend from the other, and in consequence each, enjoying a greater freedom of action, is rendered more efficient for all the purposes for which it was instituted.

It is unnecessary to treat here of the vast improvement made in the system itself by the adoption of this Constitution and of its happy effect in elevating the character and in protecting the rights of the nation as well as individuals. To what, then, do we owe these blessings? It is known to all that we derive them from the excellence of our institutions. Ought we not, then, to adopt every measure which may be necessary to perpetuate them?

President Abraham Lincoln

> " We are not enemies, but friends. We must not be enemies. Though passion may have strained it must not break our bonds of affection. "

As he stood to deliver his inaugural address on March 4, 1861, few in the crowd of dignitaries and spectators on the east lawn of the US Capitol knew what Abraham Lincoln was going to say about the policies of his new Administration toward a United States that was no longer composed of united states.

In the four months since Lincoln's election in November, seven Southern states had seceded from the Union to form the Confederate States of America. Lincoln's ineffectual predecessor, James Buchanan, had deplored secession but maintained that there was nothing the federal government could do about it. As he and Lincoln rode to

the inauguration that day, observers said that Buchanan appeared visibly relieved to be handing off a problem that he had done nothing to forestall during his term in office.

It was, however, Lincoln's very election that had brought the issue to a head. Southern slaveholders believed that the Republican Party was dominated by Northern abolitionists and that not only their economic interests but their very way of life was threatened by Lincoln's election as that new party's first occupant of the White House.

Perhaps the only man on the inauguration day platform who knew what Lincoln would say was his new secretary of state, William H. Seward. Lincoln had maintained a strict silence about his intentions toward the Confederates in public statements following his election. He had drafted his inaugural speech in Springfield, Illinois, before leaving for Washington, and had made many revisions over a period of months. He showed the draft to a few old friends, which was in itself unusual, in that Lincoln rarely consulted anyone about his speeches. Several of them made minor suggestions, but most praised the speech as written.

Lincoln Turns to Rival for Help

Seward and Lincoln were not friends, but recent rivals for the Republican presidential nomination. After Lincoln won, he reached out to Seward, a longtime political power in New York State, to join his Cabinet. After arriving in Washington ten days before the inauguration, he again reached out to Seward—a man he barely knew—for his opinion

▲ An 1860s portrait of Abraham Lincoln.

on the most important speech of his life. It was an unprecedented step.

Lincoln addressed the entire speech to the dissident Southerners, to whom he wanted to make three major points:
• First, that he intended as president to keep property belonging to the federal government—including Fort Sumter, in the seceded state of South Carolina;
• Second, that the Union under terms of the Constitution could not be dissolved, and this secession was not only illegal but impossible;
• Third, that he would never attack, but use of arms against the United States would be regarded as rebellion, and would be met with force.

The draft that Lincoln showed to Seward made those points in very strong terms, and closed with a warning to the South that, as president, he would be that day swearing a solemn oath to "preserve, protect and defend" the Union. "You can forbear the assault upon it; I can not shrink from the defense of it," read his original closing sentence, "with you, and not with me, is the solemn question of 'Shall it be peace, or a sword?'"

Seward Tells Lincoln to Soften the Tone

Seward sent back a six-page letter with forty-nine suggestions. In general, he said, he approved of the construction and of the arguments Lincoln wanted to make. His changes were mostly words designed to soften the tone and "soothe the public mind," he wrote. Seward reminded Lincoln of the situation facing Thomas Jefferson, winner of a closely contested election and faced with the anger of defeated Federalists (see the Jefferson chapter). Jefferson had successfully soothed

▲ An extract from a draft of the speech with written suggestions from Seward, perhaps the most important being his crossing out of the line "Shall it be peace, or a sword?"

the Federalists with the conciliatory tone of his inaugural address.

Lincoln's dilemma was even more dire, Seward pointed out, and Lincoln, while holding to his position about the indissolubility of the Union, should hold out an olive branch. Lincoln certainly could and should conduct his Administration according to Republican principles and make it clear that he would be unyielding in his efforts to preserve the Union, Seward counseled. However, he would not lose his party's support by being a magnanimous victor and offering soothing words to the disaffected Southerners.

Lincoln agreed with Seward, and in the few remaining days before the speech was to be delivered, he moderated the tone of the speech considerably, incorporating more than half of Seward's suggestions and making many more of his own.

Lincoln Takes to the Platform

No inauguration in the history of the country had taken place amid such uproar and disorder. Ten days earlier, Lincoln had been forced to slip stealthily into Washington to foil hostile Southern sympathizers between Illinois and Washington, who had talked openly of assassination and invasion of the nation's capital. Many hundreds of soldiers were strategically placed on the parade route to the inaugural site, and sharpshooters stood on every rooftop along Pennsylvania Avenue. Plainclothes detectives roamed the crowd, estimated at between 25,000 and 30,000 people.

After preliminary ceremonies in the Senate Chamber, the participants walked to a special inaugural platform that had been constructed on the east front of the Capitol, and in cold, blustery weather Lincoln began to speak in a clear, ringing tenor voice that was audible to the thousands who had been able to crowd in most closely.

Lincoln was a lawyer, and this was a lawyerly speech. It consisted largely of statements of his positions and logical arguments in support of those positions. His words were carefully chosen, starting with his opening salutation to "Fellow citizens of the United States." Observers noted that he emphasized the word "united." His opening words were, "In compliance with a custom as old as the government itself, I appear before you . . . to take . . . the oath prescribed by the Constitution of the United States."

In those few simple words, without rhetorical embellishment, Lincoln stressed the authority of the Constitution, and recalled the history of the nation and the continuity of the Union.

He then said that his speech would not deal with "matters of administration about which there is no special anxiety or excitement," clearly indicating that he would address a single topic—secession—and direct his remarks only toward the rebellious Southerners. In his final draft, he had removed several introductory paragraphs about the Republican platform, which Seward thought might sound too sectional and divisive.

Offering Assurances on Slavery

Lincoln then moved in lawyerly fashion to further placate the Southerners, assuring them that their "property, and their peace, and personal security" would not be threatened under his presidency. He pointed to his previous record on slavery, quoting from a speech in which he had pledged not to interfere "with the institution of slavery in the states where it exists." He referred to his target audience as "the people of the Southern States," underscoring his position that they were still part of the Union.

Lincoln also stated that he found nothing in the Constitution that specifically excluded the expansion of slavery to the territories, and that he would abide by the Constitution in upholding the legality and enforcement of fugitive slave laws.

Invoking the Constitution in regard to slavery allowed Lincoln to move on to his larger point, and to move swiftly from conciliation to firmness. Taking the oath as president, he pointed out, bound him to adhere to the precedents of the Constitution in all areas. He again referred to the continuity of the republic by pointing out that it had been seventy-two years since the first inauguration of a president under the Constitution. The republic, he said, had existed for longer than the Constitution had been in effect—since the first Articles of Association in 1774—and the purpose of the Constitution in 1787 was to "form a more perfect union," the repetition of the words "Constitution" and "Union" underscoring his points throughout the speech.

In taking the oath, he said, "I hold that in contemplation of universal law, and of the Constitution, the Union of these States is perpetual. Perpetuity is implied, if not expressed, in the fundamental law of all national governments. It is safe to assert that no government proper, ever had a provision in its organic law for its own termination."

▼ Crowds gather around the US Capitol, which is still under construction, to view the inauguration of Abraham Lincoln.

Secession Illegal, Unconstitutional

Secession, therefore, was not only illegal but also unconstitutional and impossible because of the way the Union was formed under the Constitution. Even if the Union was merely an aggregation of states, could it be dissolved by unilateral action of one or more and without the consent of all states? "Plainly," he added, "the central idea of secession is the essence of anarchy."

Lincoln buttresses this argument with further discussion of the Constitution, before pointing out that the strength of the Union under the Constitution is such that "While the people retain their virtue and vigilance, no administration, by any extreme of wickedness or folly, can very seriously injure the government in the short space of four years." In other words, do not act rashly. Calm down and give such an important matter a little time.

Lincoln then shifts dramatically from the logical tone he had used throughout the speech to a dramatic conclusion. His final two paragraphs are a challenge to the South, and a reaffirmation of faith in the Union.

The penultimate paragraph, drafted in Springfield, brings the issue from the past to the present and deals frankly with the current situation. Lincoln

▲ Seward's suggested last paragraph for the speech, in his own handwriting.

has made all of the constitutional arguments for preservation of the Union, but if logic does not prevail—as he knows it probably will not—he places the onus for Civil War on the Southern secessionists. "The government will not assail you. You can have no conflict without being yourselves the aggressors. You have no oath registered in Heaven to destroy the government, while I shall have the most solemn one to 'preserve, protect, and defend it.'"

laws of your own framing under it; while the new administration will have no imme-diate power, if it would, to change either. If it were admitted that you who are dissatisfied, hold the right side in the dispute, there still is no single good reason for precipitate action. Intelligence, patriotism, Christianity, and a firm reliance on Him, who has never yet forsaken this favored land, are still competent to adjust, in the best way, all our present difficulty.

7744   In your hands, my dissatisfied fellow countrymen, and not in *mine*, is the moment-ous issue of civil war. The government will not assail *you*. You can have no conflict, without being yourselves the aggressors. You have no oath registered in Heaven to destroy the government, while *I* shall have the most solemn one to "preserve, protect and defend" it.

but friends— We must not be enemies. We are not enemies, have strained, it must not break our bonds of affection. Though passion may the mystic chords of memory, stretching from every battle-field, and patriot grave, to every living heart and hearth-stone, all over this broad land, will yet swell the cho-rus of the Union, when again touched, as surely they will be, by the better angels of our nature.

Seward Was Good, Lincoln Was Great

One interesting development of the speech is that the final paragraph originated with Seward, and replaced Lincoln's own "peace or a sword" conclusion. Lincoln took Seward's words and recast them into his own inimitable style. Seward's ideas were good, and he was himself a noted orator. Lincoln made few changes, but they were vital. Comparing Seward's version with Lincoln's simply serves to underscore Lincoln's greatness. As with so many others of Lincoln's words, the closing is economical, poetic, powerful, and profoundly moving.

"I am loath to close," said Lincoln. "We are not enemies, but friends. We must not be enemies. Though passion may have strained, it must not break our bonds of affection. The mystic chords of memory, stretching from every battle-field, and patriot grave, to every living heart and hearth-stone, all over this broad land, will yet swell the chorus of the Union, when again touched, as surely they will be, by the better angels of our nature."

▲ A printed draft of the speech with the last paragraph added by Lincoln in his own hand.

Compare that final sentence with Seward's: "The mystic chords which, proceeding from so many battlefields, and so many patriot graves, pass through all the hearts and all of the hearths in this broad continent of ours, will yet again harmonize in their ancient music when breathed upon by the guardian angel of the nation."

As Mark Twain once observed, the difference between the almost right word and the right word is the difference between the lightning bug and the lightning. Lincoln had the gift of lightning.

The speech, of course, changed nothing. Republican politicians and newspapers praised it; Southerners excoriated it. Four more states seceded, shots were fired at Fort Sumter, and the war soon commenced. But in his inaugural address, Lincoln took the high moral ground and showed his steely resolve to hold it, over the next four bloody years, to preserve the Union.

First Inaugural Address
March 4, 1861, United States Capitol, Washington, DC

Fellow-Citizens of the United States:

In compliance with a custom as old as the Government itself, I appear before you to address you briefly and to take in your presence the oath prescribed by the Constitution of the United States to be taken by the President before he enters on the execution of this office.

I do not consider it necessary at present for me to discuss those matters of administration about which there is no special anxiety or excitement.

Apprehension seems to exist among the people of the Southern States that by the accession of a Republican Administration their property and their peace and personal security are to be endangered. There has never been any reasonable cause for such apprehension. Indeed, the most ample evidence to the

◄ A page from a printed draft of the speech with the line "I do not consider it necessary at present for me to discuss those matters of administration about which there is no special anxiety or excitement." pasted on in Lincoln's handwriting.

contrary has all the while existed and been open to their inspection. It is found in nearly all the published speeches of him who now addresses you. I do but quote from one of those speeches when I declare that–

I have no purpose, directly or indirectly, to interfere with the institution of slavery in the States where it exists. I believe I have no lawful right to do so, and I have no inclination to do so.

Those who nominated and elected me did so with full knowledge that I had made this and many similar declarations and had never recanted them; and more than this, they placed in the platform for my acceptance, and as a law to themselves and to me, the clear and emphatic resolution which I now read:

Resolved, That the maintenance inviolate of the rights of the States, and especially the right of each State to order and control its own domestic institutions according to its own judgment exclusively, is essential to that balance of power on which the perfection and endurance of our political fabric depend; and we denounce the lawless invasion by armed force of the soil of any State or Territory, no matter what pretext, as among the gravest of crimes.

I now reiterate these sentiments, and in doing so I only press upon the public attention the most conclusive evidence of which the case is susceptible that the property, peace, and security of no section are to be in any wise endangered by the now incoming Administration. I add, too, that all the protection which, consistently with the Constitution and the laws, can be given will be cheerfully given to all the States when lawfully demanded, for whatever cause – as cheerfully to one section as to another.

There is much controversy about the delivering up of fugitives from service or labor. The clause I now read is as plainly written in the Constitution as any other of its provisions:

No person held to service or labor in one State, under the laws thereof, escaping into another, shall in consequence of any law or regulation therein be discharged from such service or labor, but shall be delivered up on claim of the party to whom such service or labor may be due.

It is scarcely questioned that this provision was intended by those who made it for the reclaiming of what we call fugitive slaves; and the intention of the lawgiver is the law. All members of Congress swear their support to the whole Constitution – to this provision as much as to any other. To the proposition, then, that slaves whose cases come within the terms of this clause "shall be delivered up" their oaths are unanimous. Now, if they would make the effort in good temper, could they not with nearly equal unanimity frame and pass a law by means of which to keep good that unanimous oath?

There is some difference of opinion whether this clause should be enforced by national or by State authority, but surely that difference is not a very material one. If the slave is to be surrendered, it can be of but little consequence to him or to others by which authority it is done. And should anyone in any case be content that his oath shall go unkept on a merely unsubstantial controversy as to how it shall be kept?

Again: In any law upon this subject ought not all the safeguards of liberty known in civilized and humane jurisprudence to be introduced, so that a free man be not in any case surrendered as a slave? And might it not be well at the same time to provide by law for the enforcement of that clause in the Constitution which guarantees that "the citizens of each State shall be entitled to all privileges and immunities of citizens in the several States"?

I take the official oath to-day with no mental reservations and with no purpose to construe the Constitution or laws by any hypercritical rules; and while I do not choose now to specify particular acts of Congress as proper to be enforced, I do suggest that

It is ~~now~~ seventy-two years since the first inauguration of a President under our national Constitution. During that period fifteen different and greatly distinguished citizens, have, in succession, administered the executive branch of the *generally,* government. They have conducted it through many perils; and, ~~generally~~ with great success. Yet, with all this scope for precedent, I now enter upon the same task for the brief constitutional term of four years, under great and peculiar difficulty. A disruption of the Federal Union, *heretofore only menaced, is now formidably attempted.*

I hold, that in contemplation of universal law, and of the Constitution, the Union of these States is perpetual. Perpetuity is implied, if not expressed, in the fundamental law of all national governments. It is safe to assert that no government proper, ever had a provision in its organic law for its own termination. Continue to execute all the express provisions of our national Constitution, and the Union will endure forever—it being impossible to destroy it, except by some action not provided for in the instrument itself.

Again, if the United States be not a government proper, but an association of States in the nature of contract merely, can it, as a contract, be peaceably unmade, by less than all the parties who made it? One party to a contract may violate it—break it, so to speak; but does it not require all to lawfully rescind it?

Descending from these general principles, we find the proposition that, in legal contemplation, the Union is perpetual, confirmed by the history of the Union itself. The Union is much older than the Constitution. It was formed in fact, by the Articles of Association in 1774. It was matured and continued by the Declaration of Independ- *and the faith of all the then thirteen States expressly plighted and engaged that it should be.* ence in 1776. It was further matured perpetual, by the Articles of Confederation in 1778. And finally, in 1787, one of the declared objects for ordaining and establishing the Constitution, was "to form a more perfect union."

But if destruction of the Union, by one, or by a part only, of the States, be lawfully possible, the Union is *less* perfect than before the Constitution, *having lost the vital element of perpetuity—*

It follows from these views that no State, upon its own mere motion, can lawfully *void;* get out of the Union,—that resolves and ordinances to that effect are legally ~~~~ and that acts of violence, within any State or States, against the authority of the *revolutionary* United States, are insurrectionary or ~~~~, according to circumstances.

▲ A printed draft of the speech, with handwritten amendments added by Lincoln.

it will be much safer for all, both in official and private stations, to conform to and abide by all those acts which stand unrepealed than to violate any of them trusting to find impunity in having them held to be unconstitutional.

It is seventy-two years since the first inauguration of a President under our National Constitution. During that period fifteen different and greatly distinguished citizens have in succession administered the executive branch of the Government. They have conducted it through many perils, and generally with great success. Yet, with all this scope of precedent, I now enter upon the same task for the brief constitutional term of four years under great and peculiar difficulty. A disruption of the Federal Union, heretofore only menaced, is now formidably attempted.

I hold that in contemplation of universal law and of the Constitution the Union of these States is perpetual. Perpetuity is implied, if not expressed, in the fundamental law of all national governments. It is safe to assert that no government proper ever had a provision in its organic law for its own termination. Continue to execute all the express provisions of our National Constitution, and the Union will endure forever, it being impossible to destroy it except by some action not provided for in the instrument itself.

Again: If the United States be not a government proper, but an association of States in the nature of contract merely, can it, as a contract, be peaceably unmade by less than all the parties who made it? One party to a contract may violate it – break it, so to speak – but does it not require all to lawfully rescind it?

Descending from these general principles, we find the proposition that in legal contemplation the Union is perpetual confirmed by the history of the Union itself. The Union is much older than the Constitution. It was formed, in fact, by the Articles of Association in 1774. It was matured and continued by the Declaration of Independence in 1776. It was further matured, and the faith of all the then thirteen States expressly plighted and engaged that it should be perpetual, by the Articles of Confederation in 1778. And finally, in 1787, one of the declared objects for ordaining and establishing the Constitution was "to form a more perfect Union."

But if destruction of the Union by one or by a part only of the States be lawfully possible, the Union is less perfect than before the Constitution, having lost the vital element of perpetuity. It follows from these views that no State upon its own mere motion can lawfully get out of the Union; that resolves and ordinances to that effect are legally void, and that acts of violence within any State or States against the authority of the United States are insurrectionary or revolutionary, according to circumstances.

I therefore consider that in view of the Constitution and the laws the Union is unbroken, and to the extent of my ability, I shall take care, as the Constitution itself expressly enjoins upon me, that the laws of the Union be faithfully executed in all the States. Doing this I deem to be only a simple duty on my part, and I shall perform it so far as practicable unless my rightful masters, the American people, shall withhold the requisite means or in some authoritative manner direct the contrary. I trust this will not be regarded as a menace, but only as the declared purpose of the Union that it will constitutionally defend and maintain itself.

In doing this there needs to be no bloodshed or violence, and there shall be none unless it be forced upon the national authority. The power confided to me will be used to hold, occupy, and possess the property and places belonging to the Government and to collect the duties and imposts; but beyond what may be necessary for these objects, there will be no invasion, no using of force against or among the people anywhere. Where hostility to the United States in any interior locality shall be so great and universal as to prevent competent resident citizens from holding the Federal offices, there will be no attempt to force obnoxious strangers among the people for that object. While the strict legal right may exist in the Government to enforce the exercise of these offices, the attempt to do so would be so irritating and so nearly impracticable withal that I deem it better to forego for the time the uses of such offices.

The mails, unless repelled, will continue to be furnished in all parts of the Union. So far as possible the people everywhere shall have that sense of perfect security which is most favorable to calm thought and reflection. The course here indicated will be followed unless current events and experience shall show a modification or change to be proper, and in every case and exigency my best discretion will be exercised, according to circumstances actually existing and with a view and a hope of a peaceful solution of the national troubles and the restoration of fraternal sympathies and affections.

That there are persons in one section or another who seek to destroy the Union at all events and are glad of any pretext to do it I will neither affirm nor deny; but if there be such, I need address no word to them. To those, however, who really love the Union may I not speak?

Before entering upon so grave a matter as the destruction of our national fabric, with all its benefits, its memories, and its hopes, would it not be wise to ascertain precisely why we do it? Will you hazard so desperate a step while there is any possibility that any portion of the ills you fly from have no real existence? Will you, while the certain ills you fly to are greater than all the real ones you fly from, will you risk the commission of so fearful a mistake?

All profess to be content in the Union if all constitutional rights can be maintained. Is it true, then, that any right plainly written in the Constitution has been denied? I think not. Happily, the human mind is so constituted that no party can reach to the audacity of doing this. Think, if you can, of a single instance in which a plainly written provision of the Constitution has ever been denied. If by the mere force of numbers a majority should deprive a minority of any clearly written constitutional right, it might in a moral point of view justify revolution; certainly would if such right were a vital one. But such is not our case. All the vital rights of minorities and of individuals are so plainly assured to them by affirmations and negations, guaranties and prohibitions, in the Constitution that controversies never arise concerning them. But no organic law can ever be framed with a provision specifically applicable to every question which may occur in practical administration. No foresight can anticipate nor any document of reasonable length contain express provisions for all possible questions. Shall fugitives from labor be surrendered by national or by State authority? The Constitution does not expressly say. May Congress prohibit slavery in the Territories? The Constitution does not expressly say. Must Congress protect slavery in the Territories? The Constitution does not expressly say.

From questions of this class spring all our constitutional controversies, and we divide upon them into majorities and minorities. If the minority will not acquiesce, the majority must, or the Government must cease. There is no other alternative, for continuing the Government is acquiescence on one side or the other. If a minority in such case will secede rather than acquiesce, they make a precedent which in turn will divide and ruin them, for a minority of their own will secede from them whenever a majority refuses to be controlled by such minority. For instance, why may not any portion of a new confederacy a year or two hence arbitrarily secede again, precisely as portions of the present Union now claim to secede from it? All who cherish disunion sentiments are now being educated to the exact temper of doing this.

Is there such perfect identity of interests among the States to compose a new union as to produce harmony only and prevent renewed secession?

Plainly the central idea of secession is the essence of anarchy. A majority held in restraint by constitutional checks and limitations, and always changing easily with deliberate changes of popular opinions and sentiments, is the only true sovereign of a free people. Whoever rejects it does of necessity fly to anarchy or to despotism. Unanimity is impossible. The rule of a minority, as a permanent arrangement, is wholly inadmissible; so that, rejecting the majority principle, anarchy or despotism in some form is all that is left.

I do not forget the position assumed by some that constitutional questions are to be decided by the

Supreme Court, nor do I deny that such decisions must be binding in any case upon the parties to a suit as to the object of that suit, while they are also entitled to very high respect and consideration in all parallel cases by all other departments of the Government. And while it is obviously possible that such decision may be erroneous in any given case, still the evil effect following it, being limited to that particular case, with the chance that it may be overruled and never become a precedent for other cases, can better be borne than could the evils of a different practice. At the same time, the candid citizen must confess that if the policy of the Government upon vital questions affecting the whole people is to be irrevocably fixed by decisions of the Supreme Court, the instant they are made in ordinary litigation between parties in personal actions the people will have ceased to be their own rulers, having to that extent practically resigned their Government into the hands of that eminent tribunal. Nor is there in this view any assault upon the court or the judges. It is a duty from which they may not shrink to decide cases properly brought before them, and it is no fault of theirs if others seek to turn their decisions to political purposes.

One section of our country believes slavery is right and ought to be extended, while the other believes it is wrong and ought not to be extended. This is the only substantial dispute. The fugitive-slave clause of the Constitution and the law for the suppression of the foreign slave trade are each as well enforced, perhaps, as any law can ever be in a community where the moral sense of the people imperfectly supports the law itself. The great body of the people abide by the dry legal obligation in both cases, and a few break over in each. This, I think, can not be perfectly cured, and it would be worse in both cases after the separation of the sections than before. The foreign slave trade, now imperfectly suppressed, would be ultimately revived without restriction in one section, while fugitive slaves, now only partially surrendered, would not be surrendered at all by the other.

◀ Lincoln's re-working of a section of the speech, shown attached to a printed draft.

▲ An engraved portrait of William Henry Seward, who was instrumental in the softening of the tone of Lincoln's speech.

Physically speaking, we can not separate. We can not remove our respective sections from each other nor build an impassable wall between them. A husband and wife may be divorced and go out of the presence and beyond the reach of each other, but the different parts of our country can not do this. They can not but remain face to face, and intercourse, either amicable or hostile, must continue between them. Is it possible, then, to make that intercourse more advantageous or more satisfactory after separation than before? Can aliens make treaties easier than friends can make laws? Can treaties be more faithfully enforced between aliens than laws can among friends? Suppose you go to war, you can not fight always; and when, after much loss on both sides and no gain on either, you cease fighting, the identical old questions, as to terms of intercourse, are again upon you.

This country, with its institutions, belongs to the people who inhabit it. Whenever they shall grow weary of the existing Government, they can exercise their constitutional right of amending it or their revolutionary right to dismember or overthrow it. I can not be ignorant of the fact that many worthy and patriotic citizens are desirous of having the National Constitution amended. While I make no recommendation of amendments, I fully recognize the rightful authority of the people over the whole subject, to be exercised in either of the modes prescribed in the instrument itself; and I should, under existing circumstances, favor rather than oppose a fair opportunity being afforded the people to act upon it. I will venture to add that to me the convention mode seems preferable, in that it allows amendments to originate with the people themselves, instead of only permitting them to take or reject propositions originated by others, not especially chosen for the purpose, and which might not be precisely such as they would wish to either accept or refuse. I understand a proposed amendment to the Constitution – which amendment, however, I have not seen – has passed Congress, to the effect that the Federal Government shall never interfere with the domestic institutions of the States, including that of persons held to service. To avoid misconstruction of what I have said, I depart from my purpose not to speak of particular amendments so far as to say that, holding such a provision to now be implied constitutional law, I have no objection to its being made express and irrevocable.

The Chief Magistrate derives all his authority from the people, and they have referred none upon him to fix terms for the separation of the States. The people themselves can do this if also they choose, but the

Executive as such has nothing to do with it. His duty is to administer the present Government as it came to his hands and to transmit it unimpaired by him to his successor.

Why should there not be a patient confidence in the ultimate justice of the people? Is there any better or equal hope in the world? In our present differences, is either party without faith of being in the right? If the Almighty Ruler of Nations, with His eternal truth and justice, be on your side of the North, or on yours of the South, that truth and that justice will surely prevail by the judgment of this great tribunal of the American people.

By the frame of the Government under which we live this same people have wisely given their public servants but little power for mischief, and have with equal wisdom provided for the return of that little to their own hands at very short intervals. While the people retain their virtue and vigilance no Administration by any extreme of wickedness or folly can very seriously injure the Government in the short space of four years.

My countrymen, one and all, think calmly and well upon this whole subject. Nothing valuable can be lost by taking time. If there be an object to hurry any of you in hot haste to a step which you would never take deliberately, that object will be frustrated by taking time; but no good object can be frustrated by it. Such of you as are now dissatisfied still have the old Constitution unimpaired, and, on the sensitive point, the laws of your own framing under it; while the new Administration will have no immediate power, if it would, to change either. If it were admitted that you who are dissatisfied hold the right side in the dispute, there still is no single good reason for precipitate action. Intelligence, patriotism, Christianity, and a firm reliance on Him who has never yet forsaken this favored land are still competent to adjust in the best way all our present difficulty.

In your hands, my dissatisfied fellow-countrymen, and not in mine, is the momentous issue of civil war. The Government will not assail you. You can have no conflict without being yourselves the aggressors. You have no oath registered in heaven to destroy the Government, while I shall have the most solemn one to "preserve, protect, and defend it."

I am loath to close. We are not enemies, but friends. We must not be enemies. Though passion may have strained it must not break our bonds of affection. The mystic chords of memory, stretching from every battlefield and patriot grave to every living heart and hearthstone all over this broad land, will yet swell the chorus of the Union, when again touched, as surely they will be, by the better angels of our nature.

▲ An election poster for the Republican Party presidential candidate in the elction of 1860, showing Abraham Lincoln and his running mate, Hannibal Hamlin.

President Abraham Lincoln

"With malice toward none; with charity for all; with firmness in the right, as God gives us to see the right, let us strive on to finish the work we are in; to bind up the nation's wounds; to care for him who shall have borne the battle, and for his widow, and his orphan—to do all which may achieve and cherish a just, and a lasting peace, among ourselves, and with all nations."

Abraham Lincoln stood to speak at his second inauguration as the daylong deluge of rain stopped and the sun for the first time broke through the clouds. Many in the soggy and muddy crowd of 35,000 took this as an almost biblical omen that the storms of the past four years were nearing an end.

The gaunt and weary giant on the platform had recently been re-elected president by an overwhelming majority. The dome of the US Capitol building, half-completed at Lincoln's first inaugural, was now complete—symbolic, perhaps, of the fact that the Union stood intact as the Confederacy crumbled. Chief Justice Salmon P. Chase, Lincoln's former secretary of the treasury, administered the oath of office. The radical Republican Chase was a complete change from his pro-slavery predecessor, Roger B. Taney, who had died the year before.

Soldiers lined the streets of the capital; snipers knelt on rooftops. The disgruntled and nearly defeated South was still dangerous. Several of the conspirators in the coming assassination stood silent in the crowd. John Wilkes Booth was positioned only ten yards away from Lincoln—behind and above him.

◄ President Abraham Lincoln giving his second inaugural address on March 4, 1865.

The day began inauspiciously. Vice President-Elect Andrew Johnson had been ill with typhoid fever and had wanted to stay at home in Tennessee to recover. Lincoln, fearful for Johnson's safety in a state recently recaptured from the Confederates, insisted he come to Washington. The still-ailing Johnson made the trip. He medicated himself with whiskey the night before the inauguration and again in the morning. After taking his oath in the Senate Chamber, Johnson delivered a long, barely coherent speech that embarrassed the Republicans in attendance.

Lincoln Supported Johnson

Though Lincoln retained faith in him, after Johnson took the oath, Lincoln ordered the marshals not to let him speak outside at the inaugural. When associates expressed alarm about what would befall the country if anything happened to Lincoln and Johnson replaced him, the president replied, "I have known Andy for many years. He made a bad slip the other day, but you need not be scared. Andy ain't a drunkard."

The next few fateful weeks would test the soundness of Lincoln's judgment, as the war ended, and so did Lincoln's life. Johnson's reputation has ever since been overshadowed by his inaugural behavior and his eventual impeachment and acquittal. However, he was not nearly as bad as his enemies portrayed him. History judges that he did a creditable job of preserving the recently restored Union in the face of unrest stirred up by both vengeful radical Republicans and unrepentant Southerners.

On that March day, none but the conspirators could have predicted that Lincoln would meet his end at Ford's Theatre in a few weeks, or that Robert E. Lee would surrender at Appomattox to end the war. Nor did anyone in the crowd have an inkling what Lincoln would say.

Four years as chief executive under the most trying conditions had crystallized his thoughts and beliefs. This time, he sought no advice from William Seward or any other associate in drafting his remarks, as he had at his first inauguration. He alone spent long hours shaping his thoughts into the unforgettable phrases he was known for. And he left no preliminary drafts to trace their development.

More than one visitor to the White House in the months before the inauguration saw him working on what he said were remarks for the event, but Lincoln never shared them. Some of his thoughts are included in an 1862 musing he headed "Meditation on the Divine Will," which Lincoln never made public. Found in his papers after his death, it lays out several of the key points that later appeared in the second inaugural address. For instance he makes in the meditation an assertion he repeated in the inaugural address that both sides were praying to the same God and, "The prayers of both could not be answered. That of neither has been answered fully."

Letter to the Editor

In 1864 Lincoln wrote a public letter to Kentucky newspaper editor Albert G. Hodges that contains other passages that made their way into the speech. For example, he wrote to Hodges that, "If God now wills the removal of a great wrong, and wills also that we of the North as well as you of the South, shall pay fairly for our complicity in that wrong, impartial history will find therein new cause to attest and revere the justice and goodness of God."

Compare that with the more poetic but similar lines of the inaugural speech: "He now wills to remove, and that He gives to both North and South, this terrible war, as the woe due to those by whom the offence came, shall we discern therein any departure from those divine attributes which the believers in a Living God always ascribe to Him?"

As he had proven with the 271-word Gettysburg Address, Lincoln's ability to distill profound thoughts into few words was one of his great gifts. His second inaugural speech consisted of just 703 words, the second shortest in history. (The shortest was George Washington's second inaugural, which was a simple statement of thanks, and was delivered before the tradition of a formal address came about with Jefferson's second term.)

Lincoln's speech was about half the length of the two inaugural addresses later considered in the same rank as his: Franklin D. Roosevelt's in 1941 and John F. Kennedy's in 1960. It was no accident that Kennedy directed his speechwriter to study both Lincoln's and Roosevelt's addresses in preparing his own.

In Plain English

Lincoln began his oration plainly, with no attempt at rhetorical flourish. It was his second time taking the oath as president, he noted, which was significant because all knew that he was the first to be re-elected since Andrew Jackson thirty-six years earlier. There was little he could tell them about important events that they did not already know—including the fact that the "progress of our arms, upon which all else depends," is "reasonably satisfactory and encouraging." Although he undoubtedly knew the war was drawing to a close, he was careful to note that "no prediction is ventured."

The passive voice he used in that phrase would be unthinkable for most good orators—active voice and action verbs are two of the hallmarks of good public speaking. However, with Lincoln, it only serves to highlight a major feature of his greatest speeches: the lack of personal references. He used the pronoun "I" only once in the speech. He speaks more frequently of "we" or "both," a remarkable construct for a speech given during wartime, when "we" and "they" would be more expected. Lincoln's language is inclusive, rather than exclusive.

Another very interesting feature of the speech was its religious cast. Lincoln was frequently criticized for being insufficiently devout, because he did not regularly attend services. But the war seemed to deepen his piety, and after his matter-of-fact beginning, the remainder of the speech was packed with biblical references. In a four-paragraph address, he mentions God fourteen times, quotes the Bible four times, and invokes prayer three times.

In the second paragraph comes the first of his memorable quotes: "Both parties deprecated war, but one of them would make war rather than let the nation survive, and the other would accept war rather than let it perish, and the war came."

The real surprise of this simple and powerful quote is its conclusion, "and the war came." Not we, or they, started the war—but that the two sides had no ability to start, or stop, the war—it was inevitable. That simplicity gave the conclusion a stark power.

The second paragraph leads him to the long and eloquent third. He pinpoints the real cause of the war, and moves his language and the biblical and religious orientation of the speech into a higher gear. His first inaugural speech had been focused on making a lawyerly case for saving the Union, but now, in this powerful paragraph, he intimates that both the North and the South, despite their claims on the one side about the indissolubility of the Union and on the other about the primacy of states' rights, knew that somehow the Civil War was about slavery.

These slaves constituted "a peculiar and powerful interest," he says. One side sought to expand this interest at the cost of the Union, and the other simply to restrict it, he says. Neither anticipated the extent or duration of the conflict, or "anticipated that the cause of the conflict might cease with, or even before, the conflict itself should cease."

This is a long way forward from the conciliatory tone toward slavery he adopted in attempting to dissuade the South from secession, but still notable for its inclusiveness and lack of bitterness. Both read from the same Bible and both invoke the same God, he said.

Let Us Judge Not

Lincoln used two biblical references, one from the description of the Fall of Man in Genesis and the other the words of Jesus in Matthew 7:1, for a powerful combination of condemnation of and magnanimity toward the rebels: "It may seem strange that any men should dare to ask a just God's assistance in wringing their bread from the sweat of other men's faces, but let us judge not, that we be not judged."

The speech then becomes more like a sermon. Slavery came about, and "this terrible war" came in its appointed time to end it. God has His own purposes, he says, and they cannot be known by humankind.

He then reiterates in strong terms his determination to see the war through to the end. "Fondly and fervently" we wish for a speedy end to the war. "Yet, if God wills that it continue until all the wealth piled by the bondsman's two hundred and fifty years of unrequited toil shall be sunk,

▲ An 1865 photographic portrait of President Abraham Lincoln, pictured in the clothes he wore at his second inauguration.

and until every drop of blood drawn with the lash shall be paid by another drawn with the sword, as was said three thousand years ago, so still it must be said 'the judgments of the Lord are true and righteous altogether.'"

The last two paragraphs of the speech are among the most powerful and lyrical ever uttered by a president—or any other public speaker, American or otherwise. After thundering in the third paragraph like an Old Testament prophet, Lincoln shifted directly to forgiveness and generosity.

What Might Have Been

"With malice toward none, with charity for all, with firmness in the right as God gives us to see the right, let us strive on to finish the work we are in, to bind up the nation's wounds, to care for him who shall have borne the battle and for his widow and his orphan, to do all which may achieve and cherish a just and lasting peace among ourselves and with all nations."

In four short paragraphs, Lincoln, who had kept so much inside throughout the four years of war, revealed his deepest about slavery, and his hopes for the future of the country. The words were again inclusive. He refers to "him who shall have borne the battle and for his widow and for his orphan," by implication including the soldiers and citizens of the defeated side. That paragraph contains, perhaps, the seed of his strategies and policies for the period after the war, to "bind up the nation's wounds." Had he lived and been able to turn his words into actions, the history of the United States might have been different, and the nation might have avoided some of the troubles that resulted from the actions and inaction of lesser men in the Reconstruction period.

The words of the Second Inaugural are engraved on the Lincoln Memorial, along with those of the Gettysburg Address. The monument and the marble are impressive, but the words are the most fitting memorial to our sixteenth president.

· ·

Second Inaugural Address
March 4, 1865, United States Capitol, Washington, DC

· ·

Fellow-Countrymen:

At this second appearing to take the oath of the Presidential office there is less occasion for an extended address than there was at the first. Then a statement somewhat in detail of a course to be pursued seemed fitting and proper. Now, at the expiration of four years, during which public declarations have been constantly called forth on every point and phase of the great contest which still absorbs the attention and engrosses the energies of the nation, little that is new could be presented. The progress of our arms, upon which all else chiefly depends, is as well known to the public as to myself, and it is, I trust, reasonably satisfactory and encouraging to all. With high hope for the future, no prediction in regard to it is ventured.

On the occasion corresponding to this four years ago all thoughts were anxiously directed to an impending civil war. All dreaded it, all sought to avert it. While the inaugural address was being delivered from this place, devoted altogether to saving the Union without war, insurgent agents were in the city seeking to destroy it without war – seeking to dissolve the Union and divide effects by negotiation. Both parties deprecated war, but one of them would make war rather than let the nation survive, and the other would accept war rather than let it perish, and the war came.

One-eighth of the whole population were colored slaves, not distributed generally over the Union, but localized in the southern part of it. These slaves constituted a peculiar and powerful interest. All knew that this interest was somehow the cause of the war. To strengthen, perpetuate, and extend this interest was the object for which the insurgents would rend the Union even by war, while the Government claimed no right to do more than to restrict the territorial enlargement of it. Neither party expected for the war the magnitude or the duration which it has already attained. Neither anticipated that the cause of the conflict might cease with or even before the conflict itself should cease. Each looked for an easier triumph, and a result less fundamental and astounding. Both read the same Bible and pray to the same God, and each invokes His aid against the other. It may seem strange that any men should dare to ask a just God's assistance in wringing their bread from the sweat of other men's faces, but let us judge not, that we be not judged. The prayers of both could not be answered. That of neither has been answered fully. The Almighty has His own purposes. "Woe unto the world because of offenses; for it must needs be that offenses come, but woe to that man by whom the offense cometh." If we shall suppose that American slavery is one of those offenses which, in the providence of God, must needs come, but which, having continued through His appointed time, He now wills to remove, and that He gives to both North and South this terrible war as the woe due to those by whom the offense came, shall we discern therein any departure from those divine attributes which the believers in a living God always ascribe to Him? Fondly do we hope, fervently do we pray, that this mighty scourge of war may speedily pass away. Yet, if God wills that it continue until all the wealth piled by the bondsman's two hundred and fifty years of unrequited toil shall be sunk, and until every drop of blood drawn with the lash shall be paid by another drawn with the sword, as was said three thousand years ago, so still it must be said "the judgments of the Lord are true and righteous altogether."

▲ The last page of a copy of President Abraham Lincoln's second inaugural address in his own handwriting, with the last two lines pasted into place and an alteration made to the last two words.

With malice toward none, with charity for all, with firmness in the right as God gives us to see the right, let us strive on to finish the work we are in, to bind up the nation's wounds, to care for him who shall have borne the battle and for his widow and his orphan, to do all which may achieve and cherish a just and lasting peace among ourselves and with all nations.

President Theodore Roosevelt

"The man with the muck rake."

Theodore Roosevelt was a smallish man in height, but other than that he was in every way larger than life. The youngest man ever to become president, he occupied the national stage from the time he led his Rough Riders up San Juan Hill in Cuba in 1898 until his death at sixty in 1919.

In addition to personal courage in battle, he was utterly fearless in pursuing his beliefs, which were always strongly held. He took the fight to his opponents, and he did not shy away from even the most powerful—such as big business or the press.

Roosevelt was a prolific writer—author of some eighteen books, as well as innumerable magazine and newspaper articles—and a spellbinding orator. He and Lincoln are almost universally regarded as the finest writers ever to occupy the presidency, although Roosevelt's verbosity stands in stark contrast to Lincoln's spare and poetic style.

Roosevelt was a tireless speaker and had a gift for apt and colorful metaphor. Examples abound, such as "speak softly and carry a big stick," "the man in the arena," and many others. In one of his most famous speeches, in April 1906, he both rebuked and praised the crusading media of the period, pegging them with the name by which investigative journalists have been known ever since—muckrakers.

In that speech, Roosevelt simultaneously made a strong case for First Amendment rights and journalistic responsibility, and the speech was widely reported. The passages dealing with the press and the metaphor of the muck rake were so aggressively vivid that another aspect of the speech—strong condemnation of the era's wealthy monopolists and a call for an inheritance tax—went almost unnoticed.

Muckrakers Exposed Society's Abuses

The muckrakers of the period included Upton Sinclair, whose novel *The Jungle* had exposed horrific abuses in the meatpacking industry; Lincoln Steffens, who wrote about corruption in the New York City government and police department; and Ida Tarbell, whose

◀ Theodore Roosevelt (center left), with his men of the First Cavalry Volunteers, known as the "Rough Riders" on San Juan Hill during the Spanish-American War.

exposé of Rockefeller's Standard Oil trust was instrumental in later passage of landmark antitrust legislation.

However, by all accounts, the journalist who set Roosevelt off on his "Muckrake" speech was David Graham Phillips, who had published a series of articles in *Cosmopolitan* called "The Treason of the Senate," one of which accused Rhode Island senator Nelson Aldrich of corruption. Aldrich was a wealthy and patrician Republican, whose daughter Abby married John D. Rockefeller Jr., and whose grandson was Nelson Aldrich Rockefeller, later governor of New York and vice president under Gerald Ford. Phillips also attacked aristocratic senator Chauncey Depew and others in the articles.

Roosevelt was reportedly outraged at what he considered irresponsible and inaccurate reporting in the Phillips series. Similar articles and books were proliferating throughout the country, and Roosevelt expressed concern that the excesses of investigative reporting were becoming a destructive force.

The *Cosmopolitan* of that era specialized in such exposés, and Roosevelt was particularly incensed because its publisher, William Randolph Hearst, was at the time a congressman from New York. Hearst was already notorious for whipping up sentiment in favor of the Spanish-American War and for his sensationalist stories and headlines. Roosevelt knew Hearst was not above using his media outlets to savage his political enemies.

Roosevelt Sizzles with Moral Disdain

At a white-tie dinner of the Gridiron Club in Washington, Roosevelt boiled over. The dinner at the prestigious club was off the record, and attended by the cream of official Washington. According to one member of the audience, wrote

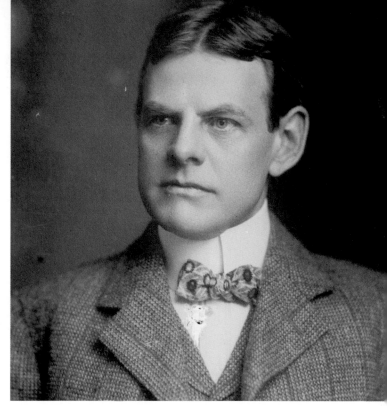

▲ A portrait photograph of David Graham Phillips, the journalist whose articles in *Cosmopolitan* outraged Roosevelt.

Roosevelt biographer Edmund Morris, Teddy "sizzled" with moral disdain for the press while making his speech.

Roosevelt chose his descriptive metaphor from John Bunyan's seventeenth-century Christian allegory, *The Pilgrim's Progress*. The passage he chose referred to "the man with the muckrake, the man who could look no way but downward with muckrake in his hand; who was offered a celestial crown for his muckrake but who would neither look up nor regard the crown he was offered but continued to rake to himself the filth of the floor."

Roosevelt expounded on the evils of the muckrakers for a good forty-five minutes, according to those in attendance, and it was clear to all that his target was Phillips. Second-hand accounts of the speech were quickly and widely reported, and distorted, in Roosevelt's opinion.

The term "muckraker" began to be generally applied to crusading reporters. Fearing that he was contributing to a backlash against legitimate exposure of social ills, Roosevelt decided to put the "Man with the Muckrake" on the record, which he did in an April 14 address marking the dedication of a House of Representatives office building.

This was familiar territory for Roosevelt. He was adept at taking his case to the people. From the first days of his presidency, he had used the media, and innumerable direct contacts with the public, to promote his beliefs and policy aims, with great success. He went on tours he described as "swings around the circle" in support of specific legislation. He elevated his press secretary to Cabinet rank, and inaugurated such practices as the strategic leaks of information, timed release of good and bad news, use of unnamed White House sources, and the staging of photo-ops and media events.

The Progressive Era

Teddy Roosevelt and the muckraking journalists were both at the heart of what has been dubbed "The Progressive Era," roughly stretching from 1900 to 1920. It was a reaction to the phenomenal growth of industry and wealth in the United States following the Civil War, and the shocking excesses, moral lapses, and sometimes outright criminality of the Robber Barons who were building US industrial might and the politicians who either came from their ranks or crawled into their pockets.

Roosevelt—dynamic, combative and absolutely incorruptible—was exactly the sort of chief executive to preside over the massive reforms the nation needed in order to overcome both the abuses of the wealthy and the plight of the poor. He called his progressive agenda "the square deal" and it was surprisingly moderate, striving to address the ills of society without harming the legitimate interests of the industrialists who provided the economic impetus to advance that society.

At the time of his "Muckrake" speech, Teddy was in the middle of a long and ultimately successful campaign to sway public opinion in favor of sweeping regulation of the railroads, overcoming politically and financially powerful interests—with the aid of some of the media. He found investigative reporters harder to handle than some of the tame mainstream reporters to whom he could hand-feed favorable news, but it was not in his interest to see the press as a whole fall out of public favor. Besides, Teddy was a restless bundle of energy who could, and did, take on more than one scuffle at a time.

Diligent Effort Improved Speaking

Roosevelt was not a natural speaker—he had little interest in debate or rhetoric at Harvard. Nevertheless, at age twenty-three his family wealth and connections helped him win election to the New York State Assembly, where his early speeches were undistinguished. He improved as a

◀ President Theodore Roosevelt speaking on a platform in front of a crowd of spectators.

speaker the same way he improved his body from childhood frailty to robust muscularity—diligent effort.

In preparing his "Muckrake" speech he followed his usual practice of outlining his ideas, dictating, then correcting and revising. He customarily read his speeches from a manuscript, the text of which was then made available to the press and public. He chose his forum for maximum exposure—the laying of the cornerstone for the House office building. He knew that the event would attract an audience of thousands—among them the most important figures in government. To ensure both a good crowd and media coverage, word was leaked days in advance that the president would be making an important statement.

The tone of the speech was intensely moralistic—cast in terms of good versus evil. The muckrakers, he said, diminish their credibility by making "indiscriminate assault" on men in business or public life. Therefore, they actually do a favor for those who really deserve exposure. These should be hunted down unsparingly, but with good judgment and common sense. Indiscriminate attacks on those already in public life discourage other good men from seeking office and leave the field to the unscrupulous and corrupt.

In Roosevelt's view, the extremes of the muckraking press were making the public cynical and unshockable, and were actually harming his efforts, and those of others, toward true reform. A free and active press was necessary to combat the "great and terrible" evils of the modern world, but to be effective they

28

fashion by keeping just within the limits of mere law-honesty. Of course no amount of charity in spending such fortunes in any way compensates for misconduct in making them. As a matter of personal conviction and without pretending to discuss the details or formulate the system, I feel that we shall ultimately have to consider the adoption of some such scheme as that of a progressive tax on all *fortunes,* beyond a certain amount, either given in life or devised or bequeathed upon death

▲ The page from the president's reading copy of the speech containing his proposal that the country "consider the adoption . . . of a progressive tax on all fortunes," with a last minute change to one word ("moneys" is replaced with "fortunes").

must move beyond "hysterical excitement" toward balance and restraint both in their choice of targets and the accuracy of their charges.

Targeting the Wealthy

Roosevelt repeats those arguments in several different ways throughout the first half of the speech, and then moves on, in the same moralistic vein, to another target—the wealthy. We are living in a time of great unrest and change, he said, and if any good is to come of it, reform should be steady, sane and measured. "Violent emotionalism leads to exhaustion," he said.

One of the most important avenues for reform, he said, is in the getting and keeping of wealth, both corporate and individual. Adopting the same tone as in the admonitions to the muckrakers, he stated, "We should discriminate in the sharpest way between fortunes well won and fortunes ill won: between those gained as an incident to performing great services to the community as a whole and those gained in evil fashion by keeping just within the limits of mere law honesty."

Then he made a suggestion that must have staggered his audience—in attendance or reading the speech later in their sumptuous clubs and mansions. The country should "consider the adoption . . . of a progressive tax on all fortunes, beyond a certain amount, either given in life or . . . upon death."

This was a Republican president talking. The Tea Party candidates taking the field in the United States today would denounce such a policy as the rankest socialism. In 1906, the Sixteenth Amendment, which made income tax a permanent feature of American life, was still seven years in the future, so such advocacy was radical for its time. It is surprising that his assault on the media drowned out his ideas on taxes in reports of the speech.

Warning the Wealthy of Dire Consequences

Roosevelt goes on to talk about his agenda for regulation of the railroads and other businesses, warning the "men of wealth" that if they were successful in blocking his efforts they would find that they had "sown the wind and would surely reap the whirlwind, for they would ultimately provoke the violent excesses which accompany a reform coming by convulsion instead of by steady and natural growth."

Overall, it was a strong and sermonic speech, and tremendously effective. The muckraking journalists themselves eagerly adopted the metaphor, turning it into a proud self-declaration that has stuck with probing journalists for more than a century. The speech might also have had as much of an impact on moves to tax the wealthy, which advanced rapidly over the next decade, as it did on restraining the media.

Roosevelt left office in 1908, but his legacy still lives. He was the first practitioner of what communication scholars Jeffrey K. Tulis and Amy L. Heyse have termed "the rhetorical presidency," and was one of the very best at it, in the same league as his cousin Franklin and Ronald Reagan. In aggressively taking his case to the people and forcefully advocating for his policies and convictions, Roosevelt set a pattern of leadership that presidents ever since have followed, and that the people of America today take for granted.

Some presidents have been as effective—a couple such as FDR and Reagan arguably more so—and some not so much. But Teddy was the very model of the modern US president, perceiving the office as "the bully pulpit" and showing his successors how to use it.

Address at the Laying of the Corner Stone of the Office Building of the House of Representatives
April 14, 1906, House of Representatives, Washington DC

Over a century ago Washington laid the corner stone of the Capitol in what was then little more than a tract of wooded wilderness here beside the Potomac. We now find it necessary to provide by great additional buildings for the business of the government. This growth in the need for the housing of the government is but a proof and example of the way in which the nation has grown and the sphere of action of the national government has grown. We now administer the affairs of a nation in which the extraordinary growth of population has been outstripped by the growth of wealth in complex interests. The material problems that face us today are not such as they were in Washington's time, but the underlying facts of human nature are the same now as they were then. Under altered external form we war with the same tendencies toward evil that were evident in Washington's time, and are helped by the same tendencies for good. It is about some of these that I wish to say a word today.

In Bunyan's "Pilgrim's Progress" you may recall the description of the Man with the Muck Rake, the man who could look no way but downward, with the muck rake in his hand; who was offered a celestial crown for his muck rake, but who would neither look up nor regard the crown he was offered, but continued to rake to himself the filth of the floor.

In "Pilgrim's Progress" the Man with the Muck Rake is set forth as the example of him whose vision is fixed on carnal instead of spiritual things. Yet he also typifies the man who in this life consistently refuses to see aught that is lofty, and fixes his eyes with solemn intentness only on that which is vile and debasing.

Now, it is very necessary that we should not flinch from seeing what is vile and debasing. There is filth on the floor, and it must be scraped up with the muck rake; and there are times and places where this

◀ The first page of the president's reading copy of the speech.

TO BE HELD IN CONFIDENCE, and no portion, synopsis, or intimation published or given out until its delivery has been begun by President Roosevelt on April 14, 1906, or a later date if for any reason its delivery should be postponed. President Roosevelt may speak upon some other occasion on this date, and special care must be taken that this speech is not by any mistake released in connection with such other remarks.

Over a century ago Washington laid the corner stone of the Capitol in what was then little more than a tract of wooded wilderness here beside the Potomac. We now find it necessary to provide by great additional buildings for the business of the Government. This growth in the need for the housing of service is the most needed of all the services that can be performed. But the man who never does anything else, who never thinks or speaks or writes, save of his feats with the muck rake, speedily becomes, not a help but one of the most potent forces for evil.

There are in the body politic, economic and social, many and grave evils, and there is urgent necessity for the sternest war upon them. There should be relentless exposure of and attack upon every evil man, whether politician or business man, every evil practice, whether in politics, business, or social life. I hail as a benefactor every writer or speaker, every man who, on the platform or in a book, magazine, or newspaper, with merciless severity makes such attack, provided always that he in his turn remembers that the attack is of use only if it is absolutely truthful.

The liar is no whit better than the thief, and if his mendacity takes the form of slander he may be worse than most thieves. It puts a premium upon knavery untruthfully to attack an honest man, or even with hysterical exaggeration to assail a bad man with untruth.

An epidemic of indiscriminate assault upon character does no good, but very great harm. The soul of every scoundrel is gladdened whenever an honest man is assailed, or even when a scoundrel is untruthfully assailed.

Now, it is easy to twist out of shape what I have just said, easy to affect to misunderstand it, and if it is slurred over in repetition not difficult really to misunderstand it. Some persons are sincerely incapable of understanding that to denounce mud slinging does not mean the endorsement of whitewashing; and both the interested individuals who need whitewashing and those others who practice mud slinging like to encourage such confusion of ideas.

One of the chief counts against those who make indiscriminate assault upon men in business or men in public life is that they invite a reaction which is sure to tell powerfully in favor of the unscrupulous scoundrel who really ought to be attacked, who ought to be exposed, who ought, if possible, to be put in the penitentiary. If Aristides is praised overmuch as just, people get tired of hearing it; and over-censure of the unjust finally and from similar reasons results in their favor.

Any excess is almost sure to invite a reaction; and, unfortunately, the reactions instead of taking the form of punishment of those guilty of the excess, is apt to take the form either of punishment of the unoffending or of giving immunity, and even strength, to offenders. The effort to make financial or political profit out of the destruction of character can only result in public calamity. Gross and reckless assaults on character, whether on the stump or in newspaper, magazine, or book, create a morbid and vicious public sentiment, and at the same time act as a profound deterrent to able men of normal sensitiveness and tend to prevent them from entering the public service at any price.

As an instance in point, I may mention that one serious difficulty encountered in getting the right type of men to dig the Panama canal is the certainty that they will be exposed, both without, and, I am sorry to say, sometimes within, Congress, to utterly reckless assaults on their character and capacity.

At the risk of repetition let me say again that my plea is not for immunity to, but for the most unsparing exposure of, the politician who betrays his trust, of the big business man who makes or spends his fortune in illegitimate or corrupt ways. There should be a resolute effort to hunt every such man out of the position he has disgraced. Expose the crime, and hunt down the criminal; but remember that even in the case of crime, if it is attacked in sensational, lurid, and untruthful fashion, the attack may do more damage to the public mind than the crime itself.

to be guilty of treason to the body politic. And, moreover, to assail
the great and admitted evils of our political and industrial life with such
crude and sweeping generalizations as to include decent men in the general
condemnation, means the searing of the public conscience. There results
a general attitude either of cynical
belief in and indifference to public corruption, or else of a distrustful
inability to discriminate between the good and the bad. Either attitude is
fraught with untold damage to the country as a whole. The fool who has
not sense to discriminate between what is good and what is bad is wellnigh
as dangerous as the man who does discriminate, and yet chooses the bad.
While there is nothing more distressing to every good patriot, to every good
American, than the hard, and scoffing spirit which treats the allegation of
dishonesty in a public man as a cause for laughter. Such laughter is worse than the crackling of thorns under a pot, for it denotes not merely the vacant mind, but the heart in which high emotions have been choked before they could grow to fruition.

▲ A page from a draft of the speech with handwritten amendments and additions by Roosevelt.

It is because I feel that there should be no rest in the endless war against the forces of evil that I ask the war be conducted with sanity as well as with resolution. The men with the muck rakes are often indispensable to the well being of society; but only if they know when to stop raking the muck, and to look upward to the celestial crown above them, to the crown of worthy endeavor. There are beautiful things above and round about them; and if they gradually grow to feel that the whole world is nothing but muck, their power of usefulness is gone.

If the whole picture is painted black there remains no hue whereby to single out the rascals for distinction from their fellows. Such painting finally induces a kind of moral color blindness; and people affected by it come to the conclusion that no man is really black, and no man really white, but they are all gray.

In other words, they neither believe in the truth of the attack, nor in the honesty of the man who is attacked; they grow as suspicious of the accusation as of the offense; it becomes well nigh hopeless to stir them either to wrath against wrongdoing or to enthusiasm for what is right; and such a mental attitude in the public gives hope to every knave, and is the despair of honest men. To assail the great and admitted evils of our political and industrial life with such crude and sweeping generalizations as to include decent men in the general condemnation means the searing of the public conscience. There results a general attitude either of cynical belief in and indifference to public corruption or else of a distrustful inability to discriminate between the good and the bad. Either attitude is fraught with untold damage to the country as a whole.

The fool who has not sense to discriminate between what is good and what is bad is well nigh as dangerous as the man who does discriminate and yet chooses the bad. There is nothing more distressing to every good patriot, to every good American, than the hard, scoffing spirit which treats the allegation of dishonesty in a public man as a cause for laughter. Such laughter is worse than the crackling of thorns under a pot, for it denotes not merely the vacant mind, but the heart in which high emotions have been choked before they could grow to fruition. There is any amount of good in the world, and there never was a time when loftier and more disinterested work for the betterment of mankind was being done than now. The forces that tend for evil are great and terrible, but the forces of truth and love and courage and honesty and generosity and sympathy are also stronger than ever before. It is a foolish and timid, no less than a wicked thing, to blink the fact that the forces of evil are strong, but it is even worse to fail to take into account the strength of the forces that tell for good.

Hysterical sensationalism is the poorest weapon wherewith to fight for lasting righteousness. The men who with stern sobriety and truth assail the many evils of our time, whether in the public press, or in magazines, or in books, are the leaders and allies of all engaged in the work for social and political betterment. But if they give good reason for distrust of what they say, if they chill the ardor of those who demand truth as a primary virtue, they thereby betray the good cause and play into the hands of the very men against whom they are nominally at war.

In his Ecclesiastical Polity that fine old Elizabethan divine, Bishop Hooker, wrote:

"He that goeth about to persuade a multitude that they are not so well governed as they ought to be shall never want attentive and favorable hearers, because they know the manifold defects whereunto every kind of regimen is subject, but the secret lets and difficulties, which in public proceedings are innumerable and inevitable, they have not ordinarily the judgment to consider."

This truth should be kept constantly in mind by every free people desiring to preserve the sanity and poise indispensable to the permanent success of self-government. Yet, on the other hand, it is vital not to permit this spirit of sanity and self-command to degenerate into mere mental stagnation. Bad though a state of hysterical excitement is, and evil though the results are which come from the violent oscillations such excitement invariably produces, yet a sodden acquiescence in evil is even worse.

At this moment we are passing through a period of great unrest-social, political, and industrial unrest. It is of the utmost importance for our future that this should prove to be not the unrest of mere rebelliousness against life, of mere dissatisfaction with the inevitable inequality of conditions, but the unrest of a resolute and eager ambition to secure the betterment of the individual and the nation.

So far as this movement of agitation throughout the country takes the form of a fierce discontent with evil, of a determination to punish the authors of evil, whether in industry or politics, the feeling is to be heartily welcomed as a sign of healthy life.

If, on the other hand, it turns into a mere crusade of appetite against appetite, of a contest between the brutal greed of the "have nots" and the brutal greed of the "haves," then it has no significance for good, but only for evil. If it seeks to establish a line of cleavage, not along the line which divides good men from bad, but along that other line, running at right

▶ A page from a draft of the speech in which the Bishop Hooker reference has first been crossed out and then a note written beside it stating "leave in."

the forces that tell for good.   Hysterical sensationalism is the very poorest weapon wherewith to ~~expect to win the victory in~~ any fight for lasting righteousness.   ~~We have a right to count upon the man who writes~~ of these *The men who with stern sobriety and truth assails the many evils of our time, whether* ~~evils~~ in the public press, ~~the man who writes of them~~ in magazines, or in books, *are* ~~as~~ the leaders and allies of all ~~those~~ engaged in the work ~~of~~ social and political ~~reform~~ *betterment. But if they give good reason for* ~~And if he so carries himself as to make man~~ distrust *of what they say, if they* ~~all that he says~~ and to chill the ardor of those who demand truth as a primary virtue, ~~he becomes a traitor~~ *they thereby betray* to the good cause, and play into the *(hands of the)* very ~~forces, which he is nominally assailing.~~ *own against whom they are nominally at war.*

~~I will now...what I have to say on...good citizenship, I wish to quote, in the first place, from the~~

IP his
"Ecclesiastical Polity", that fine old Elizabethan Divine, Bishop Hooker, *wrote*

"He that goeth about to persuade a multitude that they are not so well governed as they ought to be, shall never want attentive and favourable hearers; because they know the manifold defects whereunto every kind of regimen is subject, but the secret lets and difficulties, which in public proceedings are innumerable and inevitable, they have not ordinarily the judgment to consider."

capital than evil in the man of

and no less afford to condone evil in the man of no capital. and the reverse is equally

14

true. The wealthy man who exults because there is a failure of justice

in the effort we make to bring some trust magnate to an account for his

so-called labor leader

misdeeds, is as bad as, and no worse than, the head of a labor union who subscribes,

who endeavors to clamorously strives to excite a

or secures the subscription of money to defend other heads of labor unions

foul class feeling on behalf of some other labor leader

who is implicated in murder. One attitude is as bad

who have been guilty of murder, or other foul crime. The trust magnate who is

as the other, and no worse; in each case the accused

accused of breaking the law on a colossal scale is entitled to exact justice,

is entitled to exact justice; and in neither

to an absolutely fair trial, just as the man who is accused, whether in the

case is there need of action by others which can

course of a labor trouble or in any other fashion, of having committed murder,

be construed into an expression of sympathy

is entitled to justice and to a fair trial. But the administration of our

for crime.

criminal law is such that the danger is far greater in both cases that a

---

angles thereto, which divides those who are well off from those who are less well off, then it will be fraught with immeasurable harm to the body politic.

We can no more and no less afford to condone evil in the man of capital than evil in the man of no capital. The wealthy man who exults because there is a failure of justice in the effort to bring some trust magnate to account for his misdeeds is as bad as, and no worse than, the so-called labor leader who clamorously strives to excite a foul class feeling on behalf of some

A page from an early draft of the speech with considerable alterations in Roosevelt's handwriting.

other labor leader who is implicated in murder. One attitude is as bad as the other, and no worse; in each case the accused is entitled to exact justice; and in neither case is there need of action by others which can be construed into an expression of sympathy for crime.

It is a prime necessity that if the present unrest is to result in permanent good the emotion shall be translated into action, and that the action shall be marked by honesty, sanity, and self-restraint. There is mighty little good in a mere spasm of reform. The reform that counts is that which comes through steady, continuous growth; violent emotionalism leads to exhaustion.

It is important to this people to grapple with the problems connected with the amassing of enormous fortunes, and the use of those fortunes, both corporate and individual, in business. We should discriminate in the sharpest way between fortunes well won and fortunes ill won; between those gained as an incident to performing great services to the community as a whole and those gained in evil fashion by keeping just within the limits of mere law honesty. Of course, no amount of charity in spending such fortunes in any way compensates for misconduct in making them.

As a matter of personal conviction, and without pretending to discuss the details or formulate the system, I feel that we shall ultimately have to consider the adoption of some such scheme as that of a progressive tax on all fortunes, beyond a certain amount, either given in life or devised or bequeathed upon death to any individual-a tax so framed as to put it out of the power of the owner of one of these enormous fortunes to hand on more than a certain amount to any one individual; the tax of course, to be imposed by the national and not the state government. Such taxation should, of course, be aimed merely at the inheritance or transmission in their entirety of those fortunes swollen beyond all healthy limits. Again, the national government must in some form exercise supervision over corporations engaged in interstate business-and all large corporations engaged in interstate business-whether by license or otherwise, so as to permit us to deal with the far reaching evils of overcapitalization.

This year we are making a beginning in the direction of serious effort to settle some of these economic problems by the railway rate legislation. Such legislation, if so framed, as I am sure it will be, as to secure definite and tangible results, will amount to something of itself; and it will amount to a great deal more in so far as it is taken as a first step in the direction of a policy of superintendence and control over corporate wealth engaged in interstate commerce; this superintendence and control not to be exercised in a spirit of malevolence toward the men who have created the wealth, but with the firm purpose both to do justice to them and to see that they in their turn do justice to the public at large.

The first requisite in the public servants who are to deal in this shape with corporations, whether as legislators or as executives, is honesty. This honesty can be no respecter of persons. There can be no such thing as unilateral honesty. The danger is not really from corrupt corporations; it springs from the corruption itself, whether exercised for or against corporations.

The eighth commandment reads, "Thou shalt not steal." It does not read, "Thou shalt not steal from the rich man." It does not read, "Thou shalt not steal from the poor man." It reads simply and plainly, "Thou shalt not steal."

No good whatever will come from that warped and mock morality which denounces the misdeeds of men of wealth and forgets the misdeeds practiced at their expense; which denounces bribery, but blinds itself to blackmail; which foams with rage if a corporation secures favors by improper methods, and merely leers with hideous mirth if the corporation is itself wronged.

The only public servant who can be trusted honestly to protect the rights of the public against the misdeeds of a corporation is that public man who will just as surely protect the corporation itself from wrongful aggression.

A political cartoon featuring a caricature of President Theodore Roosevelt as he stares down a much larger, but cowering man who represents out-of-control business trusts. The original caption read, "You're a nice little man. You wouldn't hurt me, would you?"

▶ [Opposite] The last page of a draft of the speech with the closing line of the final version added in by Roosevelt.

If a public man is willing to yield to popular clamor and do wrong to the men of wealth or to rich corporations, it may be set down as certain that if the opportunity comes he will secretly and furtively do wrong to the public in the interest of a corporation.

But in addition to honesty, we need sanity. No honesty will make a public man useful if that man is timid or foolish, if he is a hot-headed zealot or an impracticable visionary. As we strive for reform we find that it is not at all merely the case of a long uphill pull. On the contrary, there is almost as much of breeching work as of collar work. To depend only on traces means that there will soon be a runaway and an upset.

The men of wealth who today are trying to prevent the regulation and control of their business in the interest of the public by the proper government authorities will not succeed, in my judgment, in checking the progress of the movement. But if they did succeed they would find that they had sown the wind and would surely reap the whirlwind, for they would ultimately provoke the violent excesses which accompany a reform coming by convulsion instead of by steady and natural growth.

On the other hand, the wild preachers of unrest and discontent, the wild agitators against the entire existing order, the men who act crookedly, whether because of sinister design or from mere puzzle headedness, the men who preach destruction without proposing any substitute for what they intend to destroy, or who propose a substitute which would be far worse than the existing evils-all these men are the most dangerous opponents of real reform. If they get their way they will lead the people into a deeper pit than any into which they could fall under the present system. If they fail to get their way they will still do incalculable harm by provoking the kind of reaction which in its revolt against the senseless evil of their teaching would enthrone more securely than ever the evils which their misguided followers believe they are attacking.

More important than aught else is the development of the broadest sympathy of man for man. The welfare of the wage worker, the welfare of the tiller of the soil, upon these depend the welfare of the entire country; their good is not to be sought in pulling down others; but their good must be the prime object of all our statesmanship.

Materially we must strive to secure a broader economic opportunity for all men, so that each shall have a better chance to show the stuff of which he is made. Spiritually and ethically we must strive to bring about clean living and right thinking. We appreciate that the things of the body are important; but we appreciate also that the things of the soul are immeasurably more important.

The foundation stone of national life is, and ever must be, the high individual character of the average citizen.

enthrone more securely than ever the very evils which their misguided followers believed they are attacking.

More important than aught else is the development of the broadest sympathy of man for man. The welfare of the wage-worker, the welfare of the tiller of the soil, upon these depend the welfare of the entire country; their good is not to be sought in pulling down others, but their good must be the prime object of all our statesmanship.

Materially we must strive to secure a broader economic opportunity for men, so that each man shall have a better chance to show the stuff of which he is made. Spiritually and ethically we must strive to bring about clean living and right thinking. We appreciate that the things of the body are important; but we appreciate also that the things of the soul are immeasurably more important. The foundation stone of national life is, and ever must be, its high individual character of the average citizen.

President Woodrow Wilson

"An evident principle ... is the principle of justice to all peoples and nationalities, and their right to live on equal terms of liberty and safety with one another, whether they be strong or weak."

◄ President Woodrow Wilson, pictured working at his desk during World War I.

Modern US presidents number their speechwriters in double digits, and most, if not all, since Washington have had at least some help in preparing speeches. But Woodrow Wilson may have set an all-time record in researching and writing his Fourteen Points speech. An estimated 150 scholars and foreign relations experts had some sort of input into the address, one of the most important of the twentieth century. The Fourteen Points formed the basis for the Armistice that ended World War I, and the final point of those fourteen proposed what became the League of Nations following the war.

The bevy of academics comprised "The Inquiry," an unofficial foreign affairs advisory group convened by Colonel Edward M. House, Wilson's chief foreign policy advisor. The group was charged with developing materials for use during peace negotiations following World War I and was led by philosopher and university president Sidney Mezes, House's brother-in-law.

The Inquiry was dominated by Ivy Leaguers, one of the most important being Walter Lippmann. At the time a twenty-eight-year-old Harvard graduate, Lippmann was already developing a reputation as an intellectual heavyweight. He served as day-to-day administrator of the group, and played a lead role in converting The Inquiry's work into the eventual speech Wilson delivered to a joint session of Congress. Lippmann went on to become one of the most important journalists and political commentators of the twentieth century, twice winning the Pulitzer Prize for his column Today and Tomorrow and writing a number of influential books.

House was himself an interesting character. He was a wealthy Texan and political kingmaker who had handpicked four successive governors of the state. Turning to the national scene, he helped Wilson get elected but refused a Cabinet appointment. He spent the years prior to US entry into World War I trying to settle the conflict through diplomacy, and then played a lead role in presenting Wilson's ideas during the peace negotiations. He eventually broke with Wilson over the latter's refusal to compromise with the Congress over the ratification of the Treaty of Versailles that ended the war.

A Web of Alliances

Wilson's unbending attitude was typical of the man. He was the son of a Presbyterian minister and an academic by profession—president of Princeton University—before entering politics to become governor of New Jersey. He was a devout believer in predestination in religion, and extended that belief into his political life. He was convinced of the destiny of the United States to be a leader in a better post-war world, and formulated a set of policies based on those beliefs. He also was firmly confident that anyone who disagreed or differed with him was wrong.

In August 1914, a stew of international intrigue that had been simmering for decades boiled over into armed conflict. On one side was an alliance called the Central Powers, consisting of Germany, the Austro-Hungarian Empire, Turkey, and other small allies. They squared off against what were termed the Entente Powers—principally Great Britain, France, and czarist Russia.

The United States remained neutral, and for a time, public opinion favored Germany nearly as much as it did Great Britain and France. Wilson, a superb and powerful speaker, although not a personally likeable man, had been elected in 1912 mainly because Teddy Roosevelt took so many votes away from incumbent Republican William Howard Taft. He was re-elected in 1916 on the slogan "he kept us out of war."

That changed in 1917 when Germany began attacking US shipping, and a number of other international calamities stemming from the long and bitter struggle made Wilson realize that US entry into the war on the side of the Entente was inevitable. At about the same time, the Bolshevik Revolution in Russia radically changed the nature of political alliances in the world. When the Bolsheviks killed the czar and took over, they gained access to the czarist government's diplomatic records, and made them all public, revealing to the world a complicated jumble of secret treaties that connected many international allies. Those secret treaties often conflicted with the public alliances and treaties among countries, and their revelation caused public outrage.

Secret Dealings Appalled Wilson

The revelation of back-channel dealings called into question any moral justification for the war. Wilson was appalled. He resolved that the ultimate aim of US involvement must be to forge a just peace, and to make international diplomacy more transparent and honest, to prevent a recurrence of the secret collusions that had led to the world war.

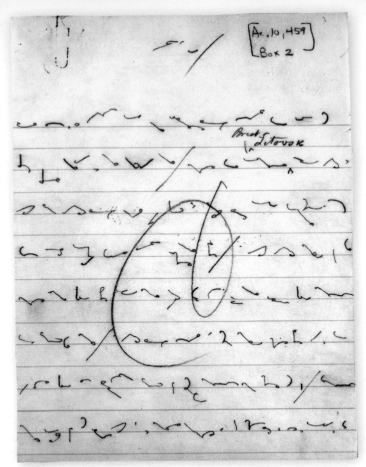

▲ The first page of Wilson's speech notes, in shorthand, for his "Fourteen Points" address.

Wilson's vehicle was the work of The Inquiry. Lippmann later said that the group's job was to "take the secret treaties, analyze the parts which were tolerable, and separate those which we regarded as intolerable, and then develop an American position which conceded as much to the Allies as it could, but took away the poison."

House took the results of The Inquiry's exhaustive studies to the White House, where he and Wilson worked to craft the speech. Wilson, typically, wrote his draft in shorthand, and he and House produced the final speech over a weekend. Then, Wilson suddenly and without warning ordered the Congress into joint session. He wanted to preserve the element of surprise.

Neither Wilson's Cabinet nor the diplomatic corps had any warning, or input. In fact, many were out of town when Wilson delivered the speech.

Nor did Wilson consult with Great Britain, France, or any other allied country before making his statement. They were locked in mortal combat with Germany and were unable to raise their eyes from the battlefield to consider the shape of the post-war world. Wilson had an vision of what that world should look like, and took the initiative.

League of Nations Was Centerpiece

The fourteenth and last point was the centerpiece—his plan for the League of Nations, which he described as "A general association of nations . . . formed under specific covenants for the purpose of affording mutual guarantees of political independence and territorial integrity to great and small states alike."

The German position weakened throughout 1918, and the end of the war seemed imminent. In October, the German imperial chancellor sent a note to Wilson through intermediaries asking for an immediate armistice and the opening of peace negotiations based on the Fourteen Points.

The British and French were less willing to accept the Fourteen Points. The British, in particular, objected to the provision on freedom of the seas. But they accepted Wilson's proposals as the basis of the negotiations, and the Armistice was signed on November 11, 1918, and a peace conference convened in Paris.

Wilson's political position was weakened that same month when the Republicans regained control of the Congress in that year's election. Nevertheless, he was determined to attend the conference and lead the battle for his principles.

Wilson was warmly received by the French, British, and Italians, but ran into strong opposition when negotiators began hammering out territorial and economic issues. He achieved his goal of launching the League of Nations as part of the peace settlement, but was forced to make many concessions. The Germans, particularly, felt betrayed by the harsh economic reparations and territorial concessions imposed on them. The resulting bitterness played a significant role in the rise of Adolf Hitler in Germany barely a decade later.

Campaigning for Treaty Ratification

While plans for the League advanced in Europe, Wilson returned to the United States to campaign for ratification of the treaty and US entry into the League. A compromise with the Congress over the treaty would have realized Wilson's fondest hopes for the post-war world: US membership in and leadership of a League of Nations to mediate international disputes. Wilson himself doomed his dream when he rejected changes to the treaty presented by his arch-foe, Republican senator Henry Cabot Lodge. They would agree to ratification of the treaty, Lodge told Wilson, but only on certain conditions, which he termed "reservations." The reservations would not require amendment of the treaty. In fact, several other countries had already attached similar reservations without the need for amendment.

Wilson refused to consider the compromise, even though House and many other advisors begged him to—pointing out that he would be giving up little to gain his greatest aim. Instead, he began a cross-country speaking campaign to whip up support for ratification of the treaty. Public opposition to the treaty was strong, particularly among German- and Irish-American Democrats who condemned terms they considered harmful to their homelands; and Republicans who were politically opposed to Wilson.

While in Colorado to give a speech, Wilson suffered a stroke, and returned to Washington to recover. He could no longer lead the fight, and the United States never ratified the treaty.

Nor did the country ever enter the League of Nations. Wilson's successor, Warren G. Harding, opposed the League and rejected all efforts to join. The League enjoyed some success and suffered some failures during more than a decade of existence, and ultimately fell apart when Germany, Italy, Japan, and others dropped out to begin arming and planning for the next war.

Wilson's Fourteen Points represented the greatest achievement of a great idealist and visionary. In the opinion of most foreign relations experts, his ideas brought about fundamental and permanent change to world diplomacy and international relations. Regrettably, for all his intellectual force and leadership, he was a flawed human being who lacked the political intuition and deftness that might have brought his vision into full flower and perhaps prevented the world's descent into another worldwide conflict.

The Inquiry later morphed into the influential Council on Foreign Relations, which exists to this day. An international think tank, it continues to offer sage advice and analysis on international issues.

▲ Influential adviser to President Woodrow Wilson, Walter Lippmann pictured in 1946.

Presidential Address to Joint Session of Congress
January 8, 1918, United States Capitol, Washington, DC

Gentlemen of the Congress:

Once more, as repeatedly before, the spokesmen of the Central Empires have indicated their desire to discuss the objects of the war and the possible basis of a general peace. Parleys have been in progress at Brest-Litovsk between Russsian representatives and representatives of the Central Powers to which the attention of all the belligerents have been invited for the purpose of ascertaining whether it may be possible to extend these parleys into a general conference with regard to terms of peace and settlement.

▼   President Woodrow Wilson reading the Armistice terms for World War I to Congress.

The Russian representatives presented not only a perfectly definite statement of the principles upon which they would be willing to conclude peace but also an equally definite program of the concrete application of those principles. The representatives of the Central Powers, on their part, presented an outline of settlement which, if much less definite, seemed susceptible of liberal interpretation until their specific program of practical terms was added. That program proposed no concessions at all either to the sovereignty of Russia or to the preferences of the populations with whose fortunes it dealt, but meant, in a word, that the Central Empires were to keep every foot of territory their armed forces had occupied -- every province, every city, every point of vantage – as a permanent addition to their territories and their power.

It is a reasonable conjecture that the general principles of settlement which they at first suggested originated with the more liberal statesmen of Germany and Austria, the men who have begun to feel the force of their own people's thought and purpose, while the concrete terms of actual settlement came from the military leaders who have no thought but to keep what they have got. The negotiations have been broken off. The Russian representatives were sincere and in earnest. They cannot entertain such proposals of conquest and domination.

The whole incident is full of significances. It is also full of perplexity. With whom are the Russian representatives dealing? For whom are the representatives of the Central Empires speaking? Are they speaking for the majorities of their respective parliaments or for the minority parties, that military and imperialistic minority which has so far dominated their whole policy and controlled the affairs of Turkey and of the Balkan states which have felt obliged to become their associates in this war?

The Russian representatives have insisted, very justly, very wisely, and in the true spirit of modern democracy, that the conferences they have been holding with the Teutonic and Turkish statesmen should be held within open, not closed, doors, and all the world has been audience, as was desired. To whom have we been listening, then? To those who speak the spirit and intention of the resolutions of the German Reichstag of the 9th of July last, the spirit and intention of the Liberal leaders and parties of Germany, or to those who resist and defy that spirit and intention and insist upon conquest and subjugation? Or are we listening, in fact, to both, unreconciled and in open and hopeless contradiction? These are very serious and pregnant questions. Upon the answer to them depends the peace of the world.

But, whatever the results of the parleys at Brest-Litovsk, whatever the confusions of counsel and of purpose in the utterances of the spokesmen of the Central Empires, they have again attempted to acquaint the world with their objects in the war and have again challenged their adversaries to say what their objects are and what sort of settlement they would deem just and satisfactory. There is no good reason why that challenge should not be responded to, and responded to with the utmost candor. We did not wait for it. Not once, but again and again, we have laid our whole thought and purpose before the world, not in general terms only, but each time with sufficient definition to make it clear what sort of definite terms of settlement must necessarily spring out of them. Within the last week Mr. Lloyd George has spoken with admirable candor and in admirable spirit for the people and Government of Great Britain.

There is no confusion of counsel among the adversaries of the Central Powers, no uncertainty of principle, no vagueness of detail. The only secrecy of counsel, the only lack of fearless frankness, the only failure to make definite statement of the objects of the war, lies with Germany and her allies. The issues of life and death hang upon these definitions. No statesman who has the least conception of his responsibility ought for a moment to permit himself to continue this tragical and appalling outpouring of blood and treasure unless he is sure beyond a peradventure that the objects of the vital sacrifice are part and parcel of the very life of Society and that the people for whom he speaks think them right and imperative as he does.

There is, moreover, a voice calling for these definitions of principle and of purpose which is, it seems to me, more thrilling and more compelling than any of the many moving voices with which the troubled air of the world is filled. It is the voice of the Russian people. They are prostrate and all but hopeless, it would seem, before the grim power of Germany, which has hitherto known no relenting and no pity. Their power, apparently, is shattered. And yet their soul is not subservient. They will not yield either in principle or in action. Their conception of what is right, of what is humane and honorable for them to accept, has been stated with a frankness, a largeness of view, a generosity of spirit, and a universal human sympathy which must challenge the admiration of every friend of mankind; and they have refused to compound their ideals or desert others that they themselves may be safe.

They call to us to say what it is that we desire, in what, if in anything, our purpose and our spirit differ from theirs; and I believe that the people of the United States would wish me to respond, with utter simplicity and frankness. Whether their present leaders believe it or not, it is our heartfelt desire and hope that some way may be opened whereby we may be privileged to assist the people of Russia to attain their utmost hope of liberty and ordered peace.

It will be our wish and purpose that the processes of peace, when they are begun, shall be absolutely open and that they shall involve and permit henceforth no secret understandings of any kind. The day of conquest and aggrandizement is gone by; so is also the day of secret covenants entered into in the interest of particular governments and likely at some unlooked-for moment to upset the peace of the world. It is this happy fact, now clear to the view of every public man whose thoughts do not still linger in an age that is dead and gone, which makes it possible for every nation whose purposes are consistent with justice and the peace of the world to avow nor or at any other time the objects it has in view.

We entered this war because violations of right had occurred which touched us to the quick and made the life of our own people impossible unless they were corrected and the world secure once for all against their recurrence. What we demand in this war, therefore, is nothing peculiar to ourselves. It is that the world be made fit and safe to live in; and particularly that it be made safe for every peace-loving nation which, like our own, wishes to live its own life, determine its own institutions, be assured of justice and fair dealing by the other peoples of the world as against force and selfish aggression. All the peoples of the world are in effect partners in this interest, and for our own part we see very clearly that unless justice be done to others it will not be done to us. The program of the world's peace, therefore, is our program; and that program, the only possible program, as we see it, is this:

I. Open covenants of peace, openly arrived at, after which there shall be no private international understandings of any kind but diplomacy shall proceed always frankly and in the public view.

II. Absolute freedom of navigation upon the seas, outside territorial waters, alike in peace and in war, except as the seas may be closed in whole or in part by international action for the enforcement of international covenants.

III. The removal, so far as possible, of all economic barriers and the establishment of an equality of trade conditions among all the nations consenting to the peace and associating themselves for its maintenance.

IV. Adequate guarantees given and taken that national armaments will be reduced to the lowest point consistent with domestic safety.

V. A free, open-minded, and absolutely impartial adjustment of all colonial claims, based upon a strict observance of the principle that in determining all such questions of sovereignty the interests of the populations concerned must have equal weight with the equitable claims of the government whose title is to be determined.

VI. The evacuation of all Russian territory and such a settlement of all questions affecting Russia as will secure the best and freest cooperation of the other nations of the world in obtaining for her an unhampered and unembarrassed opportunity for the independent determination of her own political development and national policy and assure her of a sincere welcome into the society of free nations under institutions of her own choosing; and, more than a welcome, assistance also of every kind that she may need and may herself desire. The treatment accorded Russia by her sister nations in the months to come will be the acid test of their good will, of their comprehension of her needs as distinguished from their own interests, and of their intelligent and unselfish sympathy.

▲ A page from a draft of the speech with both handwritten and typed amendments added in.

VII. Belgium, the whole world will agree, must be evacuated and restored, without any attempt to limit the sovereignty which she enjoys in common with all other free nations. No other single act will serve as this will serve to restore confidence among the nations in the laws which they have themselves set and determined for the government of their relations

MEMORANDUM OF ALLIED DIPLOMATIC STRATEGY

A Proposal

What this Proposal is Not.

The proposal here made does not call for peace negotiations with the enemy; nor for making him an "offer" in any diplomatic sense; it does not deny the necessity or desirability of "a fight to a finish"; is in no sense a plea for an early termination of the war, or an incomplete or patched up peace.

It is a necessary war measure.

The proposal is as much a factor of the successful conduct of the war itself as munitions or men or money. It is on that ground only, in so far as this memorandum is concerned, that it is urged.

Outline of Proposal.

The proposal here made is the calling now, during the war, of a Conference, or Congress, or Parliament of the Allies, of a special composition for the following object:

> To frame the international arrangements for mutual protection by which after the war the nations of the Alliance - and ultimately those of the world - are to be assured military security, national independence, and economic rights (access to raw materials and markets, equality of opportunity in undeveloped territory like Africa, Asia and South America, access to the sea for states that have insufficient, or no, ports, etc.), some plan for a League of Nations, such as that forecast by Mr. Wilson and approved by the other leading Allied statesmen.

A mere declaration of intention to be guided in the future by idealistic principles in international affairs will of course serve no end whatsoever. What is needed is the elaboration of a scheme sufficiently concrete to strike

95711

The first page of an early memo outlining a proposal for arrangements to maintain international security and economic rights after the war.

with one another. Without this healing act the whole structure and validity of international law is forever impaired.

VIII. All French territory should be freed and the invaded portions restored, and the wrong done to France by Prussia in 1871 in the matter of Alsace-Lorraine, which has unsettled the peace of the world for nearly fifty years, should be righted, in order that peace may once more be made secure in the interest of all.

IX. A readjustment of the frontiers of Italy should be effected along clearly recognizable lines of nationality.

X. The peoples of Austria-Hungary, whose place among the nations we wish to see safeguarded and assured, should be accorded the freest opportunity to autonomous development.

XI. Rumania, Serbia, and Montenegro should be evacuated; occupied territories restored; Serbia accorded free and secure access to the sea; and the relations of the several Balkan states to one another determined by friendly counsel along historically established lines of allegiance and nationality; and international guarantees of the political and economic independence and territorial integrity of the several Balkan states should be entered into.

XII. The Turkish portion of the present Ottoman Empire should be assured a secure sovereignty, but the other nationalities which are now under Turkish rule should be assured an undoubted security of life and an absolutely unmolested opportunity of autonomous development, and the Dardanelles should be permanently opened as a free passage to the ships and commerce of all nations under international guarantees.

XIII. An independent Polish state should be erected which should include the territories inhabited by indisputably Polish populations, which should be assured a free and secure access to the sea, and whose political and economic independence and territorial integrity should be guaranteed by international covenant.

XIV. A general association of nations must be formed under specific covenants for the purpose of affording mutual guarantees of political independence and territorial integrity to great and small states alike.

In regard to these essential rectifications of wrong and assertions of right we feel ourselves to be intimate partners of all the governments and peoples associated together against the Imperialists. We cannot be separated in interest or divided in purpose. We stand together until the end. For such arrangements and covenants we are willing to fight and to continue to fight until they are achieved; but only because we wish the right to prevail and desire a just and stable peace such as can be secured only by removing the chief provocations to war, which this program does remove. We have no jealousy of German greatness, and there is nothing in this program that impairs it. We grudge her no achievement or distinction of learning or of pacific enterprise such as have made her record very bright and very enviable. We do not wish to injure her or to block in any way her legitimate influence or power. We do not wish to fight her either with arms or with hostile arrangements of trade if she is willing to associate herself with us and the other peace- loving nations of the world in covenants of justice and law and fair dealing. We wish her only to accept a place of equality among the peoples of the world, -- the new world in which we now live, -- instead of a place of mastery.

Neither do we presume to suggest to her any alteration or modification of her institutions. But it is necessary, we must frankly say, and necessary as a preliminary to any intelligent dealings with her on our part, that we should know whom her spokesmen speak for when they speak to us, whether for the Reichstag majority or for the military party and the men whose creed is imperial domination.

We have spoken now, surely, in terms too concrete to admit of any further doubt or question. An evident principle runs through the whole program I have outlined. It is the principle of justice to all peoples and nationalities, and their right to live on equal terms of liberty and safety with one another, whether they be strong or weak.

Unless this principle be made its foundation no part of the structure of international justice can stand. The people of the United States could act upon no other principle; and to the vindication of this principle they are ready to devote their lives, their honor, and everything they possess. The moral climax of this the culminating and final war for human liberty has come, and they are ready to put their own strength, their own highest purpose, their own integrity and devotion to the test.

President Franklin Delano Roosevelt

" **The only thing we have to fear is fear itself.** "

When Franklin Delano Roosevelt took the oath of office for his first presidential term on March 4, 1933, America's fortunes, and the public morale, were at low ebb. In a fifteen-minute, 2,000-word speech that seems remarkably short by modern inaugural standards, FDR lifted the nation's spirits and made America's future seem brighter.

Roosevelt's first inaugural speech ranks among the very best ever by an incoming president. He put the nation's troubles into perspective and promised swift and effective action. The populist sentiments poured forth in his patrician drawl and lit up the country with hope.

Ever since, a controversy has roiled among presidential historians and scholars as to whether the words and ideas in the speech were Roosevelt's own, or were the product of the virtual assembly line of speechwriters who had worked with and for Roosevelt throughout his public life.

It was no secret that previous US presidents had help with their major addresses. George Washington received drafts of his Farewell Address from both James Madison and Alexander Hamilton. William Seward tempered the sentiments of Abraham Lincoln in his superb first inaugural. By the time Roosevelt's immediate predecessors took office in the 1920s, it was common for presidents to have speechwriters on their staffs.

But Roosevelt took the process to a higher level. He was a powerful orator with a resonant voice particularly well suited to the new medium of radio. He loved the language and possessed great off-the-cuff eloquence and wit. But coming from old money as he did, he was not accustomed to relying only on his own resources. He did not hesitate to seek out and hire the best available speechwriters.

◀ President Franklin D. Roosevelt pictured speaking at a podium.

Roosevelt's Speechwriters

Roosevelt employed at least a dozen speechwriters during his more than twelve years in office. They included poet Archibald MacLeish and playwright Robert Sherwood, each of whom had won a Pulitzer Prize in his respective field. The longest tenured of them was Samuel Rosenman, who wrote one of Roosevelt's first speeches in his campaign for governor in 1928 and was on call for the rest of FDR's life, despite being appointed a justice of the New York Supreme Court in 1936.

In 1952, Rosenman wrote a fascinating book called *Working with Roosevelt* that detailed his speechwriting and his work with colleagues to produce some of the most significant spoken words of the twentieth century. In that world, teams of speechwriters revised, transcribed, cut and pasted, then delivered multiple drafts to Roosevelt, who marked up, rewrote, or threw out their efforts. Rosenman made clear that Roosevelt was in complete control of the process, and was the equal or better of any of them as a writer.

▲ The first page of Roosevelt's initial draft of his first inauguration speech.

Speeches were routinely touched by many hands, with "no one claiming pride of authorship." Roosevelt's first inaugural speech was an exception, Rosenman said. Although some speculation has pointed to Rosenman himself as an author or contributor to the speech, he denies a role for himself or anyone else but Roosevelt.

"The speech was one of the very few of which the President wrote the very first draft in his own hand," declares Rosenman. "He wrote it on yellow legal cap paper, sitting by the fire at Hyde Park on the night of February 27. The original manuscript is now in the Roosevelt Library at Hyde Park." In a note attached to the manuscript dated March 25, 1933, FDR remarks that "A number of minor changes were made in subsequent drafts but the final draft is substantially the same as this original."

▲ President Franklin D. Roosevelt making his inaugural address to the audience before the East Portico of the Capitol.

Authorship Question Remains Unsettled

That should settle the issue of authorship, right? Except it hasn't. One of Roosevelt's early speechwriters was a prickly Columbia University law professor named Raymond Moley, who had recruited a number of other academics for Roosevelt's "brain trust" of advisors while Roosevelt was governor of New York. Although he did not like being pegged as a mere speechwriter, he nevertheless drafted many important addresses for FDR during his New York years. He continued to write speeches during Roosevelt's first term as president before breaking bitterly with the New Deal and spending the rest of his life as a right-wing Republican attacking Roosevelt's programs.

In 1966, Moley, by then a conservative elder statesman, published a memoir claiming that he had a number of conversations with Roosevelt about the Inaugural Address, and eventually delivered a draft to the incoming president at Hyde Park six days before the inauguration.

Moley claimed that Roosevelt carefully read his typed draft and then the two men spent a long evening in Roosevelt's study reworking it. Roosevelt then declared, according to Moley, that he ought to transcribe the draft into his own handwriting. The ostensible reason was that Louis Howe, Roosevelt's closest aide and political advisor for two decades, would reject any speech draft that did not come from Roosevelt himself. The previous year, Howe had had a major confrontation with Rosenman and Moley over FDR's Democratic nomination acceptance speech .

After Roosevelt finished copying the draft, Moley threw the original into the fireplace, destroying all evidence of his authorship. The ploy apparently worked—Howe left the speech largely intact. Scholars and historians have mostly accepted Moley's version, although it reflects badly on Roosevelt, and it was uncharacteristic of the man to take undeserved credit. However, the lack of proof casts at least some doubt on the account of a bitter man with an axe to grind writing decades after the fact.

It's also extremely doubtful that this wonderful speech was "substantially" crafted in one draft, whether by Moley or Roosevelt.

The Mystery of "Fear Itself"

The key omission from the Hyde Park draft was the speech's most famous phrase, the resounding assurance that "the only thing we have to fear is fear itself." Neither Rosenman, nor Moley, nor anyone else is sure exactly where that came from. It showed up in the final draft the day before the speech was to be delivered.

Maybe it's the many television montages of FDR's presidency that compress twelve years into a few minutes that cause some Americans to believe that the famous phrase comes from a World War II speech. But it does not. The fear in question was fear of poverty, not fear of invasion by foreign armies. Rosenman speculates that it may have come from a similar quote by Henry David Thoreau, "Nothing is so much to be feared as fear." Eleanor Roosevelt later said that her husband had a copy of a work by Thoreau on his bedside table in the days before the inauguration. A duller explanation is that Louis Howe saw the phrase on a department store advertisement, though the ad has never been found. Scholars have found similar phrases in other orations and writings throughout history.

Regardless of its origin, "the phrase served as a guidepost for the President in many later emergencies, as it had served him personally all his life. Although he was criticized on a great many scores, I have never heard it said that he was ever timid about taking action in an emergency," as Rosenman said.

When FDR took office, the emergency that became known as the Great Depression was more than three years old and had reached its lowest depths. Most of America's banks were closed and industrial production had dropped by more than half from its level during the boom years before the 1929 stock market crash. A quarter of the US workforce was unemployed, small farms were being foreclosed by the thousands, and one out of ten single-family homes was owned by a bank.

Roosevelt vs. Hoover

The contrast on the inaugural platform between Roosevelt and his predecessor, Herbert Hoover, was stark. Roosevelt smiled jauntily and radiated optimism. The grim Hoover looked ready to burst into tears. For five months after his defeat, Hoover had begged Roosevelt either to back his emergency plans or to propose some of his own. Roosevelt had declined, preferring to tour the country making appearances but being deliberately vague about his intentions. By the time of Roosevelt's inauguration, the public was ready to support any actions the new president proposed.

FDR began his speech with a pronouncement that he had literally added to the speech on the platform. "This is a day of national consecration," he said, using the biblical context he would employ again a few paragraphs later by assigning blame to the "money changers," elevating what was to follow above mere politics. He would reference the "money changers" more than once, assigning blame to the barons of Wall Street and the captains of industry for the country's bleak financial condition.

After promising candor, boldness, and truth, he began with a simple statement of his optimism, "This great Nation will endure as it has endured, will revive and will prosper." He could hardly be clearer or more direct.

Then he followed with the "fear" statement that gave the speech its name and that had such a visceral impact—both for those sitting in the audience and for the millions of Americans sitting at home, anxiously leaning toward their radios.

THE WHITE HOUSE
WASHINGTON

March 25, 1933.

This is the original of the Inaugural Address - March 4th, 1933 - and was used by me at the Capitol. Practically the only change, except for an occasional word, was the sentence at the opening, which I added longhand in the Senate Committee Room before the ceremonies began.

Franklin D. Roosevelt

****

▲ A note from Roosevelt accompanying his reading copy of the speech that mentions his last-minute addition of the line "This is a day of national consecration."

Roosevelt followed with a terrific line that could have been met with cries of "easy for you to say," given the president's wealth. But like the rest of the speech, it worked like a charm. The nation's troubles concerned, "thank God, only material things." The qualities of spirit, character, and faith that had sustained their forefathers through even more difficult times would bring the country through what was, after all, a mere monetary crisis, he said, simultaneously reminding Americans of their closely held religious values, the sacrifices of the Founding Fathers, and the peace the country

This is a day of consecration.

I am certain that my fellow Americans expect that on my induction into the Presidency I will address them with a candor and a decision which the present situation of our nation impels. This is preeminently the time to speak the truth, the whole truth, frankly and boldly. Nor need we shrink from honestly facing conditions in our country today. This great nation will endure as it has endured, will revive and will prosper. So first of all let me assert my firm belief that the only thing we have to fear is fear itself, - nameless, unreasoning, unjustified terror which paralyzes needed efforts to convert retreat into advance. In every dark hour of our national life a leadership of frankness and vigor has met with that understanding and support of the people themselves which is essential to victory. I am convinced that you will again give that support to leadership in these critical days.

In such a spirit on my part and on yours we face our common difficulties. They concern, thank God, only material things. Values have shrunken to fantastic levels; taxes have risen; our ability to pay has fallen; government of all kinds is faced by serious curtailment of income; the

▲ The first page of Roosevelt's reading draft, with the handwritten addition of the line "This is a day of national consecration."

had enjoyed since World War I. In a daring and successful move, FDR managed to get Americans to look on the bright side at a very dark moment in US history.

Taking the Lead

In his speech Roosevelt reminded Americans of their strength of character and refocused them on what we would today call "positive thinking." But he offered far more than that. He asserted in the most powerful terms his willingness and capacity to provide the leadership the country needed.

He would propose the measures necessary to end the Depression. The financial sector needed regulation and direction, and he would provide it. He would work with the Congress if it was willing, but if not, he would seek emergency powers to confront the national emergency.

Roosevelt offered no real specifics of the programs he would propose in this surprisingly brief speech, but he laid out his priorities clearly—putting people to work foremost among them. If the private sector could not provide jobs, the government would step in.

He also plainly foreshadowed the government's expanded role in communications and transportation. The era of an expanded, activist government was about to begin. Roosevelt also found room in the speech to speak of the need to revitalize trade and to go out into the world as a "good neighbor," a recognition that the Depression was not just an American problem, but a worldwide economic calamity.

Roosevelt later explained that his aim in the speech was to end the "fear of the present and the future which held the American people and the American spirit in its grip."

Not Just Talk, But Action

The speech was a magnificent success. For the moment, people of all political viewpoints were his allies—with the possible exception of what was left of the Wall Street establishment.

Building on the clear mandate and momentum generated by the speech, Roosevelt embarked on a whirlwind of activity during his first hundred days in office. He created government agencies that would undertake vast public works and employ hundreds of thousands, launched efforts to curb the ills and excesses of the financial sector, and proposed an alphabet soup of new regulatory agencies.

The Depression did not end overnight; it persisted for the rest of the decade. But a sense of reform and renewal had swept the country. FDR succeeded by creating a sense, or mood, that the country was moving again, and in the right direction.

During his first two terms in office, President Franklin Delano Roosevelt fundamentally altered the federal government. He massively increased its size and scope, and created a social safety net and system of economic regulation that still forms the framework of the United States government today.

During his lifetime, Roosevelt was sometimes simultaneously the most loved and most hated man in the country. And to this day, the argument continues unabated—did Roosevelt and the New Deal lead the country down the path toward its salvation or ruination? Either way, no one can deny that he led, both by his actions and by his words.

Roosevelt gave many well-crafted speeches during his time as president, but his first inaugural address in 1933 is the first and perhaps best example of his leadership style.

. . . .

First Inaugural Address
March 4, 1933, United States Capitol, Washington, DC

. . . .

This is a day of national consecration and I am certain that my fellow Americans expect that on my induction into the Presidency I will address them with a candor and a decision which the present situation of our Nation impels. This is preeminently the time to speak the truth, the whole truth, frankly and boldly. Nor need we shrink from honestly facing conditions in our country today. This great Nation will endure as it has endured, will revive and will prosper. So, first of all, let me assert my firm belief that the only thing we have to fear is fear itself--nameless, unreasoning, unjustified terror which paralyzes needed efforts to convert retreat into advance. In every dark hour of our national life a leadership of frankness and vigor has met with that understanding and support of the people themselves which is essential to victory. I am convinced that you will again give that support to leadership in these critical days.

In such a spirit on my part and on yours we face our common difficulties. They concern, thank God, only material things. Values have shrunken to fantastic levels; taxes have risen; our ability to pay has fallen; government of all kinds is faced by serious curtailment of income; the means of exchange are frozen in the currents of trade; the withered leaves of industrial enterprise lie on every side; farmers find no markets for their produce; the savings of many years in thousands of families are gone.

More important, a host of unemployed citizens face the grim problem of existence, and an equally great number toil with little return. Only a foolish optimist can deny the dark realities of the moment.

Yet our distress comes from no failure of substance. We are stricken by no plague of locusts. Compared with the perils which our forefathers conquered because they believed and were not afraid, we have still much to be thankful for. Nature still offers her bounty and human efforts have multiplied it. Plenty is at our doorstep, but a generous use of it languishes in the very sight of the supply. Primarily this is because the rulers of the exchange of mankind's goods have failed, through their own stubbornness and their own incompetence, have admitted their failure, and abdicated. Practices of the unscrupulous money changers stand indicted in the court of public opinion, rejected by the hearts and minds of men.

True they have tried, but their efforts have been cast in the pattern of an outworn tradition. Faced by failure of credit they have proposed only the lending of more money. Stripped of the lure of profit by which to induce our people to follow their false leadership, they have resorted to exhortations, pleading tearfully for restored confidence. They know only the rules of a generation of self-seekers. They have no vision, and when there is no vision the people perish.

The money changers have fled from their high seats in the temple of our civilization. We may now restore that temple to the ancient truths. The measure of the restoration lies in the extent to which we apply social values more noble than mere monetary profit.

Happiness lies not in the mere possession of money; it lies in the joy of achievement, in the thrill of creative effort. The joy and moral stimulation of work no longer must be forgotten in the mad chase of evanescent profits. These dark days will be worth all they cost us if they teach us that our true destiny is not to be ministered unto but to minister to ourselves and to our fellow men.

Recognition of the falsity of material wealth as the standard of success goes hand in hand with the abandonment of the false belief that public office and

▲ President Franklin D. Roosevelt signing the Emergency Banking Relief Act in March 1933, watched by Secretary of the Treasury William Woodin.

high political position are to be valued only by the standards of pride of place and personal profit; and there must be an end to a conduct in banking and in business which too often has given to a sacred trust the likeness of callous and selfish wrongdoing. Small wonder that confidence languishes, for it thrives only on honesty, on honor, on the sacredness of obligations, on faithful protection, on unselfish performance; without them it cannot live.

Restoration calls, however, not for changes in ethics alone. This Nation asks for action, and action now.

Our greatest primary task is to put people to work. This is no unsolvable problem if we face it wisely and courageously. It can be accomplished in part by direct recruiting by the Government itself, treating the task as we would treat the emergency of a war, but at the same time, through this employment, accomplishing greatly needed projects to stimulate and reorganize the use of our natural resources.

Hand in hand with this we must frankly recognize the overbalance of population in our industrial centers and, by engaging on a national scale in a redistribution, endeavor to provide a better use of the land for those best fitted for the land. The task can be helped by definite efforts to raise the values of agricultural products and with this the power to purchase the output of our cities. It can be helped by preventing realistically the tragedy of the growing loss through foreclosure of our small homes and our farms. It can be helped by insistence that the Federal, State, and local governments act forthwith on the demand that their cost be drastically reduced. It can be helped by the unifying of relief activities which today are often scattered, uneconomical, and unequal. It can be helped by national planning for and supervision of all forms of transportation and of communications and other utilities which have a definitely public character. There are many ways in which it can be helped, but it can never be

helped merely by talking about it. We must act and act quickly.

Finally, in our progress toward a resumption of work we require two safeguards against a return of the evils of the old order; there must be a strict supervision of all banking and credits and investments; there must be an end to speculation with other people's money, and there must be provision for an adequate but sound currency.

There are the lines of attack. I shall presently urge upon a new Congress in special session detailed measures for their fulfillment, and I shall seek the immediate assistance of the several States.

Through this program of action we address ourselves to putting our own national house in order and making income balance outgo. Our international trade relations, though vastly important, are in point of time and necessity secondary to the establishment of a sound national economy. I favor as a practical policy the putting of first things first. I shall spare no effort to restore world trade by international economic readjustment, but the emergency at home cannot wait on that accomplishment.

The basic thought that guides these specific means of national recovery is not narrowly nationalistic. It is the insistence, as a first consideration, upon the interdependence of the various elements in all parts of the United States – a recognition of the old and permanently important manifestation of the American spirit of the pioneer. It is the way to recovery. It is the immediate way. It is the strongest assurance that the recovery will endure.

In the field of world policy I would dedicate this Nation to the policy of the good

◀ The final page of Roosevelt's reading draft of the speech, signed by the President.

neighbor – the neighbor who resolutely respects himself and, because he does so, respects the rights of others – the neighbor who respects his obligations and respects the sanctity of his agreements in and with a world of neighbors.

If I read the temper of our people correctly, we now realize as we have never realized before our interdependence on each other; that we can not merely take but we must give as well; that if we are to go forward, we must move as a trained and loyal army willing to sacrifice for the good of a common discipline, because without such discipline no progress is made, no leadership becomes effective. We are, I know, ready and willing to submit our lives and property to such discipline, because it makes possible a leadership which aims at a larger good. This I propose to offer, pledging that the larger purposes will bind upon us all as a sacred obligation with a unity of duty hitherto evoked only in time of armed strife.

With this pledge taken, I assume unhesitatingly the leadership of this great army of our people dedicated to a disciplined attack upon our common problems.

Action in this image and to this end is feasible under the form of government which we have inherited from our ancestors. Our Constitution is so simple and practical that it is possible always to meet extraordinary needs by changes in emphasis and arrangement without loss of essential form. That is why our constitutional system has proved itself the most superbly enduring political mechanism the modern world has produced. It has met every stress of vast expansion of territory, of foreign wars, of bitter internal strife, of world relations.

It is to be hoped that the normal balance of executive and legislative authority may be wholly adequate to meet the unprecedented task before us. But it may be that an unprecedented demand and need for undelayed action may call for temporary departure from that normal balance of public procedure.

I am prepared under my constitutional duty to recommend the measures that a stricken nation in the midst of a stricken world may require. These measures, or such other measures as the Congress may build out of its experience and wisdom, I shall seek, within my constitutional authority, to bring to speedy adoption.

But in the event that the Congress shall fail to take one of these two courses, and in the event that the national emergency is still critical, I shall not evade the clear course of duty that will then confront me. I shall ask the Congress for the one remaining instrument to meet the crisis – broad Executive power to wage a war against the emergency, as great as the power that would be given to me if we were in fact invaded by a foreign foe.

For the trust reposed in me I will return the courage and the devotion that befit the time. I can do no less.

We face the arduous days that lie before us in the warm courage of the national unity; with the clear consciousness of seeking old and precious moral values; with the clean satisfaction that comes from the stem performance of duty by old and young alike. We aim at the assurance of a rounded and permanent national life.

We do not distrust the future of essential democracy. The people of the United States have not failed. In their need they have registered a mandate that they want direct, vigorous action. They have asked for discipline and direction under leadership. They have made me the present instrument of their wishes. In the spirit of the gift I take it.

In this dedication of a Nation we humbly ask the blessing of God. May He protect each and every one of us. May He guide me in the days to come.

President Franklin Delano Roosevelt

"In the future days, which we seek to make secure, we look forward to a world founded upon four essential human freedoms."

▼ President Franklin D. Roosevelt addressing the members of the House of Representatives.

By the start of Franklin Delano Roosevelt's third term, his previous speeches to this wounded and battered country had already set him near the top of presidential orators. On January 6, 1941, in one of the most powerful and effective addresses in US history, FDR raised the bar.

The speech prepared the country for the largest and most destructive war ever then became enshrined in history as the articulation of the "Four Freedoms," fundamental beliefs basic to all citizens of the world. Throughout the 1930s Roosevelt, appropriately preoccupied with the economy, went along with the strong isolationist

sentiments in the United States. He supported a number of neutrality measures in Congress, even as Germany, Japan, and Italy grew more aggressively militant. During his campaign for an unprecedented third term in 1940, he and opponent Wendell Willkie both pledged to keep American troops out of "foreign wars."

Though Roosevelt won by his narrowest margin he drew the support of those who favored strong measures against Hitler, while isolationists generally favored Willkie. By Election Day, the war in Europe was more than a year old and Roosevelt knew that the United States would join the fight sooner or later.

With his usual leadership and guile, FDR nudged a reluctant nation toward preparedness. He beefed up and modernized the armed forces and dramatically increased manufacture of armaments, on the very valid grounds that they could well be needed to defend the country against eventual invasion.

Persuading a Reluctant Congress

After the outbreak of war in Europe in 1939, Roosevelt asked the Congress to revise the Neutrality Act to permit the United States to sell arms to countries at war—chiefly Britain and France on a "cash and carry" basis. After France fell, the United States stepped up arms sales to Britain until, in November 1940, a desperate Winston Churchill wrote Roosevelt that Britain was running out of money to pay for arms shipments.

Congress would not support a loan to Britain. The solution reportedly came to Roosevelt while he was on a cruise, in what Labor Secretary Frances Perkins called "a flash of almost clairvoyant knowledge and understanding." The United States would not sell arms to Britain; it would lend them. Roosevelt dubbed the program "lend-lease" and set about selling it to the press and public.

He first broached the topic at a press conference on December 17, 1940, using what longtime aide Samuel Rosenman called "his talent for homely simile." If I have a garden hose, Roosevelt said, and my neighbor's house catches fire, I don't ask him to pay for its use in advance. I let him use it and he returns it afterward. We'll lend our neighbors (Britain) the materiel to meet the threat of Adolf Hitler, and get it back afterwards. Arch-isolationist Senator Robert Taft said lending ships, planes, and other weaponry would be like lending chewing gum: "you don't want it back

afterwards." But Roosevelt's arguments proved more persuasive.

In late December 1940, he further advanced the issue in one of his famous fireside chats, adopting a phrase coined by French diplomat Jean Monnet. America must be "the great arsenal of democracy," Monnet told Roosevelt, persuading him to further increase arms production.

Roosevelt prepared to lay out the entire case for lend-lease to the Congress in his Annual Message to Congress—what we know now as the State of the Union Address. The team assembled to prepare the speech consisted of Rosenman, Harry Hopkins, and Robert Sherwood.

Rosenman had been with Roosevelt since his gubernatorial campaign in 1928. Hopkins had succeeded Louis Howe as Roosevelt's closest aide after Howe's death in 1936. Hopkins carried out a variety of diplomatic assignments, including a detailed assessment of how determined the British were to continue the war. His assessment led Roosevelt to an even deeper commitment to keep Britain afloat.

Sherwood, two-time Pulitzer Prize winner for drama, was a recent addition. A glamorous name, he was courted by the president to join the team. A liberal and an advocate of US entry into the war, Sherwood eagerly accepted. Some combination of Sherwood, Hopkins, and Rosenman would produce just about every major speech Roosevelt gave for the rest of his life.

In his book *Working with Roosevelt*, Rosenman described a chaotic but effective working process, with, on a typical night, the speechwriters assembling in the White House Cabinet Room after regular working hours to "put together" the speeches. The president frequently poured cocktails and the group worked through dinner. They would cut and paste, hand-write notes onto

◀ Author of the original draft of the "Four Freedoms" speech Adolf Berle, pictured leaving the American Embassy in England, 1943.

the typed drafts and, in general, swap ideas. The president would go to bed around 11:00 p.m., and the speechwriters would keep working—fueled by whiskey for Sherwood, black coffee for Hopkins, and Coke for Rosenman—until they had produced a draft suitable for the night stenographers to type up so it was ready for President Roosevelt when he arose.

An Unprecedented Threat

Such was the process they followed with the Four Freedoms speech, which had started out as "a very good draft" sent over from the State Department and written by Adolf Berle, the assistant secretary of state for Latin American affairs who frequently contributed to foreign policy addresses. This draft referenced the European threats that led to the 1823 Monroe Doctrine, which until World War I had been largely successful in protecting US interests from European threats and entanglements. But even that conflict could not compare with the threat posed by dictators like Hitler, a psychopath whose vision was to conquer the world.

The Monroe Doctrine references were cut before the final draft, but the "unprecedented nature" of the threat became one of Roosevelt's core themes as he worked to make Americans understand the imminent danger and the need for a unified response. (He uses the word "unprecedented" twice in the first paragraph of the delivered version.)

The trio of White House speechwriters took Berle's draft apart and put it back together, with considerable help from Roosevelt. "The President himself dictated five pages, and worked on it very hard through the [seven] drafts," recalls Rosenman, "filling each of them with his handwritten corrections and insertions."

In the final speech, Roosevelt takes considerable time and effort to describe the nature and extent of the threat—and in the strongest terms dismisses isolationist arguments about the invulnerability of the United States to foreign invasion. The invasion would not be direct, he warned, in part because of a powerful British fleet in the Atlantic. Reminding his audience of Great Britain's role in protecting US shores was another way of arguing for sending help in the form of lend-lease. The first phase of the invasion would be sneaky and accomplished by "secret agents and their dupes" who might already be at work, he said, in the United States and throughout Latin America.

He also slams isolationists and other appeasers who undermined US security by seeking to do business with Hitler. Sherwood wrote the sentence that condemned them as a "small group of selfish men who would clip the wings of the American eagle in order to feather their own nests." The speechwriters believed this phrase would be the most memorable of the speech. It passed unnoticed.

Envisioning the US as World Protector

What became immortal, and what elevated the speech above a basic cry of alarm, was the section dictated by Roosevelt. Here were the President's ambitious and visionary aims for the

United States as a protector of rights around the world—the Four Freedoms.

Toward the end of the fourth draft, Rosenman recounts, the president announced that he had an idea for the *peroration* (which is, formally, the powerful ending of a speech in which ideas are summed up and the audience is exhorted to action). Roosevelt then dictated the Four Freedoms passages, which survived into the speech almost exactly as he pronounced them, according to Rosenman.

Here Roosevelt outlined his vision of a world founded on four essential freedoms: freedom of speech and expression, freedom of religion, freedom from want, and freedom from fear.

Roosevelt's speechwriters were generally enthusiastic about the president's addition to the speech, though Hopkins was concerned that phrases like "everywhere in the world" covered a lot of territory, adding "I don't know how interested Americans are going to be in the people of Java."

"I'm afraid they'll have to be some day, Harry," replied Roosevelt. "The world is getting so small that even the people in Java are getting to be our neighbors now."

Within a year Roosevelt would be proven right. Java—the most populous island of Indonesia—was soon well known to American military strategists working to halt Japanese domination of that part of the world.

Roosevelt also took care in the message to explain to Americans why they were fighting by outlining the objectives of a democracy—essentially restating the objectives of the New Deal. It served to give "our fighting men and those who produced behind the lines . . . additional stamina and courage from the

The peroration dictated by Roosevelt and written down by Sam Rosenman.

very knowledge that they were defending that way of life," Rosenman pointed out.

A Lasting Legacy

Lend-lease passed through Congress the next month, and Roosevelt put Harry Hopkins in charge of it. It sustained the British for the rest of the year until Pearl Harbor brought the United States into the war in December 1941.

The Four Freedoms became a key element of Allied war propaganda, illustrated by a famous series of Norman Rockwell paintings that were widely reproduced as posters.

The goals of the Four Freedoms also represented the basis of the Atlantic Charter signed by Roosevelt and Winston Churchill in 1941. Later, in 1948, they were the foundation of the United Nations Universal

Declaration of Human Rights, championed by Eleanor Roosevelt. Six decades later, President George W. Bush's speechwriters drew on the Four Freedoms in framing his remarks to the Congress following the September 11 attacks.

Like many of Roosevelt's words, the Four Freedoms have entered history as among the most memorable and effective declarations ever uttered by an American president. The speech remains one of the most important State of the Union adesses.

State of the Union Address
January 6, 1941, United States Capitol, Washington, DC

Mr. President, Mr. Speaker, members of the 77th Congress:

I address you, the members of this new Congress, at a moment unprecedented in the history of the union. I use the word "unprecedented" because at no previous time has American security been as seriously threatened from without as it is today.

Since the permanent formation of our government under the Constitution in 1789, most of the periods of crisis in our history have related to our domestic affairs. And, fortunately, only one of these – the four-year war between the States – ever threatened our national unity. Today, thank God, 130,000,000 Americans in 48 States have forgotten points of the compass in our national unity.

It is true that prior to 1914 the United States often has been disturbed by events in other continents. We have even engaged in two wars with European nations and in a number of undeclared wars in the West Indies, in the Mediterranean and in the Pacific, for the maintenance of American rights and for the principles of peaceful commerce. But in no case had a serious threat been raised against our national safety or our continued independence.

What I seek to convey is the historic truth that the United States as a nation has at all times maintained opposition – clear, definite opposition – to any attempt to lock us in behind an ancient Chinese wall while the procession of civilization went past. Today, thinking of our children and of their children, we oppose enforced isolation for ourselves or for any other part of the Americas.

That determination of ours, extending over all these years, was proved, for example, in the early days during the quarter century of wars following the French Revolution. While the Napoleonic struggles did threaten interests of the United States because of the French foothold in the West Indies and in Louisiana, and while we engaged in the War of 1812 to vindicate our right to peaceful trade, it is nevertheless clear that neither France nor Great Britain nor any other nation was aiming at domination of the whole world.

And in like fashion, from 1815 to 1914 – ninety-nine years – no single war in Europe or in Asia constituted a real threat against our future or against the future of any other American nation.

Except in the Maximilian interlude in Mexico, no foreign power sought to establish itself in this hemisphere. And the strength of the British fleet in the Atlantic has been a friendly strength; it is still a friendly strength.

Even when the World War broke out in 1914, it seemed to contain only small threat of danger to

MESSAGE TO CONGRESS
1941

───────────────

I address you the Members of the Seventy-Seventh
Congress at a moment unprecedented in our history. I
use the word "unprecedented", because at no previous time
has the future of American security been more greatly
threatened from without.

Since the permanent formation of the government
under the Constitution in 1789, most of the periods of
crisis in our history have related to the domestic scene.
Fortunately, only one of these -- the four year war
between the States -- has threatened continued national
unity.

It is true that up to 1914 the United States was
often disturbed by events in other Continents, and we
even engaged in wars with other nations. In no case,
however, was a serious threat raised against our national
safety.

▶ The first page of the second draft of the speech with changes written in by Roosevelt.

our own American future. But as time went on, as we remember, the American people began to visualize what the downfall of democratic nations might mean to our own democracy.

We need not overemphasize imperfections in the peace of Versailles. We need not harp on failure of the democracies to deal with problems of world reconstruction. We should remember that the peace of 1919 was far less unjust than the kind of pacification which began even before Munich, and which is being carried on under the new order of tyranny that seeks to spread over every continent today. The American people have unalterably set their faces against that tyranny.

I suppose that every realist knows that the democratic way of life is at this moment being directly assailed in every part of the world – assailed either by arms or by secret spreading of poisonous propaganda by those who seek to destroy unity and promote discord in nations that are still at peace. During 16 long months this assault has blotted out the whole pattern of democratic life in an appalling number of independent nations, great and small. And the assailants are still on the march, threatening other nations, great and small.

Therefore, as your President, performing my constitutional duty to "give to the Congress information of the state of the union," I find it unhappily necessary to report that the future and the safety of our country and of our democracy are overwhelmingly involved in events far beyond our borders.

Samuel Rosenman (left) with Harry S. Truman (right) at the 1956 Democratic Convention.

Armed defense of democratic existence is now being gallantly waged in four continents. If that defense fails, all the population and all the resources of Europe and Asia, and Africa and Austral-Asia will be dominated by conquerors. And let us remember that the total of those populations in those four continents, the total of those populations and their resources greatly exceed the sum total of the population and the resources of the whole of the Western Hemisphere – yes, many times over.

In times like these it is immature – and, incidentally, untrue – for anybody to brag that an unprepared America, single-handed and with one hand tied behind its back, can hold off the whole world.

No realistic American can expect from a dictator's peace international generosity, or return of true independence, or world disarmament, or freedom of expression, or freedom of religion – or even good business. Such a peace would bring no security for us or for our neighbors. Those who would give up essential liberty to purchase a little temporary safety deserve neither liberty nor safety.

As a nation we may take pride in the fact that we are soft-hearted; but we cannot afford to be soft-headed. We must always be wary of those who with sounding brass and a tinkling cymbal preach the "ism" of appeasement. We must especially beware of that small group of selfish men who would clip the wings of the American eagle in order to feather their own nests.

I have recently pointed out how quickly the tempo of modern warfare could bring into our very midst the physical attack which we must eventually expect if the dictator nations win this war.

There is much loose talk of our immunity from immediate and direct invasion from across the seas. Obviously, as long as the British Navy retains its power, no such danger exists. Even if there were no British Navy, it is not probable that any enemy would be stupid enough to attack us by landing troops in the United States from across thousands of miles of ocean, until it had acquired strategic bases from which to operate.

But we learn much from the lessons of the past years in Europe – particularly the lesson of Norway, whose essential seaports were captured by treachery and surprise built up over a series of years. The first phase of the invasion of this hemisphere would not be the landing of regular troops. The necessary strategic points would be occupied by secret agents and by their dupes – and great numbers of them are already here and in Latin America. As long as the aggressor nations maintain the offensive they, not we, will choose the time and the place and the method of their attack.

And that is why the future of all the American Republics is today in serious danger. That is why this annual message to the Congress is unique in our history. That is why every member of the executive branch of the government and every member of the Congress face great responsibility, great accountability. The need of the moment is that our actions and our policy should be devoted primarily – almost exclusively – to meeting this foreign peril. For all our domestic problems are now a part of the great emergency.

Just as our national policy in internal affairs has been based upon a decent respect for the rights and the dignity of all our fellow men within our gates, so our national policy in foreign affairs has been based on a decent respect for the rights and the dignity of all nations, large and small. And the justice of morality must and will win in the end.

Our national policy is this:

First, by an impressive expression of the public will and without regard to partisanship, we are committed to all-inclusive national defense.

Secondly, by an impressive expression of the public will and without regard to partisanship, we are committed to full support of all those resolute people everywhere who are resisting aggression and are thereby keeping war away from our hemisphere. By this support we express our determination that the democratic cause shall prevail, and we strengthen the defense and the security of our own nation.

Third, by an impressive expression of the public will and without regard to partisanship, we are committed to the proposition that principles of morality and considerations for our own security will never permit us to acquiesce in a peace dictated by aggressors and sponsored by appeasers. We know that enduring peace cannot be bought at the cost of other people's freedom.

In the recent national election there was no substantial difference between the two great parties in respect to that national policy. No issue was fought out on this line before the American electorate. And today it is abundantly evident that American citizens everywhere are demanding and supporting speedy and complete action in recognition of obvious danger.

Therefore, the immediate need is a swift and driving increase in our armament production. Leaders of industry and labor have responded to our summons. Goals of speed have been set. In some cases these goals are being reached ahead of time. In some cases we are on schedule; in other cases there are slight but not serious delays. And in some cases – and, I am sorry to say, very important cases – we are all concerned by the slowness of the accomplishment of our plans.

The Army and Navy, however, have made substantial progress during the past year. Actual experience is improving and speeding up our methods of production with every passing day. And today's best is not good enough for tomorrow.

I am not satisfied with the progress thus far made. The men in charge of the program represent the best in training, in ability, and in patriotism. They are not satisfied with the progress thus far made. None of us will be satisfied until the job is done.

No matter whether the original goal was set too high or too low, our objective is quicker and better results.

To give you two illustrations:

We are behind schedule in turning out finished airplanes. We are working day and night to solve the innumerable problems and to catch up.

We are ahead of schedule in building warships, but we are working to get even further ahead of that schedule.

To change a whole nation from a basis of peacetime production of implements of peace to a basis of wartime production of implements of war is no small task. And the greatest difficulty comes at the beginning of the program, when new tools, new plant facilities, new assembly lines, new shipways must first be constructed before the actual material begins to flow steadily and speedily from them.

The Congress of course, must rightly keep itself informed at all times of the progress of the program. However, there is certain information, as the Congress itself will readily recognize, which, in the interests of our own security and those of the nations that we are supporting, must of needs be kept in confidence.

New circumstances are constantly begetting new needs for our safety. I shall ask this Congress for greatly increased new appropriations and authorizations to carry on what we have begun.

I also ask this Congress for authority and for funds sufficient to manufacture additional munitions and war supplies of many kinds, to be turned over to those nations which are now in actual war with aggressor nations. Our most useful and immediate role is to act as an arsenal for them as well as for ourselves. They do not need manpower, but they do need billions of dollars' worth of the weapons of defense.

The time is near when they will not be able to pay for them all in ready cash. We cannot, and we will not, tell them that they must surrender merely because of present inability to pay for the weapons which we know they must have.

I do not recommend that we make them a loan of dollars with which to pay for these weapons – a loan to be repaid in dollars. I recommend that we make it possible for those nations to continue to obtain war materials in the United States, fitting their orders into our own program. And nearly all of their material would, if the time ever came, be useful in our own defense.

Taking counsel of expert military and naval authorities, considering what is best for our own security, we are free to decide how much should be kept here and how much should be sent abroad to our friends who, by their determined and heroic resistance, are giving us time in which to make ready our own defense.

For what we send abroad we shall be repaid, repaid within a reasonable time following the close of hostilities, repaid in similar materials, or at our option in other goods of many kinds which they can produce and which we need.

Let us say to the democracies: "We Americans are vitally concerned in your defense of freedom. We are putting forth our energies, our resources, and our organizing powers to give you the strength to regain and maintain a free world. We shall send you in

ever-increasing numbers, ships, planes, tanks, guns. That is our purpose and our pledge."

In fulfillment of this purpose we will not be intimidated by the threats of dictators that they will regard as a breach of international law or as an act of war our aid to the democracies which dare to resist their aggression. Such aid – Such aid is not an act of war, even if a dictator should unilaterally proclaim it so to be.

And when the dictators – if the dictators – are ready to make war upon us, they will not wait for an act of war on our part.

They did not wait for Norway or Belgium or the Netherlands to commit an act of war. Their only interest is in a new one-way international law, which lacks mutuality in its observance and therefore becomes an instrument of oppression. The happiness of future generations of Americans may well depend

▲ President Franklin D. Roosevelt and British Prime Minister Winston Churchill seated on the deck of an English battleship during talks in February 1941, which preceded the signing of the Atlantic Charter.

on how effective and how immediate we can make our aid felt. No one can tell the exact character of the emergency situations that we may be called upon to meet. The nation's hands must not be tied when the nation's life is in danger.

Yes, and we must prepare, all of us prepare, to make the sacrifices that the emergency – almost as serious as war itself – demands. Whatever stands in the way of speed and efficiency in defense, in defense preparations of any kind, must give way to the national need.

A free nation has the right to expect full cooperation from all groups. A free nation has the right to look to the leaders of business, of labor, and

~~PERORATION~~

~~We must look forward to a world based on four essential~~ human freedoms.

The first is freedom of speech and expression everywhere in the world.

The second is freedom of every person to worship God in his own way everywhere in the world.

The third is freedom from want -- which translated into international terms means economic understandings which will secure to every nation everywhere a healthy peace time life for its inhabitants.

The fourth is freedom from fear -- which translated into international terms means a world-wide reduction of armaments to such a point and in such a thorough fashion that no nation anywhere will be in a position to commit an act of physical aggression against any neighbor.

That kind of a world is the very antithesis of the "so-called "new order" which ~~being~~ ~~by~~ the dictators seek to ~~for Europe and Asia~~ create ~~by~~ ~~first~~ the point of a gun in Europe and in Asia

-18- 178

The first is freedom of speech and expression everywhere in the world.

The second is freedom of every person to worship God in his own way everywhere in the world.

The third is freedom from want — which translated into ~~international~~ *world* terms means economic understandings which will secure to every nation ~~everywhere~~ a healthy peace time life for its inhabitants. *Everywhere in the world*

The fourth is freedom from fear — which translated into ~~international~~ *world* terms means a world-wide reduction of armaments to such a point and in such a thorough fashion that no nation ~~anywhere~~ will be in a position to commit an act of physical aggression against any neighbor. *Anywhere in the world.*

A-17A. That kind of a world is the very antithesis of the so-called "new order" which the dictators seek to create ~~at the point of a gun~~ *with the crash of a bomb* in Europe and in Asia.

To that "new order" we oppose the greater conception, the moral order. A good society is able to face schemes of world domination and foreign revolutions alike without fear. It has no need either for the one or for the other.

◄▲ Pages from the fourth (left) and fifth (above) drafts with handwritten amendments by Roosevelt.

of agriculture to take the lead in stimulating effort, not among other groups but within their own group.

The best way of dealing with the few slackers or trouble-makers in our midst is, first, to shame them by patriotic example, and if that fails, to use the sovereignty of government to save government.

As men do not live by bread alone, they do not fight by armaments alone. Those who man our defenses and those behind them who build our defenses must have the stamina and the courage which come from unshakable belief in the manner of life which they are defending. The mighty action that we are calling for cannot be based on a disregard of all the things worth fighting for.

The nation takes great satisfaction and much strength from the things which have been done to make its people conscious of their individual stake in the preservation of democratic life in America. Those things have toughened the fiber of our people, have renewed their faith and strengthened their devotion to the institutions we make ready to protect.

Certainly this is no time for any of us to stop thinking about the social and economic problems which are the root cause of the social revolution which is today a supreme factor in the world. For there is nothing mysterious about the foundations of a healthy and strong democracy.

The basic things expected by our people of their political and economic systems are simple. They are:

Equality of opportunity for youth and for others.

Jobs for those who can work.

Security for those who need it.

The ending of special privilege for the few.

The preservation of civil liberties for all.

The enjoyment – The enjoyment of the fruits of scientific progress in a wider and constantly rising standard of living.

These are the simple, the basic things that must never be lost sight of in the turmoil and unbelievable complexity of our modern world. The inner and abiding strength of our economic and political systems is dependent upon the degree to which they fulfill these expectations.

Many subjects connected with our social economy call for immediate improvement. As examples:

We should bring more citizens under the coverage of old-age pensions and unemployment insurance.

We should widen the opportunities for adequate medical care.

We should plan a better system by which persons deserving or needing gainful employment may obtain it.

I have called for personal sacrifice, and I am assured of the willingness of almost all Americans to respond to that call. A part of the sacrifice means the payment of more money in taxes. In my budget message I will recommend that a greater portion of this great defense program be paid for from taxation than we are paying for today. No person should try, or be allowed to get rich out of the program, and the principle of tax payments in accordance with ability to pay should be constantly before our eyes to guide our legislation.

If the Congress maintains these principles the voters, putting patriotism ahead of pocketbooks, will give you their applause.

In the future days, which we seek to make secure, we look forward to a world founded upon four essential human freedoms.

The first is freedom of speech and expression – everywhere in the world.

The second is freedom of every person to worship God in his own way – everywhere in the world.

The third is freedom from want, which, translated into world terms, means economic understandings which will secure to every nation a healthy peacetime life for its inhabitants – everywhere in the world.

The fourth is freedom from fear, which, translated into world terms, means a world-wide reduction of armaments to such a point and in such a thorough fashion that no nation will be in a position to commit an act of physical aggression against any neighbor – anywhere in the world.

That is no vision of a distant millennium. It is a definite basis for a kind of world attainable in our own time and generation. That kind of world is the very antithesis of the so-called "new order" of tyranny which the dictators seek to create with the crash of a bomb.

To that new order we oppose the greater conception – the moral order. A good society is able to face schemes of world domination and foreign revolutions alike without fear.

Since the beginning of our American history we have been engaged in change, in a perpetual, peaceful revolution, a revolution which goes on steadily, quietly, adjusting

itself to changing conditions without the concentration camp or the quicklime in the ditch. The world order which we seek is the cooperation of free countries, working together in a friendly, civilized society.

This nation has placed its destiny in the hands and heads and hearts of its millions of free men and women, and its faith in freedom under the guidance of God. Freedom means the supremacy of human rights everywhere. Our support goes to those who struggle to gain those rights and keep them. Our strength is our unity of purpose.

To that high concept there can be no end save victory.

▼ President Franklin D. Roosevelt signing the Lend-Lease Bill at the White House.

President Franklin Delano Roosevelt

A date which will live in infamy.

On December 8, 1941, Franklin Delano Roosevelt addressed the US Congress and the largest radio audience in history—eighty-one percent of the American people. They were stunned, grieving, and afraid. The day before, the Japanese had without warning attacked Pearl Harbor, and the future was uncertain.

Roosevelt had faced many tests of his leadership during nearly nine years as president. His jaunty optimism had buoyed Americans throughout the grindingly grim decade of the 1930s. He had fought the Depression not only with innovative government programs, but also with a torrent of sometimes overblown rhetoric. That battle was not yet completely won, but listening to Roosevelt gave the people hope that it would be.

Now he was faced with a much different situation—a devastating attack from an unexpected source. Not that he was entirely unready. Since 1939, he had been, sometimes covertly, preparing America for war—but in Europe. War across the Atlantic was inevitable, he believed, and his close alliance with Winston Churchill led him to build up American defenses, which proved fortuitous sooner than he had anticipated.

▲   President Franklin D. Roosevelt making his address to the Joint Session of Congress on December 8, 1941.

FDR had taken note of Japan's increasing belligerency and the empire's formal alliance with Germany and Italy. He also was well aware of Japan's increased deployment of men and arms throughout the Pacific region. Nevertheless, Roosevelt was convinced the Japanese were bluffing.

Roosevelt Responded Quickly

He was wrong, of course, as December 7, 1941, graphically and tragically proved. The unprecedented strike on American soil, the devastation to the Pacific fleet, and the loss of so many young servicemen in one day spread panic throughout the country. The president needed to respond, quickly and effectively, to right the reeling country and galvanize it for the coming war. And although his words would be pointed toward the Japanese threat, he knew that the attack also heralded the start of war with the Nazis and the Fascists in Europe.

How to respond to an event that suddenly placed the fate of the world in the balance? Supreme Court justice Oliver Wendell Holmes famously said Roosevelt possessed "a second-rate intellect but a first-rate temperament." The slight to his intellectual gifts is debatable, but the

▲ Black smoke and flames pour out of a battleship on fire in Pearl Harbor after the surprise attack by the Japanese that brought America into World War II.

question of his temperament had long since been decided by his response to economic disaster. His coolness served the country equally well when presented with military disaster.

Roosevelt famously employed a group of high-profile speechwriters, and they quickly mobilized at the White House. He set them to work crafting a speech that would explain the situation to the American people. He had, however, already decided what he needed to do immediately, and what he should say.

"The President had decided to go to Congress the next day," wrote longtime speechwriter and aide Sam Rosenman, in his book *Working with Roosevelt*, "and we learned later that evening [of December 7] that he had already prepared most

▲ Saburo Kurusu, Japan's special envoy for a "final attempt at peace," Secretary of State Cordell Hull, and Kichisaburo Nomura, Japanese Ambassador to the United States, arriving at the White House for a conference with President Roosevelt, on November 17, 1941.

of the speech. He had dictated it to [secretary] Grace [Tully] between his many conferences of the day with military leaders, and with scores of other people."

FDR Resisted Calls for History Lesson

Roosevelt, naturally, was receiving advice from all quarters. Secretary of State Cordell Hull wanted him to lay out in detail the history of relations between the United States and Japan and the efforts to find a peaceful solution to Japanese expansionist moves in the Far East.

The President rejected Hull's advice. The precedent for a reasoned and full explanation lay with President Woodrow Wilson's speech to the Congress making the case for US entry into World War I. Master of symbolism that Roosevelt was, he underscored the parallel by inviting Wilson's widow, Edith Bolling Wilson, to attend the speech.

But FDR correctly perceived that the sneak attack on Pearl Harbor had been a vicious and deceitful act and deserved an outraged and visceral reply. No justification was required, he knew—just a pledge of vengeance. He did include a nod to Hull's suggestion by noting in his second paragraph that the two nations had been at peace and were still in negotiations over a solution to Japanese expansionism. An hour after the planes hit Pearl Harbor, he noted, the Japanese ambassador had visited the secretary of state, and had given no hint of war or attack—underscoring the depth of the Japanese treachery.

Other than that reference, however, he stuck to the bare facts of the attack and the resultant death and destruction. Roosevelt the superb communicator knew that the events of December 7 spoke for themselves, and that simplicity and brevity would be more effective than eloquence and bombast.

Superb Rhetorical Instincts on Display

Roosevelt's superb instincts as a wordsmith were on display, under the most trying circumstances. Replacing just three words turned a strong sentence into an immortal one—one that has indeed lived on in world history. In addition, his use of the passive voice, saying "the United States was attacked by Japan" instead of "Japan attacked the United States" cast his country as the aggrieved victim of a deceitful and unprovoked assault. Though speechwriters typically avoid the passive voice because it sounds weak, in this case it enhanced the image Roosevelt was trying to create, and added another dimension to the growing American outrage.

Roosevelt made handwritten changes to the draft as he received new information. He added one sentence each to reflect the incoming intelligence on five more Japanese attacks—Hong Kong, Guam, the Philippines, Wake Island, and Midway—and torpedo attacks on American ships between Honolulu and San Francisco.

The sentences were intoned one by one as a litany of the Japanese aggression, using the rhetorical technique of repetition to heighten the impact, hammering home each separate incident by repeating the words, "last night."

Roosevelt made no attempt to minimize the harm the attacks had caused, or the gravity of the threat. Presenting the facts in the starkest possible terms would bring his people more rapidly through the stages of shock and fear and toward the outrage necessary to unite behind him as he led them into World War II.

Yesterday the Japanese Government also launched an attack against Malaya.

Last night Japanese forces attacked Hong Kong.

Last night Japanese forces attacked Guam.

Last night Japanese forces attacked the Philippine Islands.

Last night the Japanese attacked Wake Island.

This morning the Japanese attacked Midway Island.

Japan has, therefore, undertaken a surprise offensive extending throughout the Pacific area. The facts of yesterday speak for themselves. The people of the United States have already formed their opinions and well understand the implications to the very life and safety of our nation.

As Commander-in-Chief of the Army and Navy I have directed that all measures be taken for our defense.

Always will be remembered the character of the onslaught against us.

No matter how long it may take us to overcome this premeditated invasion, the American people will in their righteous might win through to absolute victory.

I believe I interpret the will of the Congress and of the people when I assert that we will not only defend ourselves to the uttermost but will make very certain that this form of treachery shall never endanger us again.

Hostilities exist. There is no blinking at the fact that our people, our territory and our interests are in grave danger.

▲ The second page of Roosevelt's reading copy of the speech, with last minute alterations in the President's own handwriting.

Speech Was Strikingly Brief

The speech was strikingly brief at just 520 words, taking less than seven minutes to deliver. There was no attempt at persuasion. He made no attempt to build a case for going to war, or to appease the still considerable isolationist sentiments that had kept the United States from entering the war in Europe for more than two years. He made no appeal for support from the people. It was a given that every American would provide total support and total commitment to defeat a vicious and powerful enemy.

Roosevelt injected no personal opinions into the speech, other than his characterization of "infamy" and one reference to "treachery." One of his only forays into rhetoric came when he inverted the order of a sentence to say "always will our nation remember the character of the onslaught against us."

-4-

Hostilities exist. There is no mincing the fact that our people, our territory and our interests are in grave danger.

I, therefore, ask that the Congress declare that since the unprovoked and dastardly attack by Japan on Sunday, December seventh, a state of war has existed between the United States and the Japanese Empire.

****

◄ The final page of the draft of the speech in which Harry Hopkins added a handwritten note suggesting the addition of the "gain the inevitable triumph—so help us God" line.

steeled his audience to take the hard and bitter steps that would lead to that victory.

Harry Hopkins was responsible for one final flourish just before the final draft was completed. Roosevelt, not notably religious, had nevertheless taken care to invoke the Almighty in many of his speeches. In the heat of the moment, he neglected to do so in his address to Congress. Hopkins persuaded Roosevelt to add a pledge that the United States would "gain the inevitable triumph—so help us God."

That construction underscored the historic nature of the offense, and indeed, for those alive and aware on that day in December, it became a defining moment in their history.

Roosevelt pledged nothing less than "absolute victory," presaging a struggle that would end with the obliteration of two Japanese cities by atomic bombs, and Germany in ruins. His strength and resolve

Republicans Joined in Applause

There were no party politics or partisan divisions in the chamber of the House of Representatives that day. "On most of the President's personal appearances before the Congress," recalls Rosenman, "we found the applause coming largely from one side—the Democratic side. But this day was different. The applause, the spirit of cooperation, came equally from both sides of the chamber. . . . The new feeling of unity which suddenly welled up in the chamber on December 8, the common purpose behind the leadership of the President, the joint determination to see things through, were typical of what was taking place throughout the country."

Thirty-three minutes after the president concluded his speech, the Congress almost unanimously approved a resolution declaring war on Japan. The only dissenting vote was in the House, from pacifist representative Jeannette Rankin, a Republican from Montana. Three days later, Japan's Axis allies Germany and Italy declared war on the United States, and the country was fully engaged in the global war that would occupy it for the next four years. Roosevelt would not live to see the "absolute victory" he had pledged to win.

The White House was immediately inundated with telegrams praising the president's stance. Typical of them is this one: "On that Sunday we were dismayed and frightened, but your unbounded courage pulled us together." Recruiting stations were jammed with volunteers and had to go on twenty-four-hour duty to handle the crowds seeking to sign up. The numbers were reported to be twice as high as after Woodrow Wilson's declaration of war in 1917. The anti-war and isolationist movement collapsed in the aftermath of the speech, and even the president's fiercest critics began pledging their support. Charles Lindbergh, for example, an icon of the isolationist movement and an admirer of Adolf Hitler, issued a statement of unqualified support for the government, adding that, "We must now turn every effort to building the greatest and most efficient Army, Navy and Air Force in the world."

Political scientists and scholars of presidential rhetoric alike have declared Roosevelt's brief, uncomplicated speech one of the greatest by any US president and one of the one hundred or so most important documents in American history. Roosevelt in effect created a template for facing and surmounting a crisis. His few words to the Congress on that December 8 resonate to this day. They have unquestionably affected every presidential statement since at moments of national crisis, with the most vivid example being President George W. Bush's statements in the wake of the September 11, 2001, attacks, which drew direct parallels between the two events.

▲ President Franklin D. Roosevelt signing the declaration of war against Japan, wearing a black armband.

Presidential Address to Joint Session of Congress
December 8, 1941, United States Capitol, Washington, DC

Mr. Vice President, Mr. Speaker, members of the Senate and the House of Representatives:

Yesterday, December 7th, 1941 – a date which will live in infamy – the United States of America was suddenly and deliberately attacked by naval and air forces of the Empire of Japan.

The United States was at peace with that nation, and, at the solicitation of Japan, was still in conversation with its government and its Emperor looking toward the maintenance of peace in the Pacific.

Indeed, one hour after Japanese air squadrons had commenced bombing in the American island of Oahu, the Japanese Ambassador to the United States and his colleague delivered to our Secretary of State a formal reply to a recent American message. And, while this reply stated that it seemed useless to continue the existing diplomatic negotiations, it contained no threat or hint of war or of armed attack.

It will be recorded that the distance of Hawaii from Japan makes it obvious that the attack was deliberately planned many days or even weeks ago. During the intervening time the Japanese Government has deliberately sought to deceive the United States by false statements and expressions of hope for continued peace.

The attack yesterday on the Hawaiian Islands has caused severe damage to American naval and military forces. I regret to tell you that very many American lives have been lost. In addition, American ships have been reported torpedoed on the high seas between San Francisco and Honolulu.

Yesterday the Japanese Government also launched an attack against Malaya.

Last night Japanese forces attacked Hong Kong. Last night Japanese forces attacked Guam. Last night Japanese forces attacked the Philippine Islands. Last night the Japanese attacked Wake Island. And this morning the Japanese attacked Midway Island.

Japan has therefore undertaken a surprise offensive extending throughout the Pacific area. The facts of yesterday and today speak for themselves. The people of the United States have already formed their opinions and well understand the implications to the very life and safety of our nation.

As Commander-in-Chief of the Army and Navy I have directed that all measures be taken for our defense, that always will our whole nation remember the character of the onslaught against us.

No matter how long it may take us to overcome this premeditated invasion, the American people, in their righteous might, will win through to absolute victory.

I believe that I interpret the will of the Congress and of the people when I assert that we will not only defend ourselves to the uttermost but will make it very certain that this form of treachery shall never again endanger us.

Hostilities exist. There is no blinking at the fact that our people, our territory and our interests are in grave danger.

With confidence in our armed forces, with the unbounding determination of our people, we will gain the inevitable triumph. So help us God.

I ask that the Congress declare that since the unprovoked and dastardly attack by Japan on Sunday, December 7th, 1941, a state of war has existed between the United States and the Japanese Empire.

PROPOSED MESSAGE TO THE CONGRESS

Yesterday, December 7, 1941, a date which will live in ~~world history~~ *infamy* ~~of Japan~~

the United States of America was *suddenly* ~~simultaneously~~ and deliberately attacked

by naval and air forces of the Empire of Japan ~~without warning~~ .

The United States was at the moment at peace with that nation and was

still in ~~continuing the~~ conversation with its Government and its Emperor looking

toward the maintenance of peace in the Pacific. Indeed, one hour after

Japanese air squadrons had commenced bombing in *Oahu* ~~the American island of~~

the Japanese Ambassador to the United States and his colleague delivered

to the Secretary of State a formal reply to a *recent American* ~~former~~ message. ~~from the~~

~~Secretary.~~ *While* This reply ~~contained a statement~~ *stated* *it seemed useless* that diplomatic negotiations

~~must be considered at an end, but~~ *it* contained no threat ~~and no~~ *or* hint of *war or*

armed attack.

It will be recorded that the distance ~~of Hawaii from Japan~~ of

Hawaii from Japan make~~s~~ it obvious that the~~y~~ attack *was* ~~planned~~ deliberately

planned many days *or even weeks* ago. During the intervening time the Japanese Govern-

ment has deliberately sought to deceive the United States by false

statements and expressions of hope for continued peace.

▲ The draft of the speech in which Roosevelt added the key word "infamy" to the lead paragraph.

President Harry S. Truman

> "I believe that we must assist free peoples to work out their own destinies in their own way."

Branded as the puppet of a Missouri political boss, Harry Truman entered the US Senate under a cloud. Yet he soon proved he was his own man, and a tough one at that.

During his presidency, one of the most dangerous periods in world history ended, and another began. His Truman Doctrine, delivered in a speech to the Congress on March 12, 1947, essentially launched the Cold War that concluded more than forty years later with the collapse of the Soviet Union.

Truman was an unlikely choice to be Franklin D. Roosevelt's vice presidential running mate in the 1944 election—replacing the erratic Henry A. Wallace. Truman loved the Senate and agreed to be on the ticket only after a personal appeal from Roosevelt. As vice president, Truman met with the president only twice before Roosevelt died eighty-two days into his term, and he took office knowing little of the Administration's policies and plans.

Nevertheless, he had important decisions to make immediately. In his first months in office, he made arrangements for the San Francisco charter-writing conference of the United Nations, helped arrange Germany's unconditional surrender on May 8, and left in July for his first

▲   President Harry S. Truman making his address to the joint session of Congress in which he outlined the Truman Doctrine.

international summit with Winston Churchill and Stalin at Potsdam, where the three leaders discussed a peace settlement. Then he ordered the dropping of atomic bombs on Hiroshima and Nagasaki, ending the war with Japan.

The Russians Are No Longer Our Friends

Truman barely had time to turn his attention back to domestic matters—launching an unpopular series of economic reforms designed to prevent a return to the pre-war Depression—when it became apparent that the Soviets were quickly turning from allies to adversaries.

In short order, the Soviets either annexed outright or occupied the countries that they had crossed to reach Germany, creating the Eastern Bloc and prompting Churchill's famous "Iron Curtain" warning in March 1946 (interestingly, delivered to a Missouri college audience). From this base of captive countries, the Russians advanced aggressively, encouraging and supporting communist uprisings in the protective ring of countries bordering the USSR.

Truman had been suspicious of the Soviets since Potsdam, and his concerns were only heightened by a delay in the Soviet departure from Iran. The Allies' power-sharing agreement in Germany was also breaking down.

Truman began to see a Soviet strategy of movement toward the oil-rich Middle East and warm-water ports in the region. The suspicion was heightened by Soviet backing of communist insurgencies in Greece and Turkey.

We Won't Baby the Communists Anymore

In 1946, US diplomat George Kennan sent what became known as "The Long Telegram" from

▲ US diplomat George Kennan (left) being sworn in as Ambassador to the Soviet Union by Raymond Muir, as Kennan's wife and daughter look on, 1952.

Moscow, an influential analysis asserting that the Soviets would only respond to force, and advocating a long-term strategy of containment of their geographical expansion. Even prior to the Kennan paper, Truman had advocated a hard-line policy, complaining to Secretary of State James M. Byrnes that "I am tired of babying the Soviets." The United States prompted the recently formed United Nations to pass a resolution directing the Soviets to leave Iran. Early in 1947, Truman replaced Byrnes with General George C. Marshall.

Throughout 1946 and into 1947, the Soviets increased their efforts in both Greece and Turkey. Great Britain had been offering assistance to both countries, but on February 24, 1947, the British Ambassador warned Marshall that his country was in dire financial straits and could no longer afford to help either country. Marshall relayed the news to Truman and other top officials, and they quickly decided that the United States should promptly take over from Britain in supplying financial aid to both Greece and Turkey to help them to fend off the communists.

March 12, 1947

MEMORANDUM FOR THE FILE

The Drafting of the President's Message to Congress
on the Greek Situation
Delivered before a Joint Session of Congress
March 12, 1947.

The early part of this record is hearsay from Acheson and others concerned. When the message came from the British Ambassador on February 24, Secretary Marshall took up the matter promptly with the President, with the Secretaries of War and of the Navy, and with the Chiefs of Staff, and it was decided that prompt and vigorous action was necessary.

The next step was the calling of Congressional leaders to the White House on February 27. At that meeting (according to Mr. Acheson) Mr. Acheson and the Secretary, in the presence of the President, presented the problem to Congressional leaders in outline form. The reaction of the Congressional leaders was rather trivial. At that point Mr. Acheson then launched into a full analysis of just what Greece and Turkey meant to the security of the United States. He apparently reviewed the situation throughout the world, the pressure of communist parties everywhere, and the necessity, in the interest of the security of the United States, in taking a firm stand.

Most of the Congressional leaders were greatly shaken and impressed with this analysis and promised to support whatever measures should be necessary, on the condition that the President should explain the situation fully to Congress in a special message, and to the people by radio. They felt that they could support such a program only if the public were apprised of the grim facts. The President promised to go to the Congress and the people in this manner. He also promised to have a program, including the details of what would be required, prepared for a meeting of the Congressional leaders which he would call eight days thereafter, on Friday, March 7th.

Truman called in congressional leaders for a briefing and he, Marshall, and Undersecretary of State Dean Acheson made a compelling case for the importance of Greece and Turkey to US security, and the severity of the threat of communist expansionism. Barring US aid, the fall of Greece and Turkey to the communists was

▲ The opening paragraphs of a memo giving details of the president's meeting with congressional leaders during which they were informed of the importance of Greece and Turkey to US security.

only weeks away, and these would be the first of a series of crises that could lead to the eventual communist domination of Europe, the Middle East, and Asia. They were describing what quickly became known as "the domino theory" of communist world takeover.

Congressional leaders were "very shaken and upset" according to a report relayed from Acheson. Truman needed congressional action to provide the aid to Greece and Turkey. That presented a problem for him, since his domestic policies had helped Republicans gain control of both houses of Congress.

Buoyed by Republican Support

Fortunately for Truman, the influential Senator Arthur Vandenberg supported him and was able to assure him of Republican votes, on the condition that the president explain the situation to the Congress in a special message, and to the people by radio. Truman quickly agreed and set the State Department to work on both the message and a detailed program to contain the Soviets, both to be ready within two weeks. He went even further, deciding to deliver the message as an address to a joint session of the Congress, eliminating the need for a separate radio address to the people. The public would hear of the problem at the same time the Congress did.

The following day, Acheson convened a meeting of key officials at the State Department and they got to work. Joseph H. Jones, a State Department speechwriter, records that one of the top State Department officials ended the meeting by calling the crisis "the most important thing that had happened since Pearl Harbor," and that all in attendance were "bowled over by the gravity of the situation."

The speechwriters retreated to their offices and worked over the weekend, several producing complete drafts, a few others papers establishing the tone of what was to be said. One of the early drafts used the phrase "a page has turned," indicating that because of Great Britain's postwar economic troubles and inability to continue aid to Greece and Turkey, the United States would be replacing the United Kingdom as the great defender of freedom in the world. That idea disappeared quickly, deemed both too boastful by the United States and insulting to Great Britain.

A first draft was cobbled together over the next few days, while Truman was on a goodwill trip to Mexico. When he returned on March 7, he looked it over and found it too long and technical. It opened with a reference to Greece and Turkey, then digressed into a discussion of the general world situation, before returning to the specific problems of those two countries.

Greeks Make Plea for Aid

Truman's aide, Clark Clifford, presumably relaying the president's views, suggested that they reorder the speech to begin with a detailed discussion of the problems of Greece and Turkey, since relief for those countries was the main reason for Truman's speech. The rationale for leading off the speech with a description of the Greek problem was provided by a March 3 letter from the Greek prime minister containing a desperate appeal to the United States for help. Truman could now emphasize that he was responding to a specific request from the legally constituted government of Greece, shifting focus away from the diplomatic powder keg of moving in to replace Great Britain.

The speech, said the White House, should emphasize the threat that Greek and Turkish collapse posed for the rest of the world, and the necessity for acting quickly, and finish with specific actions Truman wanted Congress to take to shore up Greece and Turkey economically, thereby safeguarding them from communist takeover.

The speech went through several more drafts. Arguments were polished, but the basic structure remained as the White House had wanted it. A last-minute addition came from the State Department just before the speech was made final, adding two paragraphs providing a rationale for unilateral action by the United States, as opposed to an appeal to the United Nations to provide aid. "We have considered how the United Nations might assist in this crisis," read the lines in the speech supplied by State. "But the situation we must meet is an urgent one requiring immediate action, and the United Nations and its related organizations are not yet in a position to extend assistance of the kind that is required."

Truman spoke to the Congress for just eighteen minutes, and most of the speech was devoted to the specifics of the Greek economic crisis, and to a lesser extent to Turkey. Greece had been devastated by war, and did not possess the resources to recover. Armed insurgents were threatening to topple Greece's legitimately elected government and take over the country by force.

Unnamed Threat Clear to All

Truman did not ever mention the Soviet Union by name in the speech, but the source of the threat was clear to all. Once Truman had laid out a strong

DEPARTMENT OF STATE
WASHINGTON

March 10, 1947

MEMORANDUM FOR COMMANDER ELSEY

Here is the paragraph on United Nations that you requested:

For insertion after first full paragraph on page 12 ending with "principles of the charter".

"We have considered how the United Nations might assist in this crisis. But the situation we must meet is an urgent one requiring immediate action, and the United Nations and its related organizations are not yet in a position to extend assistance of the kind that is required.

"The extension of direct aid by the United States to Greece and Turkey means that the United States is stepping into the breach in order to help maintain conditions in which the United Nations can grow in international confidence and authority. The United States has already taken the lead in the establishment of international agencies designed for the rehabilitation of devastated areas and for long-term economic reconstruction. We will continue to study ways and means through which the United Nations and related international agencies might undertake financial and economic responsibilities in such areas."

C. H. Humelsine,
Director, Executive Secretariat.

▲ The memo from the State Department containing two paragraphs providing a rationale for unilateral action by the United States, as opposed to an appeal to the United Nations to provide aid.

case for aid to the specific countries, he turned to the general world situation.

"I am fully aware of the broad implications involved if the United States extends assistance to Greece and Turkey, and I shall discuss these implications with you at this time," he said. "One of the primary objectives of the foreign policy of the

United States is the creation of conditions in which we and other nations will be able to work out a way of life free from coercion. This was a fundamental issue in the war with Germany and Japan. Our victory was won over countries which sought to impose their will, and their way of life, upon other nations.

"At the present moment in world history nearly every nation must choose between alternative ways of life. The choice is too often not a free one.

"One way of life is based upon the will of the majority, and is distinguished by free institutions, representative government, free elections, guarantees of individual liberty, freedom of speech and religion, and freedom from political oppression.

"The second way of life is based upon the will of a minority forcibly imposed upon the majority. It relies upon terror and oppression, a controlled press and radio; fixed elections, and the suppression of personal freedoms.

"I believe that it must be the policy of the United States to support free peoples who are resisting attempted subjugation by armed minorities or by outside pressures.

"I believe that we must assist free peoples to work out their own destinies in their own way.

"I believe that our help should be primarily through economic and financial aid which is essential to economic stability and orderly political processes."

Truman Sets Course for Cold War

In those few paragraphs, he laid out the essence of the Truman Doctrine, and set the course of US actions over the next four decades. The Congress quickly voted $400 million in aid to Greece and Turkey.

The Truman Administration followed up with the four-year, $17 billion Marshall Plan of 1948 to bring economic recovery to Western Europe and keep communist ideology from taking firm root. He also formed the North Atlantic Treaty

▲ President Harry S. Truman signing the Foreign Assistance Act of 1948, more popularly known as the Marshall Plan, which provided a program of foreign aid to Greece and Turkey.

Organization (NATO) to provide collective security for noncommunist European nations.

When China came under communist control in 1949, Truman's containment policies were extended to include that enormous nation. He also established the Central Intelligence Agency, instituted the Berlin Airlift in 1948 when the Soviets blockaded the former German capital, began a broad program of support for underdeveloped countries, and ordered development of the hydrogen bomb in 1950 to stay ahead of the Soviets after they had stolen US atomic secrets. He also sent US troops to Korea, under UN auspices, to fight the Chinese-backed North Koreans as they invaded South Korea.

The Truman Doctrine meant meeting the Soviet—and later Chinese—threat at every turn and in every country where they attempted to establish influence. There were successes and failures, but always action and decision. The sign on Truman's desk read "The Buck Stops Here." He believed it and lived it. Whatever else history judges about Harry Truman, there is no doubt that his strong and decisive actions in Greece, Turkey, and elsewhere thwarted Stalin's ambitions for world domination, and did a great service for the cause of freedom.

Drafted over snowy week-end march 2-3. JmJ — in effort to arrive at a tone.

Suggestions for the President's message to Congress in regard to the Greek situation.

I lay before you today one of the gravest problems of national

security ever to confront the nation. We are face to face with a crisis

in foreign policy. It is a crisis less serious than a crisis of arms

only because there is still time to work out a program of peaceful

salvation. But upon the decisions that must be made now will depend the

security and well-being of the American people.

The British Government, through its Ambassador in Washington, has

informed the Government of the United States that as of March 31 it will

be obliged to discontinue its program of economic assistance to Greece.

The British Government has also informed us that it will not be in

position to extend further financial or economic aid to Turkey.

The Greek Gov't on mar. 3 informed us that —

The setting in which these developments must be viewed is one of

acute economic weakness and financial stringency in Great Britain, which

imposes upon that country the necessity of reducing or liquidating its

commitments not only in Greece and Turkey but in other parts of the world,

notably in Egypt, Palestine, India and Burma.

The situation with which we have to deal, therefore, is no sudden

and limited occurence. It is the culminating development in a long

historical

Presidential Address to Joint Session of Congress
March 12, 1947, United States Capitol, Washington, DC

Mr. President, Mr. Speaker, Members of the Congress of the United States:

The gravity of the situation which confronts the world today necessitates my appearance before a joint session of the Congress. The foreign policy and the national security of this country are involved.

One aspect of the present situation, which I wish to present to you at this time for your consideration and decision, concerns Greece and Turkey.

The United States has received from the Greek Government an urgent appeal for financial and economic assistance. Preliminary reports from the American Economic Mission now in Greece and reports from the American Ambassador in Greece corroborate the statement of the Greek Government that assistance is imperative if Greece is to survive as a free nation.

I do not believe that the American people and the Congress wish to turn a deaf ear to the appeal of the Greek Government.

Greece is not a rich country. Lack of sufficient natural resources has always forced the Greek people to work hard to make both ends meet. Since 1940, this industrious and peace loving country has suffered invasion, four years of cruel enemy occupation, and bitter internal strife.

When forces of liberation entered Greece they found that the retreating Germans had destroyed virtually all the railways, roads, port facilities, communications, and merchant marine. More than a thousand villages had been burned. Eighty-five

◀ The first page of an early draft of the speech dated March 3, 1947.

per cent of the children were tubercular. Livestock, poultry, and draft animals had almost disappeared. Inflation had wiped out practically all savings.

As a result of these tragic conditions, a militant minority, exploiting human want and misery, was able to create political chaos which, until now, has made economic recovery impossible.

Greece is today without funds to finance the importation of those goods which are essential to bare subsistence. Under these circumstances the people of Greece cannot make progress in solving their problems of reconstruction. Greece is in desperate need of financial and economic assistance to enable it to resume purchases of food, clothing, fuel and seeds. These are indispensable for the subsistence of its people and are obtainable only from abroad. Greece must have help to import the goods necessary to restore internal order and security, so essential for economic and political recovery.

The Greek Government has also asked for the assistance of experienced American administrators, economists and technicians to insure that the financial and other aid given to Greece shall be used effectively in creating a stable and self-sustaining economy and in improving its public administration.

The very existence of the Greek state is today threatened by the terrorist activities of several thousand armed men, led by Communists, who defy the government's authority at a number of points, particularly along the northern boundaries. A Commission appointed by the United Nations security Council is at present investigating disturbed conditions in northern Greece and alleged border violations along the frontier between Greece on the

- 4 -

territory, it must have supplies and equipment to permit its

reorganization and it must be supported by a sound economy.

If Greece is to have help in this critical situation, the

United States must supply it. The United States has already extended

to Greece certain types of relief and economic assistance, but these

are inadequate.

There is no other country to which democratic Greece can

turn.

No other nation is willing and able to provide the necessary

support for a democratic Greek government.

The British Government, which has been assisting Greece, can

give no further financial or economic aid after March 31. Great Britain

finds itself under the necessity of reducing or liquidating its commit-

ments in several parts of the world, including Greece.

We have considered how the United Nations might assist in

this crisis. But the situation is an urgent one requiring immediate

action, and the United Nations and its related organizations are not

in a position to extend assistance of the kind that is required.

SECRET

▲ A page from a draft of the speech
dated March 10, 1947.

one hand and Albania, Bulgaria, and Yugoslavia on the other.

Meanwhile, the Greek Government is unable to cope with the situation. The Greek army is small and poorly equipped. It needs supplies and equipment if it is to restore the authority of the government throughout Greek territory. Greece must have assistance if it is to become a self-supporting and self-respecting democracy.

The United States must supply that assistance. We have already extended to Greece certain types of relief and economic aid but these are inadequate.

There is no other country to which democratic Greece can turn.

No other nation is willing and able to provide the necessary support for a democratic Greek government.

The British Government, which has been helping Greece, can give no further financial or economic aid after March 31. Great Britain finds itself under the necessity of reducing or liquidating its commitments in several parts of the world, including Greece.

We have considered how the United Nations might assist in this crisis. But the situation is an urgent one requiring immediate action and the United Nations and its related organizations are not in a position to extend help of the kind that is required.

It is important to note that the Greek Government has asked for our aid in utilizing effectively the financial and other assistance we may give to Greece, and in improving its public administration. It is of the utmost importance that we supervise the use of any funds made available to Greece; in such a manner that each dollar spent will count toward making Greece self-supporting, and will help to build an economy in which a healthy democracy can flourish.

No government is perfect. One of the chief virtues of a democracy, however, is that its defects are always visible and under democratic processes can be pointed out and corrected. The Government of Greece is not perfect. Nevertheless it represents eighty-five per cent of the members of the Greek Parliament who were chosen in an election last year. Foreign observers, including 692 Americans, considered this election to be a fair expression of the views of the Greek people.

The Greek Government has been operating in an atmosphere of chaos and extremism. It has made mistakes. The extension of aid by this country does not mean that the United States condones everything that the Greek Government has done or will do. We have condemned in the past, and we condemn now, extremist measures of the right or the left. We have in the past advised tolerance, and we advise tolerance now.

Greece's neighbor, Turkey, also deserves our attention.

The future of Turkey as an independent and economically sound state is clearly no less important to the freedom-loving peoples of the world than the future of Greece. The circumstances in which Turkey finds itself today are considerably different from those of Greece. Turkey has been spared the disasters that have beset Greece. And during the war, the United States and Great Britain furnished Turkey with material aid.

Nevertheless, Turkey now needs our support.

Since the war Turkey has sought financial assistance from Great Britain and the United States for the purpose of effecting that modernization necessary for the maintenance of its national integrity.

That integrity is essential to the preservation of order in the Middle East.

The British government has informed us that, owing to its own difficulties can no longer extend financial or economic aid to Turkey.

As in the case of Greece, if Turkey is to have the assistance it needs, the United States must supply it. We are the only country able to provide that help.

I am fully aware of the broad implications involved if the United States extends assistance to Greece and Turkey, and I shall discuss these implications with you at this time.

One of the primary objectives of the foreign policy of the United States is the creation of conditions in which we and other nations will be able to work out a way of life free from coercion. This was a fundamental issue in the war with Germany and Japan. Our victory was won over countries which sought to impose their will, and their way of life, upon other nations.

To ensure the peaceful development of nations, free from coercion, the United States has taken a leading part in establishing the United Nations, The United Nations is designed to make possible lasting freedom and independence for all its members. We shall not realize our objectives, however, unless we are willing to help free peoples to maintain their free institutions and their national integrity against aggressive movements that seek to impose upon them totalitarian regimes. This is no more than a frank recognition that totalitarian regimes imposed on free peoples, by direct or indirect aggression, undermine the foundations of international peace and hence the security of the United States.

The peoples of a number of countries of the world have recently had totalitarian regimes forced upon them against their will. The Government of the United States has made frequent protests against coercion and intimidation, in violation of the Yalta agreement, in Poland, Rumania, and Bulgaria. I must also state that in a number of other countries there have been similar developments.

At the present moment in world history nearly every nation must choose between alternative ways of life. The choice is too often not a free one.

One way of life is based upon the will of the majority, and is distinguished by free institutions, representative government, free elections, guarantees of individual liberty, freedom of speech and religion, and freedom from political oppression.

The second way of life is based upon the will of a minority forcibly imposed upon the majority. It relies upon terror and oppression, a controlled press and radio; fixed elections, and the suppression of personal freedoms.

I believe that it must be the policy of the United States to support free peoples who are resisting attempted subjugation by armed minorities or by outside pressures.

I believe that we must assist free peoples to work out their own destinies in their own way.

I believe that our help should be primarily through economic and financial aid which is essential to economic stability and orderly political processes.

The world is not static, and the status quo is not sacred. But we cannot allow changes in the status quo in violation of the Charter of the United Nations by such methods as coercion, or by such subterfuges as political infiltration. In helping free and independent

▲ President Harry S. Truman signing the Greece-Turkish Aid Bill on May 22, 1947.

nations to maintain their freedom, the United States will be giving effect to the principles of the Charter of the United Nations.

It is necessary only to glance at a map to realize that the survival and integrity of the Greek nation are of grave importance in a much wider situation. If Greece should fall under the control of an armed minority, the effect upon its neighbor, Turkey, would be immediate and serious. Confusion and disorder might well spread throughout the entire Middle East.

Moreover, the disappearance of Greece as an independent state would have a profound effect upon those countries in Europe whose peoples are struggling against great difficulties to maintain their freedoms and their independence while they repair the damages of war.

It would be an unspeakable tragedy if these countries, which have struggled so long against overwhelming odds, should lose that victory for which they sacrificed so much. Collapse of free institutions and loss of independence would be disastrous not only for them but for the world. Discouragement and possibly failure would quickly be the lot of neighboring peoples striving to maintain their freedom and independence.

Should we fail to aid Greece and Turkey in this fateful hour, the effect will be far reaching to the West as well as to the East.

We must take immediate and resolute action.

I therefore ask the Congress to provide authority for assistance to Greece and Turkey in the amount of $400,000,000 for the period ending June 30, 1948. In requesting these funds, I have taken into consideration the maximum amount of relief assistance which would be furnished to Greece out of the $350,000,000 which I recently requested that the Congress authorize for the prevention of starvation and suffering in countries devastated by the war.

In addition to funds, I ask the Congress to authorize the detail of American civilian and military personnel to Greece and Turkey, at the request of those countries, to assist in the tasks of reconstruction, and for the purpose of supervising the use of such financial and material assistance as may be furnished. I recommend that authority also be provided for the instruction and training of selected Greek and Turkish personnel.

Finally, I ask that the Congress provide authority which will permit the speediest and most effective use, in terms of needed commodities, supplies, and equipment, of such funds as may be authorized.

If further funds, or further authority, should be needed for purposes indicated in this message, I shall not hesitate to bring the situation before the Congress. On this subject the Executive and Legislative branches of the Government must work together.

This is a serious course upon which we embark.

I would not recommend it except that the alternative is much more serious. The United States contributed $341,000,000,000 toward winning World War II. This is an investment in world freedom and world peace.

The assistance that I am recommending for Greece and Turkey amounts to little more than 1 tenth of 1 per cent of this investment. It is only common sense that we should safeguard this investment and make sure that it was not in vain.

The seeds of totalitarian regimes are nurtured by misery and want. They spread and grow in the evil soil of poverty and strife. They reach their full growth when the hope of a people for a better life has died. We must keep that hope alive.

The free peoples of the world look to us for support in maintaining their freedoms.

If we falter in our leadership, we may endanger the peace of the world—and we shall surely endanger the welfare of our own nation.

Great responsibilities have been placed upon us by the swift movement of events.

I am confident that the Congress will face these responsibilities squarely.

◀ US President Harry S. Truman shaking hands with Secretary of State George Marshall upon Marshall's return from the Big Four Minister's conference held in Moscow in 1947.

President Dwight David Eisenhower

> "In the councils of government, we must guard against the acquisition of unwarranted influence, whether sought or unsought, by the military-industrial complex."

The eight years of Dwight D. Eisenhower's presidency were among the most deeply paradoxical in the history of the United States. So was the man himself.

Eisenhower's two terms spanned the very harshest period of the Cold War with the Soviet Union—an escalation in arms capability unprecedented in human history. Each of the two superpowers built a nuclear arsenal big enough to obliterate all life on the planet many times over.

Despite the constant threat of the big bang, life in the United States went on smoothly. The country grew wealthier and more powerful by the year. Television sitcoms like "Leave it to Beaver" and "Ozzie and Harriet" reflected the national mood of button-down, buttoned-up self-satisfaction. Problems there were aplenty, but the lid stayed on until well into the next decade.

Presiding over both the international turmoil and the domestic prosperity was the smiling, affable Ike; a war hero of tremendous stature but also a slightly bumbling, bemused presence. He was not a good communicator. He stumbled over words and delivered his remarks in a flat, Mid-American twang. But he projected confidence and calm. The enduring image was of Ike flashing his famous grin, or strolling down the fairway on one of his many golf outings. A safe, reassuring presence but not, to the public, a man who would shake things up or accomplish much.

▲ President Dwight D. Eisenhower preparing to make his Farewell Address, January 17, 1961.

Yet this was the same man who planned and carried out the Normandy Invasion and led the Allies to victory in Europe—a man with a tough, strategic military mind. His record as President reflected those capabilities. He ended the Korean War, blunted Soviet expansion, kicked off the interstate highway system, initiated the Space Race, greatly expanded Social Security, backed racial equality with Federal troops and generally held things together during a dangerous period in the world.

A Gutsy and Prophetic Warning

This flawed orator also delivered one of the great speeches in the history of the Presidency—a blunt, gutsy, prophetic, and eloquent warning to the American people that is still talked about more than half a century later. Eisenhower's farewell speech also coined the enduring phrase by which it has become known: the Military-Industrial Complex.

There are obvious parallels between Eisenhower and the nation's first president, George Washington—chiefly their military backgrounds and enormous personal popularity. They also gave what are considered the two finest Presidential farewell addresses in the history of the country. Washington warned of the dangers and divisiveness of political parties, the importance of the Constitution at a time when it was a new and largely untested document, of foreign entanglements and many other topics that had tremendous influence during the formative years of the new republic.

It was no accident that Eisenhower decided to follow Washington's example and give a parting statement. His advisors held up the Washington farewell as a model and his speechwriters were directed to study the address in preparing the Eisenhower version.

Speech Development Started Early

As early as May 1959—twenty months before Eisenhower was to leave office—a memo from Presidential speechwriter Malcolm Moos began the process of preparation. Moos said the President "mentioned in an aside" that he hoped Congress would invite him to address them before he left office. Moos considered it "a brilliant idea if it can be carried off with a minimum of fanfare and emotionalism." Moos

THE WHITE HOUSE
WASHINGTON
April 5, 1960

MEMORANDUM TO: Mac Moos

As the time for the President's retirement draws near, I recommend to your re-reading the "Farewell Address" of George Washington. It is a beautifully wise and modest piece by a faithful public servant who loved his country.

I was struck by its relevance to our day: the call for Constitutional obedience; the warnings about sectionalism; the dangers of "overgrown military establishments" but the necessity of maintaining "a respectable defensive posture"; the realistic attitude toward "that love of power and proneness to abuse it which predominate in the human heart"; the unhappy tendency of mankind "to seek security and repose in the absolute power of an individual"; the necessity for an enlightened public opinion; the generous habit of one generation to spend beyond its means and to throw "upon posterity the burden which we ourselves ought to bear"; the broad diplomatic advice. And much more.

This Address could furnish some fine ammunition over the year -- and perhaps serve as a guide for a final statement in January 1961?

Frederic Fox

▲ A memo from Staff Assistant to President Dwight D. Eisenhower Frederic Fox to Malcolm Moos, highlighting George Washington's Farewell Address as a point of reference for the speech.

told his fellow staffers "we should be dropping ideas into a bin" to get ready.

Before starting the process, Eisenhower had been discussing the idea of a farewell with his brother, Milton, president of Johns Hopkins University. Milton had always been a close and trusted advisor to his older brother, and as Ike's second term neared its end, he and some others met and drafted a list of speech and

31 October 1960

MEMORANDUM FOR FILE

Subject: State of the Union 1961

Conversation with Dr. Moos this morning produced following preliminary guide lines:

1. The problem of militarism -- for the first time in its history, the United States has a permanent war-based industry -- aircraft, 90% -- missiles, 100%, etc. Not only that but flag and general officers retiring at an early age take positions in war based industrial complex shaping its decisions and guiding the direction of its tremendous thrust. This creates a danger that what the Communists have always said about us may become true. We must be very careful to insure that the "merchants of death do not come to dictate national policy".

2. Over the past year there has been a world wide tendency for orderly societies to break down into mob ridden anarchies, e.g. student riots, the Congo, Cuba, etc. In our own country we see instances where political decisions are first on the barricades instead of normal governmental processes. It is easy to wave banners to riot, to protest, but the difficult thing is to work a constructive change so that society is strengthened rather than weakened and divided.

3. Analyze previous major addresses of DDE. (Get Eisenhower's ~~speaks~~ from Military Aide's office)

Ralph E. Williams

▲ A memo from Ralph E. Williams, speechwriter and assistant to Eisenhower's Naval Aid, Captain Evan P. Aurand, outlining some preliminary guidelines for the speech.

topic recommendations for the President for the remainder of his term.

Ike replied to Milton that he was wary of the idea of an address to Congress while it was controlled by the other party. He could not talk about any topics that were partisan or divisive,

he said. The speech might still be worth giving if he could express some "home truths" about the "responsibilities and duties of government that must be responsive to the will of majorities." That theme might have been reflected in some of the preliminary language of the earliest drafts, but did not make it into the final speech. If it had, it would be well worth quoting to the deeply divided and antagonistic politicians of recent years.

The speech itself proceeded through twenty-one drafts over more than a year, undergoing many changes and a lot of polishing by Eisenhower's speechwriters, and his brother.

Military-Industrial Phrase Evolved

Early drafts also broadened the speech's most famous phrase into a warning against a "military-industrial-congressional complex" and the influence of that three-headed monster. Only two heads of the monster survived into the final form of the speech. Eisenhower was worried about offending Congress and eliminated the references to the Congressional appropriations process as an element of the "potential for the disastrous rise of misplaced power." The key phrase itself evolved from warnings against a "war-based industrial complex" to a "vast military-industrial complex" and eventually was pared down to the final version.

Washington had worried in his farewell address, which Ike's advisors were studying, about the need to avoid "those overgrown military establishments which, under any form of government, are inauspicious to liberty, and which are to be regarded as particularly hostile to republican liberty." As a military man, Washington knew he could issue such a warning and be taken seriously. The same was true of Eisenhower.

And while the specific warning about the military-industrial complex was extremely powerful coming from a president and five-star general, it was far from a new concept. The exact phrase had been in use by academics since at least the late 1940s. Even earlier, Eisenhower could look across the battle lines during World War II and see that Germany had very efficiently employed its industrial might to create its war machine.

The same was true of Japan. Industries in both countries enjoyed extraordinary prosperity—using slave labor and other advantages of collaboration with the military. The lesson, not lost on the industrialists of the Cold War period, was that war was good for business . . . provided your side didn't lose.

Warning about "Big Science"

The military-industrial admonition is the one most remembered by history, but Eisenhower had other points he wanted to make. An early draft from Moos said he "planned to go from here"—the military-industrial point—to "the twin dangers of government dominating scientific research through purse power and of the generalists becoming captives of the technical specialists." Those points were made in a warning against "Big Science"—the replacement of the "solitary inventor tinkering in his shop" by enormous and costly government projects. "A government contract becomes virtually a substitute for intellectual curiosity," Eisenhower fretted. The point is valid. In the decades since Ike left office, not only government but mega-corporations have taken the lead in scientific research. University science programs across the country are kept afloat by corporate and government grants—and directed toward finding useful products and processes for the sponsors, rather than "tinkering."

Eisenhower also warns that the complex of the technological revolution could bring as much influence over public policy to a scientific and technological elite as to the military-industrial complex. The whole warning against the evils of Big Science started out as a lengthy section, but later drafts cut it down considerably—to just five paragraphs in the final speech.

A Limited Role for Government

Bigger is badder, is the basic Eisenhower thesis in both the military-industrial and Big Science admonitions, and early in the speech he makes a similar conservative observation regarding the role of government. We have faced crises, he says, we will continue to face them, but don't overreact.

Eisenhower warned of "the recurring temptation to feel that some spectacular and costly action could become the miraculous solution to all current difficulties." He counseled a balanced—meaning limited—approach to problems. This section comes near the beginning of the speech, before the military-industrial point, and only appears in the latest drafts. It is very likely that Eisenhower added it himself, and it clearly stems from his dislike and distrust of John F. Kennedy. Ike personally disliked and distrusted Kennedy, regarding him as a dangerous, activist liberal. The dislike may have had its roots with JFK's father, the wealthy and controversial Joseph P. Kennedy—a Democrat whose isolationist views as Ambassador to Great Britain at the outset of World War II ended his public career.

Human Rights Section Disappears

One interesting development as the speech evolved was the inclusion, and then disappearance, of a section on independence and human rights in the international community. A very early memo by Malcolm Moos makes it clear that this is to be a major point. "Last point," he writes in May 1959, "the new concept of equality among nations, which only came into existence in the Eisenhower half-century [of public service]—its implications for

THE WHITE HOUSE
WASHINGTON

Mac -

This is my start. Plan to go from here to the Scientific Revolution and the twin dangers of government dominating scientific research through purse power, and of the generalists becoming captives of the technical specialists. Last point: the new concept of equality among nations, which only came into existence in the Eisenhower half-century--its implications for world order and our support of nations holding these ideals.

▲ An early memo from Eisenhower to Malcolm Moos outlining some of his thoughts on the speech.

world order and our support for nations holding these ideals."

As late as the December 21, 1960, draft this statement of support for equality among nations took up the last two pages of an eight-page draft. It had largely disappeared in the draft dated January 7, 1961, and by the final speech there remained only the single ambiguous statement that "the weakest [nations] must come to the conference table with the same confidence as we do, protected as we are by our moral, economic, and military strength."

The January 7 draft contained several pages of handwritten changes, and was initialed at the top "MSE", indicating that Ike's brother Milton had weighed in with some heavy late input—presumably in collaboration with both the President and his speechwriters. This draft established the final main points of the speech, and thereafter it was a matter of pruning and polishing.

A Plea for Moderation

In place of the pledge of support for captive and emerging nations, Eisenhower made another plea for moderation, this time in national consumption. "We . . . must avoid the impulse to live only for plundering, for our own ease and convenience, the precious resources of tomorrow," he said. "We cannot mortgage the material assets of our grandchildren without risking the loss of their political and spiritual heritage." Some analysts of the speech consider those words an eloquent and forward-looking warning, others dismiss them as mere political platitudes. Whatever the opinion, it is clear from the succeeding fifty years of ever-mounting consumption and soaring use of energy and other natural resources that this particular warning went unheeded.

Since Eisenhower spoke much of what he warned about has come to pass. The US defense establishment now spends nearly $700 billion dollars a year—well over half of the global total of military spending. Government and industry now fund nearly ninety percent of scientific and technological research. Both strongly favor applied research—development of useful products and processes—over pure research. And one need not look further than the energy industries to conclude that the U.S., and the rest of the developed world are depleting natural resources at the expense of future generations.

So did anyone pay attention? Were Eisenhower's warnings fruitless? The temptation is to say that they had no impact. But Eisenhower's words, particularly in debates over military spending, have been quoted countless times over the past half-century. It is possible—even likely—that his warning has prevented even worse excesses. The same is true to a lesser extent in the debate over the role of government and industry in scientific research.

The bottom line is that Eisenhower's speech has helped frame the debate for more than five decades since he delivered it. Eisenhower successfully and powerfully delivered his "home truths," as much as they changed between initial conception and final delivery, and the result is one of the more important and positive features of his legacy as President.

Farewell Address to the American People
January 17, 1961, White House, Washington DC

Good evening, my fellow Americans.

First, I should like to express my gratitude to the radio and television networks for the opportunities they have given me over the years to bring reports and messages to our nation. My special thanks go to them for the opportunity of addressing you this evening.

Three days from now, after half century in the service of our country, I shall lay down the responsibilities of office as, in traditional and solemn ceremony, the authority of the Presidency is vested in my successor. This evening, I come to you with a message of leave-taking and farewell, and to share a few final thoughts with you, my countrymen.

Like every other – Like every other citizen, I wish the new President, and all who will labor with him, Godspeed. I pray that the coming years will be blessed with peace and prosperity for all.

Our people expect their President and the Congress to find essential agreement on issues of great moment, the wise resolution of which will better shape the future of the nation. My own relations with the Congress, which began on a remote and tenuous basis when, long ago, a member of the Senate appointed me to West Point, have since ranged to the intimate during the war and immediate post-war period, and finally to the mutually interdependent during these past eight years. In this final relationship, the Congress and the Administration have, on most vital issues, cooperated well, to serve the nation good, rather than mere partisanship, and so have assured that the business of the nation should go forward. So, my official relationship with the Congress ends in a feeling – on my part – of gratitude that we have been able to do so much together.

▲ President Dwight D. Eisenhower presenting his farewell address to the Nation.

We now stand ten years past the midpoint of a century that has witnessed four major wars among great nations. Three of these involved our own country. Despite these holocausts, America is today the strongest, the most influential, and most productive nation in the world. Understandably proud of this pre-eminence, we yet realize that America's leadership and prestige depend, not merely upon our unmatched material progress, riches, and military strength, but on how we use our power in the interests of world peace and human betterment.

Throughout America's adventure in free government, our basic purposes have been to keep the peace, to foster progress in human achievement, and to enhance liberty, dignity, and integrity among peoples and among nations. To strive for less would be unworthy of a free and religious people. Any failure traceable to arrogance, or our lack of comprehension, or readiness to sacrifice would inflict upon us grievous hurt, both at home and abroad.

Progress toward these noble goals is persistently threatened by the conflict now engulfing the world. It commands our whole attention, absorbs our very beings. We face a hostile ideology global in scope, atheistic in character, ruthless in purpose, and insiduous [insidious] in method. Unhappily, the danger it poses promises to be of indefinite duration. To meet it successfully, there is called for, not so much the emotional and transitory sacrifices of crisis, but rather those which enable us to carry forward steadily, surely, and without complaint the burdens of a prolonged and complex struggle with liberty the stake. Only thus shall we remain, despite every provocation, on our charted course toward permanent peace and human betterment.

Crises there will continue to be. In meeting them, whether foreign or domestic, great or small, there is a recurring temptation to feel that some spectacular and costly action could become the miraculous solution to all current difficulties. A huge increase in newer elements of our defenses; development of unrealistic programs to cure every ill in agriculture; a dramatic expansion in basic and applied research – these and many other possibilities, each possibly promising in itself, may be suggested as the only way to the road we wish to travel.

But each proposal must be weighed in the light of a broader consideration: the need to maintain balance in and among national programs, balance between the private and the public economy, balance between the cost and hoped for advantages, balance between the clearly necessary and the comfortably desirable, balance between our essential requirements as a nation and the duties imposed by the nation upon the individual, balance between actions of the moment and the national welfare of the future. Good judgment seeks balance and progress. Lack of it eventually finds imbalance and frustration. The record of many decades stands as proof that our people and their Government have, in the main, understood these truths and

The prospect of domination of the nation's scholars by Federal employment, project allocations, and contracts is ever present -- and is gravely to be regarded.

Yet, in holding scientific research and discovery in respect, as we should, we must also be alert to the equal and opposite danger that public policy could itself become the captive of a scientific-technological elite.

It is the task of statesmanship to mold, to balance, and to integrate these and other forces, new and old, within the principles of our democratic system -- ever aiming toward the supreme goals of our free society.

~~Elsewhere there is yet another new development -- perhaps the most momentous of all in shaping the patterns of tomorrow. In the past fifteen years, while eight hundred million persons were being (pushed) into submission by the Communists, almost a billion others were winning political independence. Spurring this emancipation movement is the concept of equality among nations which, for the first time in history, has come to be recognized as a basic principle in international affairs. Acceptance of this principle is as yet imperfect. But even~~

have responded to them well, in the face of threat and stress.

But threats, new in kind or degree, constantly arise. Of these, I mention two only.

A vital element in keeping the peace is our military establishment. Our arms must be mighty, ready for instant action, so that no potential aggressor may

▲ A page from a draft (dated January 7, 1961) showing the removal of the human rights section of the speech.

be tempted to risk his own destruction. Our military organization today bears little relation to that known of any of my predecessors in peacetime, or, indeed, by the fighting men of World War II or Korea.

Until the latest of our world conflicts, the United States had no armaments industry. American makers of plowshares could, with time and as required, make swords as well. But we can no longer risk emergency improvisation of national defense. We have been compelled to create a permanent armaments industry of vast proportions. Added to this, three and a half million men and women are directly engaged in the defense establishment. We annually spend on military security alone more than the net income of all United States corporations.

Now this conjunction of an immense military establishment and a large arms industry is new in the American experience. The total influence – economic, political, even spiritual – is felt in every city, every Statehouse, every office of the Federal government. We recognize the imperative need for this development. Yet, we must not fail to comprehend its grave implications. Our toil, resources, and livelihood are all involved. So is the very structure of our society.

In the councils of government, we must guard against the acquisition of unwarranted influence, whether sought or unsought, by the military-industrial complex. The potential for the disastrous rise of misplaced power exists and will persist. We must never let the weight of this combination endanger our liberties or democratic processes. We should take nothing for granted. Only an alert and knowledgeable citizenry can compel the proper meshing of the huge industrial and military machinery of defense with our peaceful methods and goals, so that security and liberty may prosper together.

Akin to, and largely responsible for the sweeping changes in our industrial-military posture, has been the technological revolution during recent decades. In this revolution, research has become central; it also becomes more formalized, complex, and costly. A steadily increasing share is conducted for, by, or at the direction of, the Federal government.

Today, the solitary inventor, tinkering in his shop, has been overshadowed by task forces of scientists in laboratories and testing fields. In the same fashion, the free university, historically the fountainhead of free ideas and scientific discovery, has experienced a revolution in the conduct of research. Partly because of the huge costs involved, a government contract becomes virtually a substitute for intellectual curiosity. For every old blackboard there are now hundreds of new electronic computers. The prospect of domination of the nation's scholars by Federal employment, project allocations, and the power of money is ever present – and is gravely to be regarded.

Yet, in holding scientific research and discovery in respect, as we should, we must also be alert to the equal and opposite danger that public policy could itself become the captive of a scientific-technological elite.

It is the task of statesmanship to mold, to balance, and to integrate these and other forces, new and old, within the principles of our democratic system -- ever aiming toward the supreme goals of our free society.

Another factor in maintaining balance involves the element of time. As we peer into society's future, we – you and I, and our government – must avoid the impulse to live only for today, plundering for our own ease and convenience the precious resources of tomorrow. We cannot mortgage the material assets of our grandchildren without risking the loss also of their political and spiritual heritage. We want democracy to survive for all generations to come, not to become the insolvent phantom of tomorrow.

During the long lane of the history yet to be written, America knows that this world of ours, ever growing smaller, must avoid becoming a community of dreadful fear and hate, and be, instead, a proud confederation of mutual trust and respect. Such a confederation must be one of equals. The weakest must come to the conference table with the same confidence as do we, protected as we are by our moral, economic, and military strength. That table,

▲ Ex-President Dwight D. Eisenhower passes some admirers with a placard following President John F. Kennedy's inauguration ceremony on January 20, 1961.

though scarred by many fast frustrations – past frustrations, cannot be abandoned for the certain agony of disarmament – of the battlefield.

Disarmament, with mutual honor and confidence, is a continuing imperative. Together we must learn how to compose differences, not with arms, but with intellect and decent purpose. Because this need is so sharp and apparent, I confess that I lay down my official responsibilities in this field with a definite sense of disappointment. As one who has witnessed the horror and the lingering sadness of war, as one who knows that another war could utterly destroy this civilization which has been so slowly and painfully built over thousands of years, I wish I could say tonight that a lasting peace is in sight.

Happily, I can say that war has been avoided. Steady progress toward our ultimate goal has been made. But so much remains to be done. As a private citizen, I shall never cease to do what little I can to help the world advance along that road.

So, in this, my last good night to you as your President, I thank you for the many opportunities you have given me for public service in war and in peace. I trust in that – in that – in that service you find some things worthy. As for the rest of it, I know you will find ways to improve performance in the future.

You and I, my fellow citizens, need to be strong in our faith that all nations, under God, will reach the goal of peace with justice. May we be ever unswerving in devotion to principle, confident but humble with power, diligent in pursuit of the Nations' great goals.

To all the peoples of the world, I once more give expression to America's prayerful and continuing aspiration: We pray that peoples of all faiths, all races, all nations, may have their great human needs satisfied; that those now denied opportunity shall come to enjoy it to the full; that all who yearn for freedom may experience its few spiritual blessings. Those who have freedom will understand, also, its heavy responsibility; that all who are insensitive to the needs of others will learn charity; and that the sources -- scourges of poverty, disease, and ignorance will be made [to] disappear from the earth; and that in the goodness of time, all peoples will come to live together in a peace guaranteed by the binding force of mutual respect and love.

Now, on Friday noon, I am to become a private citizen. I am proud to do so. I look forward to it.

Thank you, and good night.

President John Fitzgerald Kennedy

"Ask not what your country can do for you—
ask what you can do for your country."

▼ President John F. Kennedy at the
podium giving his inaugural speech.

John F. Kennedy's inaugural address is undisputedly one of the greatest ever, ranking almost by acclamation of scholars and laymen alike with Lincoln's second inaugural speech and two of Franklin Delano Roosevelt's four. The speech launched Kennedy's Administration into a stratosphere of public approval from which it never slipped.

But did those lofty sentiments spring from the mind of Kennedy himself? The murky question of whether the president actually wrote most, or any, of his memorable inaugural address has been hashed out by scholars and political friends and foes in the decades since its delivery.

Kennedy's many detractors have never stopped circulating tales of his extramarital activities and other purported failings. Among them are allegations that he was nothing more than a rich man's son who bought the flights of rhetorical brilliance that carried him to the presidency just as he might have bought a yacht or a Palm Beach home. Those who do not subscribe to the Kennedy myth have branded him a dilettante who surrounded himself with brilliant and talented underlings. His speeches, they say, were almost exclusively the work of his speechwriter and alter ego, the brilliant and self-effacing Ted Sorensen.

Claims Don't Hold Up

The claims that Kennedy had minimal input into the speech do not stand up under even the most cursory examination. Two full-length books, and innumerable articles, have examined the speech. Both of the books concluded that the speech was a close collaboration between Kennedy and Sorensen. Sorensen was amused by the fact that one writer concluded that Kennedy was mainly responsible, while the other thought that the bulk of the speech was Sorensen's work.

Sorensen himself was the soul of discretion. He simply replied to queries about authorship with a shorter version of the most famous line of the speech. "Ask not," he would say with a smile.

The "smoking gun" of the matter is the question of who wrote the first draft of the speech. Both Sorensen and Kennedy produced handwritten first drafts. Sorensen's, written on or about January 9, 1961, predated Kennedy's by several days. Sorensen quoted several paragraphs of it in his 1965 book, *Kennedy*, showing the development of several of the central ideas of the speech. But Sorensen later destroyed his first draft out of concern that history might not credit Kennedy as the true author of the speech.

That concern was well founded. Kennedy had won a Pulitzer Prize for his book *Profiles in Courage* in 1957, a factor in his rapid ascent to presidential contention in 1960. Muckraking syndicated columnist Drew Pearson alleged that Sorensen wrote the book and that Kennedy was, essentially, a fraud. Pearson later was forced to issue a retraction, but doubts remained.

Speech Origins Complicated

The true origins of the inaugural speech are much more convoluted. Both Sorensen's account and the consensus of independent scholars agree that the themes of the speech echo many that were developed during the 1960 presidential campaign. These were ideas and policies conceived and honed by a back-and-forth dialogue between Kennedy and Sorensen.

Analysts of the speech also conclude that Kennedy was active in shaping not only the substance but the form of the speech from the outset. He directed Sorensen to research previous inaugural speeches, with particular attention to the rhetorical strategies and cadences of Lincoln's

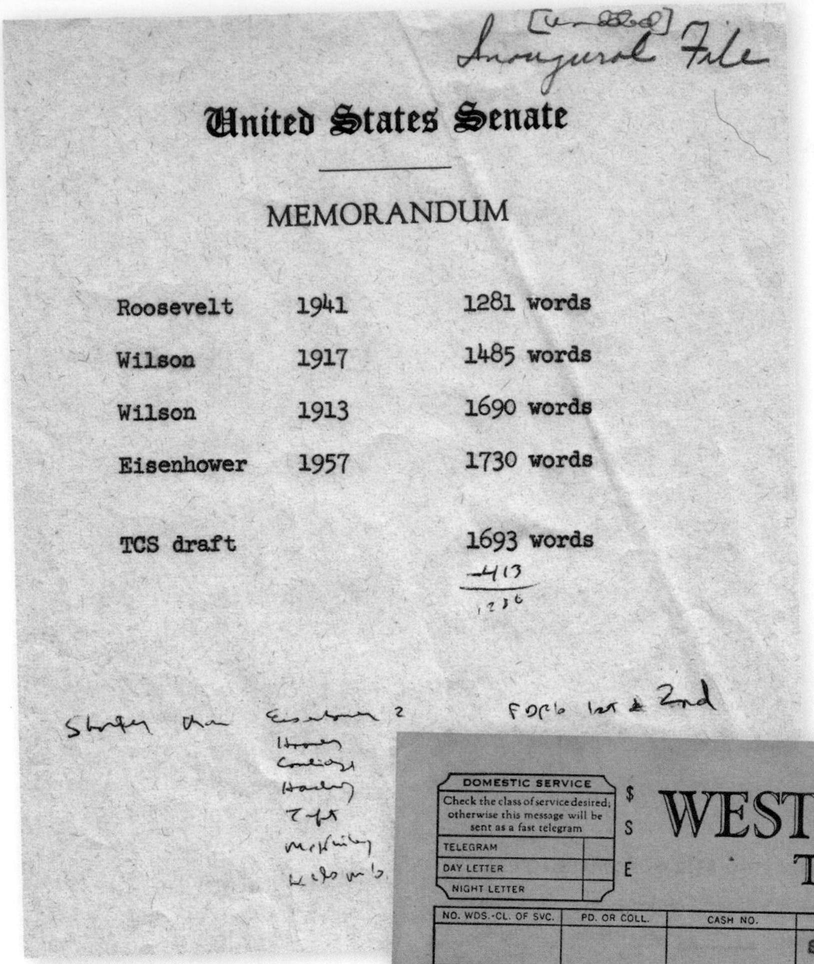

[Inaugural File] (handwritten at top)

United States Senate

MEMORANDUM

Roosevelt	1941	1281 words
Wilson	1917	1485 words
Wilson	1913	1690 words
Eisenhower	1957	1730 words
TCS draft		1693 words
		—413 (handwritten)
		1230 (handwritten)

(handwritten notes at bottom left) Shorter than Eisenhower 2, Hoover, Coolidge, Harding, Taft, McKinley, Webster's

(handwritten) FDR's 1st & 2nd

▲ A memo from Ted Sorensen listing the word counts of previously successful inauguration speeches.

superb second inaugural. Kennedy also concerned himself with length, realizing that the hallmark of the most successful inaugural speeches had been brevity. Lincoln's first inaugural speech ran to just 703 words, and FDR's 1941 speech around 1,300. The most recent, Eisenhower's, was just 1,730 words. In the end, Kennedy spoke just 1,345 words at his inauguration and took fewer than fourteen minutes to deliver his speech.

That was a remarkable compression, given the amount of advice Kennedy was given in the weeks and months before January 20. Kennedy directed Sorensen to seek contributions from ten major Democratic Party figures, including

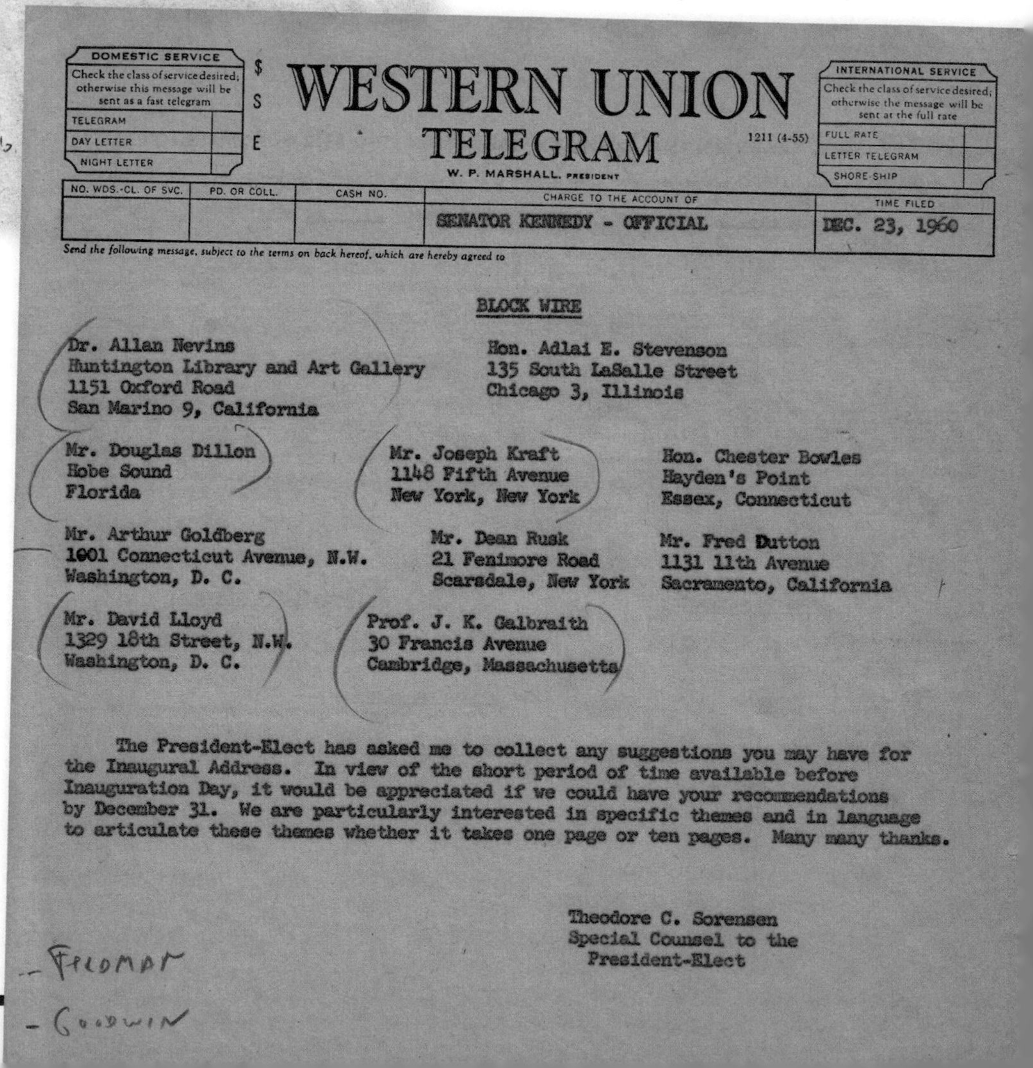

▶ A telegram from Ted Sorensen to ten major Democratic Party figures seeking suggestions for the upcoming inaugural address.

WESTERN UNION TELEGRAM

W. P. MARSHALL, PRESIDENT

1211 (4-55)

DOMESTIC SERVICE — Check the class of service desired; otherwise this message will be sent as a fast telegram
TELEGRAM / DAY LETTER / NIGHT LETTER

INTERNATIONAL SERVICE — Check the class of service desired; otherwise the message will be sent at the full rate
FULL RATE / LETTER TELEGRAM / SHORE-SHIP

NO. WDS.-CL. OF SVC.	PD. OR COLL.	CASH NO.	CHARGE TO THE ACCOUNT OF	TIME FILED
			SENATOR KENNEDY – OFFICIAL	DEC. 23, 1960

Send the following message, subject to the terms on back hereof, which are hereby agreed to

BLOCK WIRE

Dr. Allan Nevins
Huntington Library and Art Gallery
1151 Oxford Road
San Marino 9, California

Hon. Adlai E. Stevenson
135 South LaSalle Street
Chicago 3, Illinois

Mr. Douglas Dillon
Hobe Sound
Florida

Mr. Joseph Kraft
1148 Fifth Avenue
New York, New York

Hon. Chester Bowles
Hayden's Point
Essex, Connecticut

Mr. Arthur Goldberg
1001 Connecticut Avenue, N.W.
Washington, D. C.

Mr. Dean Rusk
21 Fenimore Road
Scarsdale, New York

Mr. Fred Dutton
1131 11th Avenue
Sacramento, California

Mr. David Lloyd
1329 18th Street, N.W.
Washington, D. C.

Prof. J. K. Galbraith
30 Francis Avenue
Cambridge, Massachusetts

The President-Elect has asked me to collect any suggestions you may have for the Inaugural Address. In view of the short period of time available before Inauguration Day, it would be appreciated if we could have your recommendations by December 31. We are particularly interested in specific themes and in language to articulate these themes whether it takes one page or ten pages. Many many thanks.

Theodore C. Sorensen
Special Counsel to the
President-Elect

(handwritten at bottom) — FREEDMAN / — GOODWIN

two-time presidential candidate Adlai Stevenson and economist John Kenneth Galbraith. All responded at length, with five offering full drafts, but their efforts played at best minor roles in the shaping of the speech.

Sorensen played a much more substantial role. Like any good speechwriter, he always carefully described himself as an artisan who helped craft speeches that reflected Kennedy's ideas in Kennedy's words. By the time of the inaugural, he had been working for Kennedy for eight years, and had drafted and polished hundreds of speeches for the Senate and the campaign trail. His knowledge of Kennedy's favored topics, likes and dislikes, and speech cadences ran bone deep.

Sorensen Admits Some Authorship

Despite his insistence that the substance of the speeches came from Kennedy, Sorensen made an interesting admission in his autobiography, *Counselor*. "Traces of some themes in the inaugural," he wrote, "can be found in themes evoked by my father many years earlier, which I may have heard from him more than once. In 1934, my father deplored 'the poverty, misery and disease facing large masses of people' around the world. In 1961 [in the inaugural address], JFK deplored 'the common enemies of man: tyranny, poverty, disease and war itself.' C. A. Sorensen had said that 'The years have taught me patience. I no longer complain if things go slowly. God did not make a tree in a day; it took Him millions of years. . . So what if it does take a century to accomplish a reform. If we are on the right road, it matters not that the road is long . . .' Those words, written by C. A. the year before I was born, foreshadowed JFK: 'all this will not be finished in the first 100 days . . . nor even perhaps in our lifetime on this planet—but let us begin.'"

That passage may be intended as a tribute to Sorensen's father, a crusading Republican politician from Nebraska, whom he placed beside Kennedy in his pantheon of heroes. But it also indicates that Sorensen was more than a typist—he came into the process with a brain and a political philosophy that left its imprint on the inaugural speech, and on many others.

Kennedy's own stamp on the speech, according to Sorensen, began with the central question of what the speech should accomplish. Kennedy realized that he remained an unknown quantity. His aim from the outset was to deliver a speech that would transform him in the eyes of the world—and of the Democratic Party establishment—from a young politician elected by a razor-thin margin to a confident leader and statesman.

Focus on Foreign Policy

From the earliest drafts, the speech dealt almost exclusively with foreign policy. Kennedy believed that domestic issues were too complex for a short speech. He wanted a speech focused on international affairs and stressing his capacity for leadership in finding solutions to the world's problems and the Cold War standoff with the Soviet Union. Kennedy wanted a forward-looking and unifying message that would set a positive tone for his Administration, so he needed to steer clear of divisive rhetoric.

Aside from the fragments quoted by Sorensen in his *Kennedy* book, the earliest surviving draft of the speech is the "TCS draft," a typewritten document found in Kennedy's files, produced around ten days before the inaugural. Sorensen's initials are, of course, TCS. The five-page draft is missing the first page, but otherwise conforms quite well to later versions. Kennedy dictated his own version of the speech to his secretary, Evelyn

Lincoln, sometime after January 10, but no copy of that draft survives. Evelyn Lincoln's shorthand notes still exist, and were transcribed in Richard J. Tofel's book, *Sound the Trumpet*. Mrs. Lincoln recalls that Kennedy was referring to the TCS draft while he dictated.

The bulk of the TCS draft made it into the final speech, but Kennedy made some important additions. Sorensen noted in his autobiography that the famous section about the passing of the torch to a new generation, "born in this century, tempered by war," had been added by Kennedy and reflected his wartime experiences—"with which I had no firsthand experience."

Late Changes

Kennedy's dictated draft also added a number of new phrases, including an expansion and improvement of the "Ask Not" section. He expanded it to include not only a plea to Americans to ask what they could do for their country, but also to, "My fellow citizens of the world, ask not what America or any other country will do for you, but rather what you yourself can do for freedom."

In addition to his dictated version, Kennedy himself produced a handwritten draft, also found in his files, and including his own scrawl of "Ask not what your country can do for you." This draft was produced only a few days before the inauguration, and was clearly intended to establish Kennedy's authorship of the speech and preempt accusations of the sort that still dogged him about *Profiles in Courage*.

Both the tone and the content of the speech were basically set in the TCS draft, but there were many changes still to come. One of the most important late changes produced the only reference to domestic policy in a speech that had been exclusively devoted to foreign policy. On the day before the inauguration,

Sorensen recalls, he met with Kennedy's chief civil rights advisors, Harris Wofford and Louis Martin. They suggested that the reference near the beginning of the speech to "those human rights to which this nation has always been committed and to which we are committed today" be expanded by the phrase "at home and around the world." That brief declaration put Kennedy on record, in the most important speech of his life, in support of the civil rights struggle that would become one of the dominant issues of the 1960s and beyond.

The speech continued to undergo word changes right up to the time of delivery, notes Sorensen, including some that Kennedy made on the platform. "A host of joint ventures," which Galbraith said sounded like a mining company, became "cooperative ventures"; and "We shall join to prevent aggression . . . in the Americas" became the more realistic "We shall join to oppose aggression." Sorensen admitted authorship of the phrase about making the United Nations "more than a forum for invective." He acknowledged that the change of the phrase to "prevent it from becoming merely a forum for invective" was an improvement.

Many Memorable Lines

The "Ask not" construction may be the most famous, but any one of a number of other memorable lines might have been the highlight of a lesser politician's career. Among them was Kennedy's powerful observation that "man holds in his mortal hands the power to abolish all forms of human poverty and all forms of human life."

Among many other notable phrases are:
• "Let every nation know . . . that we shall pay any price, bear any burden, meet any hardship, support any friend, oppose any foe to assure the survival and the success of liberty."

• "Let us never negotiate out of fear. But let us never fear to negotiate."

• "For only when our arms are sufficient beyond doubt can we be certain beyond doubt that they will never be used."

• "All this will not be finished in the first 100 days. Nor will it be finished in the first one thousand days, nor in the life of this Administration, nor even perhaps in our lifetime on this planet. But let us begin."

Whoever actually authored them, Kennedy's phrases sang and soared, with dozens that deserved a place in anthologies of great quotations.

In the end, whatever the contributions of Kennedy, Sorensen, or the others to the language, the job of actually saying the words was solely Kennedy's responsibility, and his performance was exceptionally good. Standing coatless in the bright, frigid sunshine of that January day, he exuded dynamism. He made the words his own for all time, uttering one after another the ringing phrases that have far outlasted his regrettably brief presidency and life. He would build his presidency around the themes set out in the speech, gaining

the common enemies of war: tyranny, poverty, disease and war itself.

Can we forge against these enemies a grand and global alliance, North and South, East and West, that can assure a more fruitful life for all mankind? Will you join in that historic effort?

To few generations in the long history of the world have time and events granted the role of chief defenders of freedom at an hour of maximum danger. I do not shrink from this responsibility -- I welcome it -- and I do not believe that any of us would exchange places with any other people or any other generation. The energy, the faith and the devotion which we bring to this endeavor will light our country and all who serve it -- and the glow from that fire can truly light the world. For "when a man's ways please the Lord, he maketh even his enemies to be at peace with him."

And so, my fellow Americans: ask not what your country will do for you -- ask what you can do for your country.

My fellow citizens of the world: ask not what America will do for you but what you can do for freedom.

Finally, whether you are citizens of America or the world, ask of me and those who serve with me the same high standards of strength and sacrifice that we will ask of you; while asking the Lord above to grant us all the strength and wisdom we shall need. With a good conscience our only sure reward, with history the final judge of our deeds, let us go forth to lead the land we love, asking His blessing and help, but knowing that here on earth God's work must truly be our own.

▲ A page from a typed draft of the speech with handwritten amendments by Kennedy.

steadily in stature and the esteem of the world, until tragedy intervened.

Inaugural Address
January 20, 1961, United States Capitol, Washington, DC

Vice President Johnson, Mr. Speaker, Mr. Chief Justice, President Eisenhower, Vice President Nixon, President Truman, reverend clergy, fellow citizens, we observe today not a victory of party, but a celebration of freedom—symbolizing an end, as well as a beginning—signifying renewal, as well as change. For I have sworn before you and Almighty God the same solemn oath our forebears prescribed nearly a century and three quarters ago.

The world is very different now. For man holds in his mortal hands the power to abolish all forms of human poverty and all forms of human life. And yet the same revolutionary beliefs for which our forebears fought are still at issue around the globe—the belief that the rights of man come not from the generosity of the state, but from the hand of God.

We dare not forget today that we are the heirs of that first revolution. Let the word go forth from this time and place, to friend and foe alike, that the torch has been passed to a new generation of Americans— born in this century, tempered by war, disciplined by a hard and bitter peace, proud of our ancient heritage—and unwilling to witness or permit the slow undoing of those human rights to which this Nation has always been committed, and to which we are committed today at home and around the world.

Let every nation know, whether it wishes us well or ill, that we shall pay any price, bear any burden, meet any hardship, support any friend, oppose any foe, in order to assure the survival and the success of liberty.

This much we pledge—and more.

To those old allies whose cultural and spiritual origins we share, we pledge the loyalty of faithful friends. United, there is little we cannot do in a host of cooperative ventures. Divided, there is little we can do—for we dare not meet a powerful challenge at odds and split asunder.

To those new States whom we welcome to the ranks of the free, we pledge our word that one form of colonial control shall not have passed away merely to be replaced by a far more iron tyranny. We shall not always expect to find them supporting our view. But we shall always hope to find them strongly supporting their own freedom—and to remember that, in the past, those who foolishly sought power by riding the back of the tiger ended up inside.

To those peoples in the huts and villages across the globe struggling to break the bonds of mass misery, we pledge our best efforts to help them help themselves, for whatever period is required—not because the Communists may be doing it, not because we seek their votes, but because it is right. If a free society cannot help the many who are poor, it cannot save the few who are rich.

To our sister republics south of our border, we offer a special pledge—to convert our good words into good deeds—in a new alliance for progress—to assist free men and free governments in casting off the chains of poverty. But this peaceful revolution of hope cannot become the prey of hostile powers. Let all our neighbors know that we shall join with them to oppose aggression or subversion anywhere in the Americas. And let every other power know that this Hemisphere intends to remain the master of its own house.

To that world assembly of sovereign states, the United Nations, our last best hope in an age where the instruments of war have far outpaced the instruments of peace, we renew our pledge of support—to prevent

it from becoming merely a forum for invective—to strengthen its shield of the new and the weak—and to enlarge the area in which its writ may run.

Finally, to those nations who would make themselves our adversary, we offer not a pledge but a request: that both sides begin anew the quest for peace, before the dark powers of destruction unleashed by science engulf all humanity in planned or accidental self-destruction.

We dare not tempt them with weakness. For only when our arms are sufficient beyond doubt can we be certain beyond doubt that they will never be employed.

But neither can two great and powerful groups of nations take comfort from our present course—both

▲ A view of the crowd from behind President John F. Kennedy as he gives his inaugural speech.

sides overburdened by the cost of modern weapons, both rightly alarmed by the steady spread of the deadly atom, yet both racing to alter that uncertain balance of terror that stays the hand of mankind's final war.

So let us begin anew—remembering on both sides that civility is not a sign of weakness, and sincerity is always subject to proof. Let us never negotiate out of fear. But let us never fear to negotiate.

Let both sides explore what problems unite us instead of belaboring those problems which divide us.

ADLAI E. STEVENSON
135 So. LaSalle Street
Chicago

December 30, 1960

Mr. Theodore C. Sorensen
c/o Hon. John F. Kennedy
United States Senate
Washington 25, D. C.

Dear Mr. Sorensen:

In response to your telegram of December 24 requesting suggestions for the Inaugural by December 31, I will confine my comments to foreign affairs. Due to a myriad of other pressing "priorities" just now, I have had little time for this, but my first reaction is that it would be well for Senator Kennedy to include the following:

1. A frank acknowledgement of the changing equilibrium in the world and the grave dangers and difficulties which the West faces for the first time.

2. The assertion that our objective is the peace, the progress and the independence of all people, everywhere. We want to end, not prolong the cold war. Hence, all-out support of the UN, (a) as the protector of the new nations against involvement in the cold war; (b) as the ideal instrument for fostering economic development; (c) as the agency which will have to be strengthened in order that it may be able to keep the peace and enforce world law.

3. An unequivocal commitment to disarmament.

4. Recognition that the first order of business is to halt the proliferation of nuclear powers and to reduce the ever growing danger of war by accident.

5. An unequivocal commitment to the Western defensive alliance to deter aggression and keep the peace.

▲ The first page of Adlei Stevenson's reply to Ted Sorensen's telegram requesting suggestions for the upcoming inaugural address.

Let both sides, for the first time, formulate serious and precise proposals for the inspection and control of arms—and bring the absolute power to destroy other nations under the absolute control of all nations.

Let both sides seek to invoke the wonders of science instead of its terrors. Together let us explore the stars, conquer the deserts, eradicate disease, tap the ocean depths, and encourage the arts and commerce.

Let both sides unite to heed in all corners of the earth the command of Isaiah—to "undo the heavy burdens ... and to let the oppressed go free."

And if a beachhead of cooperation may push back the jungle of suspicion, let both sides join in creating a new endeavor, not a new balance of power, but a new world of law, where the strong are just and the weak secure and the peace preserved.

All this will not be finished in the first 100 days. Nor will it be finished in the first 1,000 days, nor in the life of this Administration, nor even perhaps in our lifetime on this planet. But let us begin.

In your hands, my fellow citizens, more than in mine, will rest the final success or failure of our course. Since this country was founded, each generation of Americans has been summoned to give testimony to its national loyalty. The graves of young Americans who answered the call to service surround the globe.

Now the trumpet summons us again—not as a call to bear arms, though arms we need; not as a call to battle, though embattled we are—but a call to bear the burden of a long twilight struggle, year in and year out, "rejoicing in hope, patient in tribulation"—a struggle against the common enemies of man: tyranny, poverty, disease, and war itself.

Can we forge against these enemies a grand and global alliance, North and South, East and West, that can assure a more fruitful life for all mankind? Will you join in that historic effort?

In the long history of the world, only a few generations have been granted the role of defending freedom in its hour of maximum danger. I do not shrink from this responsibility—I welcome it. I do not believe that any of us would exchange places with any other people or any other generation. The energy, the faith, the devotion which we bring to this endeavor will light our country and all who serve it—and the glow from that fire can truly light the world.

And so, my fellow Americans: ask not what your country can do for you—ask what you can do for your country.

My fellow citizens of the world: ask not what America will do for you, but what together we can do for the freedom of man.

Finally, whether you are citizens of America or citizens of the world, ask of us the same high standards of strength and sacrifice which we ask of you. With a good conscience our only sure reward, with history the final judge of our deeds, let us go forth to lead the land we love, asking His blessing and His help, but knowing that here on earth God's work must truly be our own.

◀ The last page of a draft of the speech in Kennedy's own handwriting, featuring a version of the "ask not what your country can do for you" line.

President John Fitzgerald Kennedy

"We choose to go to the moon in this decade and do the other things, not because they are easy, but because they are hard "

When John F. Kennedy was elected president in 1960, the United States was losing the race to space. Kennedy gave space a high priority from the day he took office, mentioning its importance in a number of speeches. Thanks to his new commitment, in September 1961 construction of the Manned Space Center (now called the Johnson Space Center) began on one thousand acres donated by Rice University. The following year Kennedy visited the center and made his case for why America needed to invest in space exploration.

Texas had always been somewhat hostile to John F. Kennedy. After all, he had beaten favorite son Lyndon Johnson for the 1960 Democratic nomination. The conservative state also was highly suspicious of Eastern liberals. The trip to Houston to tour the new Manned Space Center was designed partly to draw attention to the space program, but also with an eye to the 1964 election. The same political considerations, regrettably, led to Kennedy's fatal visit to Dallas in November 1963.

The Soviet Union grabbed and held the lead in the space race from the time it launched Sputnik in 1957. Their efforts—and their failures—were muffled by Iron Curtain secrecy. The US space program operated in the glare of media attention. When it stumbled in its efforts to catch up, everyone on Earth knew about it and the Soviets gloated. The highly public failure of the first US satellite launch, *Vanguard*, was a major

▲ **President John F. Kennedy delivering his address at Rice University.**

embarrassment. The United States eventually managed to put satellites into orbit, but then the Soviets greeted President Kennedy with their first manned orbital flight, by cosmonaut Yuri Gagarin, less than three months after he took office. The United States answered feebly with the sub-orbital flight of astronaut Alan Shepard, and it was nearly a year before the world saw the first orbiting American, John Glenn.

Cold War in Space

The Kennedy Administration saw the race to space as an important component of the Cold War, and a component in which the United States had clearly fallen behind. Superiority in space grabbed worldwide headlines and conveyed great prestige to the Soviets. Behind the scenes the stakes were even higher. Satellites leant a new dimension to spying. Moreover, rockets that could put a man in orbit could reach enemy territory—or place weapons into those same orbits. The United States was desperately fearful of Soviet military occupation of space, and vice versa.

Kennedy issued behind the scenes orders to catch and surpass the Soviets. His advisors told him that the Soviets had bigger, heavier rockets more adapted to sending large objects, such as manned space capsules, into orbit. It would be years before the United States could match their rocketry and payloads. Only a month after JFK's speech at Rice, the Soviet Union placed some of those larger, heavier rockets in Cuba, where they could easily reach any point in the United States. The raw fact of superiority in rocketry, of which the space program was symbolic, was a very real worry in 1962.

So how could we quickly gain the advantage? What about going to the moon, Kennedy wanted to know? Advisors were doubtful, but the prospect excited the restless Kennedy, who desperately wanted to outflank the rival superpower. While seeking money from Congress for an expanded space program in mid-1961, he first pledged that America would reach the moon by the end of the decade, and reach it before the Soviet Union.

On that occasion, he was straightforward in setting out the goal, declaring simply, "I believe that this nation should commit itself to achieving the goal, before this decade is out, of landing a man on the moon and returning him safely to the Earth."

Kennedy Makes Compelling Case

In his speech at Rice University, he was much more eloquent in his statement that "We choose to go to the moon," and made a compelling case for the space program.

Sorensen, as usual, wrote the speech, and it went through only four drafts, with Kennedy tightening the final version considerably. The president was greeted by a large and enthusiastic crowd. In campaign mode, he loaded the speech with positive references to the state and its people, and with local inside jokes to build rapport with the crowd. Some of these he improvised on the platform, and others appear in draft copies in his illegible scrawl.

In explaining why the nation should set its sights on the moon, Kennedy set up the biggest laugh in the speech by asking, rhetorically, why climb the highest mountain, and why [referring to Lindbergh's solo flight] fly the Atlantic. He followed that by asking, "Why does Rice play Texas?"

The crowd erupted in laughter and applause, because they knew that the chronically weak Rice football team annually was trounced by powerful Texas, usually by lopsided scores.

Kennedy followed up the laughter with the most famous line of the speech, "We choose to go to the moon . . . and do the other things, not because they are easy, but because they are hard." That was an example of the vaunted Kennedy ability to deliver historic phrases, and it is the sound bite seen countless times in news accounts and documentaries on space.

Compressing Human History to Half a Century

Kennedy began his speech with the familiar rhetorical technique of compressing a timeline to dramatize it. How many times have we heard a speaker say that if the history of the world were expressed as twenty-four hours, man would occupy only the last few seconds? Kennedy did the same with human history, expressing it in terms of half a century. He used that compression as a way of saying the human race was moving fast, but it was necessary and not unprecedented when cast in terms of recent versus ancient history. And again, he alluded to Texas in his argument: "This city of Houston, this State of Texas, this country of the United States was not built by those who waited and rested and wished to look behind them. This country was conquered by those who moved forward—and so will space [be]."

Both the transcript and the recording of the speech show that the fastidiousness that marked some of Kennedy's earlier efforts was missing, as evidenced by the grammatical lapse in the above sentence. He followed that reference with an obtuse and confusing quote from Plymouth Colony governor William Bradford in 1630, to the effect that difficult undertakings must be "enterprised and overcome with answerable courage." The Bradford quote did not appear in Sorensen's earlier drafts, and in the draft material available from the Kennedy Library a version of it appears on a piece of paper bearing the logo of the Avis

▲ The note with the William Bradford quote written in pencil and remarks from Kennedy in black pen.

car rental company. The handwriting is neat and round and decidedly not Kennedy's, although a couple of scrawls on the paper do appear to be in his hand.

Mistakes on the Platform

In all probability, Kennedy asked an aide to research the Bradford quote and added it himself at the last minute because the occasion for his presence at Rice was that the university was making him an honorary visiting professor. Kennedy was a history buff who liked to show off his knowledge in his speeches. Nevertheless, the quote was labored, and misplaced. In using it, Kennedy committed the speaker's cardinal sin of making the audience stop and think about what he meant. Some speech communications scholars call those "stop signs" and claim that they reduce the audience's ability to absorb the message. Kennedy rarely made those mistakes, but this was one.

Kennedy later ended the speech with a rather weak analogy between going to the moon and the wishes of British explorer George Mallory, who said he wanted to climb Mount Everest "because it is there." Mallory died on Mount Everest—not the best example to use when sending men to the moon.

The speech also suffered from some substandard staff work. Not only did the above-mentioned grammatical error creep in, but so did another puzzling gaffe. In the official transcript as provided by the Kennedy Library there was a reference to the "$5,400 million" per year NASA budget. The usual American style would be to refer to $5.4 billion. Additionally, US Office of Management and Budget figures show that the NASA budget for 1962 was about $1.25 billion, and would not exceed Kennedy's "$5,400 million" for another four years.

One wonders why the error was not caught and corrected before delivery of the speech, and why it has remained uncorrected all these years. In later White Houses, heads rolled for errors far less egregious. It should also be noted that early drafts of the speech referred to the venue as "Rice Institute," although it had changed its name to "Rice University" two years earlier. That error was caught just in time.

The speech had its moments, and the high points were strong enough to overcome Kennedy's gaffes. It was much more substantive than his Inaugural Address, which attempted only to set the tone and direction of his Administration. Here was a working executive, selling a costly program that proposed an outlandishly ambitious goal to a less-than-friendly audience.

In the speech, Kennedy raised the spectre of the military competition for space as justification for going forward. He pointed to American progress, noting that the United States was as of 1962 now putting far more—and more sophisticated—satellites into orbit than the Soviets.

Selling the Program

The United States probably had not failed more than the Soviets had failed, he said. Rumors of launching pad explosions and crashed rockets killing Soviet cosmonauts and observers circulated widely at the time, and have since been at least partly confirmed.

Kennedy also talked about the considerable cost of the program. That was a major sticking point both with fiscal conservatives and with liberals who thought the money could be used more effectively to alleviate poverty.

Before this audience, as an astute politician, Kennedy made sure to recount the positive economic impact of the new space center on the city and state, even as candidates do to this day. It would create jobs in Houston, across Texas, and throughout the Southwest, to the tune of "more than $1 billion from this Center in this City."

"What was once the farthest outpost of the old frontier of the West will be the heart of the new frontier of science and space," he said, deftly getting in a plug for the "New Frontier" umbrella slogan for his programs.

The Kennedy Legacy

Despite the errors and gaffes, the speech as delivered showcased Kennedy at his charismatic best, received wide and positive coverage, and effectively highlighted US commitment to the space program.

The Congress was then in the midst of budget debates and voted NASA much of its requested money. Within the next four budget years, the money targeted for space exploration quadrupled. And, of course, the United States did achieve Kennedy's goal by the end of the decade, reaching the moon in July 1969. Sadly, Kennedy did not live to see it.

Sorensen counts the space program among Kennedy's greatest achievements in his 1,000-day presidency. Others agree.

"I believe posterity will note," Sorensen writes in his autobiography, *Counselor*, "that three of the most significant events in American history were the Cuban missile crisis, when he peacefully resolved the world's first nuclear confrontation, his reversal of this country's centuries-old subjugation of blacks, and his establishment of a robust space program enabling the human race to travel beyond the limits of the Earth. That is the Kennedy legacy having an impact on all today."

Address at Rice University
September 12, 1962, Houston, Texas

President Pitzer, Mr. Vice President, Governor, Congressman Thomas, Senator Wiley, and Congressman Miller, Mr. Webb, Mr. Bell, scientists, distinguished guests, and ladies and gentlemen:

I appreciate your president having made me an honorary visiting professor, and I will assure you that my first lecture will be very brief.

I am delighted to be here, and I'm particularly delighted to be here on this occasion.

We meet at a college noted for knowledge, in a city noted for progress, in a State noted for strength, and we stand in need of all three, for we meet in an hour of change and challenge, in a decade of hope and fear, in an age of both knowledge and ignorance. The greater our knowledge increases, the greater our ignorance unfolds.

Despite the striking fact that most of the scientists that the world has ever known are alive and working today, despite the fact that this Nation's own scientific manpower is doubling every 12 years in a rate of growth more than three times that of our population as a whole, despite that, the vast stretches of the unknown and the unanswered and the unfinished still far outstrip our collective comprehension.

No man can fully grasp how far and how fast we have come, but condense, if you will, the 50,000 years of man's recorded history in a time span of but a half-century. Stated in these terms, we know very little about the first 40 years, except at the end of them advanced man had learned to use the skins of animals to cover them. Then about 10 years ago, under this standard, man emerged from his caves to construct other kinds of shelter. Only five years ago man learned to write and use a cart with wheels. Christianity began less than two years ago. The printing press came this year, and then less than two months ago, during this whole 50-year span of human history, the steam engine provided a new source of power.

Newton explored the meaning of gravity. Last month electric lights and telephones and automobiles and airplanes became available. Only last week did we develop penicillin and television and nuclear power, and now if America's new spacecraft succeeds in reaching Venus, we will have literally reached the stars before midnight tonight.

This is a breathtaking pace, and such a pace cannot help but create new ills as it dispels old, new ignorance, new problems, new dangers. Surely the opening vistas of space promise high costs and hardships, as well as high reward.

So it is not surprising that some would have us stay where we are a little longer to rest, to wait. But this city of Houston, this State of Texas, this country of the United States was not built by those who waited and rested and wished to look behind them. This country was conquered by those who moved forward—and so will space.

William Bradford, speaking in 1630 of the founding of the Plymouth Bay Colony, said that all great and honorable actions are accompanied with great difficulties, and both must be enterprised and overcome with answerable courage.

If this capsule history of our progress teaches us anything, it is that man, in his quest for knowledge and progress, is determined and cannot be deterred. The exploration of space will go ahead, whether we join in it or not, and it is one of the great adventures of all time, and no nation which expects to be the leader of other nations can expect to stay behind in the race for space.

Those who came before us made certain that this country rode the first waves of the industrial revolutions, the first waves of modern invention, and

-4-

I do not say that we should or will go unprotected against the hostile misuse of space -- any more than we would go unprotected against the hostile misuse of land or sea or sky. But I do say that space can be explored and *mastered* ~~exploited~~ without taking what belongs to others -- without feeding the fires of war and imperialism -- without repeating the mistakes man made in extending his writ around the earth. There is no strife, no prejudice, no hate in outer space. Its hazards are hostile to all. Its conquest deserves the best of us all. Its ~~allure~~ *And* opportunity for peaceful cooperation ~~just~~ may never come again.

But why, some say, the moon? Why choose this as our goal? And they may as well ask: why climb the highest mountain? *Why 35 years ago fly the Atlantic?* ~~Why take on the toughest team?~~ Why set your sights on a ~~4 minute mile~~? We choose to go to the moon in this decade, not because that will be easy, but because it will be hard -- because that goal will serve to organize and measure the best of our energies and skills -- because that challenge is one we are willing to accept, one we are unwilling to postpone, and one we intend to win.

It is for these reasons that I regard the decision last year to shift our efforts in space from low to high-gear as among the most important decisions I expect to make in the office of President.

In these last 24 hours I have seen the vast facilities now being created for the greatest and most complex exploration in man's history. I have felt the ground quake ~~and the ear shattered~~ *And* the air shattered by the testing of a Saturn *C-1* booster rocket, *many* times as powerful as the Atlas which

▲ A page from an early draft of the speech with changes in Kennedy's handwriting, in pencil, and that of an unidentified presidential aide in black pen.

the first wave of nuclear power, and this generation does not intend to founder in the backwash of the coming age of space. We mean to be a part of it—we mean to lead it. For the eyes of the world now look into space, to the moon and to the planets beyond, and we have vowed that we shall not see it governed by a hostile flag of conquest, but by a banner of freedom and peace. We have vowed that we shall not see space filled with weapons of mass destruction, but with instruments of knowledge and understanding.

Yet the vows of this Nation can only be fulfilled if we in this Nation are first, and, therefore, we intend to be first. In short, our leadership in science and

strife, no prejudice, no hate in outer space.
Its hazards are hostile to us all. Its conquest
deserves the best of us all. and its opportunity
for peaceful cooperation may never come again.

But why, some say, the moon? Why choose
this as our goal? And they may as well ask: why
climb the highest mountain? Why 35 years ago
fly the Atlantic? *Why does Rice play Texas* We choose to go to the moon
in this decade, not because that will be easy,
but because it will be hard -- because that goal
will serve to organize and measure the best of
our energies and skills -- because that challenge
is one we are willing to accept, one we are
unwilling to postpone, and one we intend to win.

It is for these reasons that I regard the
decision last year to shift our efforts in space
from low to high-gear as among the most important

◄ A page from a later draft of the speech with handwritten changes by Kennedy as well as words underlined for emphasis.

in industry, our hopes for peace and security, our obligations to ourselves as well as others, all require us to make this effort, to solve these mysteries, to solve them for the good of all men, and to become the world's leading space-faring nation.

We set sail on this new sea because there is new knowledge to be gained, and new rights to be won, and they must be won and used for the progress of all people. For space science, like nuclear science and all technology, has no conscience of its own. Whether it will become a force for good or ill depends on man, and only if the United States occupies a position of pre-eminence can we help decide whether this new ocean will be a sea of peace or a new terrifying theater of war. I do not say the we should or will go unprotected against the hostile misuse of space any more than we go unprotected against the hostile use of land or sea, but I do say that space can be explored and mastered without feeding the fires of war, without repeating the mistakes that man has made in extending his writ around this globe of ours.

There is no strife, no prejudice, no national conflict in outer space as yet. Its hazards are hostile to us all. Its conquest deserves the best of all mankind, and its opportunity for peaceful cooperation many never come again. But why, some say, the moon? Why choose this as our goal? And they may well ask why climb the highest mountain? Why, 35 years ago, fly the Atlantic? Why does Rice play Texas?

We choose to go to the moon. We choose to go to the moon in this decade and do the other things, not because they are easy, but because they are hard, because that goal will serve to organize and measure the best of our energies and skills, because that challenge is one that we are willing to accept, one we are unwilling to postpone, and one which we intend to win, and the others, too.

It is for these reasons that I regard the decision last year to shift our efforts in space from low to high gear as among the most important decisions that will be made during my incumbency in the office of the Presidency.

In the last 24 hours we have seen facilities now being created for the greatest and most complex exploration in man's history. We have felt the ground shake and the air shattered by the testing of a Saturn C-1 booster rocket, many times as powerful as the Atlas which launched John Glenn, generating power equivalent to 10,000 automobiles with their accelerators on the floor. We have seen the site where the F-1 rocket engines, each one as powerful as all eight engines of the Saturn combined, will be clustered together to make the advanced Saturn missile, assembled in a new building to be built at Cape Canaveral as tall as a 48 story structure, as wide as a city block, and as long as two lengths of this field.

Within these last 19 months at least 45 satellites have circled the earth. Some 40 of them were "made in the United States of America" and they were far more sophisticated and supplied far more knowledge to the people of the world than those of the Soviet Union.

The Mariner spacecraft now on its way to Venus is the most intricate instrument in the history of space science. The accuracy of that shot is comparable to firing a missile from Cape Canaveral and dropping it in this stadium between the 40-yard lines.

Transit satellites are helping our ships at sea to steer a safer course. Tiros satellites have given us unprecedented warnings of hurricanes and storms, and will do the same for forest fires and icebergs.

We have had our failures, but so have others, even if they do not admit them. And they may be less public.

To be sure, we are behind, and will be behind for some time in manned flight. But we do not intend to stay behind, and in this decade, we shall make up and move ahead.

The growth of our science and education will be enriched by new knowledge of our universe and environment, by new techniques of learning and mapping and observation, by new tools and computers for industry, medicine, the home as well as the school. Technical institutions, such as Rice, will reap the harvest of these gains.

And finally, the space effort itself, while still in its infancy, has already created a great number of new companies, and tens of thousands of new jobs. Space and related industries are generating new demands in investment and skilled personnel, and this city and this State, and this region, will share greatly in this growth. What was once the furthest outpost on the old frontier of the West will be the furthest outpost on the new frontier of science and space. Houston, your City

President John F. Kennedy with astronaut Walter Shirra and a military official in front of the Mercury Satellite installation during a visit to the Space Center.

$1 billion from this Center in this City.

To be sure, all this costs us all a good deal of money. This year's space budget is three times what it was in January 1961, and it is greater than the space budget of the previous eight years combined. That budget now stands at $5,400 million a year—a staggering sum, though somewhat less than we pay for cigarettes and cigars every year. Space expenditures will soon rise some more, from 40 cents per person per week to more than 50 cents a week for every man, woman and child in the United Stated, for we have given this program a high national priority—even though I realize that this is in some measure an act of faith and vision, for we do not now know what benefits await us.

of Houston, with its Manned Spacecraft Center, will become the heart of a large scientific and engineering community. During the next 5 years the National Aeronautics and Space Administration expects to double the number of scientists and engineers in this area, to increase its outlays for salaries and expenses to $60 million a year; to invest some $200 million in plant and laboratory facilities; and to direct or contract for new space efforts over

But if I were to say, my fellow citizens, that we shall send to the moon, 240,000 miles away from the control station in Houston, a giant rocket more than 300 feet tall, the length of this football field, made of new metal alloys, some of which have not yet been invented, capable of standing heat and stresses several times more than have ever been experienced, fitted together with a precision better than the finest watch, carrying all the equipment needed for propulsion, guidance, control, communications, food and survival, on an untried mission, to an unknown celestial body, and then return it safely to earth, re-entering the atmosphere at speeds of over 25,000 miles per hour, causing heat about half that of the temperature of the sun—almost as hot as it is here today—and do all this, and do it right, and do it first before this decade is out—then we must be bold.

I'm the one who is doing all the work, so we just want you to stay cool for a minute.

However, I think we're going to do it, and I think that we must pay what needs to be paid. I don't think we ought to waste any money, but I think we ought to do the job. And this will be done in the decade of the sixties. It may be done while some of you are still here at school at this college and university. It will be done during the term of office of some of the people who sit here on this platform. But it will be done. And it will be done before the end of this decade.

I am delighted that this university is playing a part in putting a man on the moon as part of a great national effort of the United States of America.

Many years ago the great British explorer George Mallory, who was to die on Mount Everest, was asked why did he want to climb it. He said, "Because it is there."

Well, space is there, and we're going to climb it, and the moon and the planets are there, and new hopes for knowledge and peace are there. And,

▲ The last page of a draft of the speech with handwritten amendments by Kennedy.

therefore, as we set sail we ask God's blessing on the most hazardous and dangerous and greatest adventure on which man has ever embarked.

Thank you.

President Lyndon Baines Johnson

> "We shall overcome."

Lyndon Johnson entered the White House under tragic circumstances following John Kennedy's assassination, and left it five years later in frustration over Vietnam. In between, he amassed some great and lasting achievements in civil rights and the ambitious social legislation of his "Great Society" plan, including Medicare, education funding, and other programs.

Arguably his finest hour, though, came on March 15, 1965, when he addressed a joint session of Congress to reintroduce voting rights legislation.

Johnson was not a great, or even good, speaker. He was incomparably persuasive with individuals or small groups, as many legislators and others whose arms he twisted into submission would attest. But on the platform, he was wooden and seemed oddly morose.

▲ President Lyndon B. Johnson making an address at a podium flanked by two flags.

When he became president, many doubted whether a Southern man who had opposed some civil rights legislation while in the House and Senate would pursue Kennedy's civil rights agenda. In 1964, he proposed a tough voting rights bill and renewed his call for passage in his State of the Union Message in January 1965.

The bill went nowhere until, on March 7, a line of peaceful civil rights marchers singing "We Shall Overcome" approached the Edmund Pettus Bridge in Selma, Alabama. As America watched on the nightly news, they were savagely beaten by police wielding billy clubs. In his speech a week later, Johnson underscored his support for voting rights by using the phrase "we shall overcome," one of the few times LBJ would electrify an audience from the speaker's platform.

Marchers' Beatings Created National Outrage

The national outrage over the Selma beatings gave Johnson the chance he wanted to advance the legislation. He strongly condemned the atrocity but declined to respond immediately, telling aides that "if I just send in federal troops with their big black boots and rifles, it'll look like Reconstruction all over again." Instead, he used a meeting with segregationist Alabama governor George Wallace to browbeat Wallace into asking for federal help. Johnson used that leverage, and the continuing outrage over Selma, to request an invitation to speak before Congress.

Johnson summoned congressional leaders to a meeting at the White House on Sunday, March 14, and used his legendary persuasive powers to elicit an invitation to address a joint session the following day.

Aside from the annual State of the Union Message, US presidents rarely address the Congress directly, and then only on the most important and solemn occasions. Examples include Woodrow Wilson's two important speeches declaring war on Germany and outlining his fourteen points for the post-war world, and Franklin Delano Roosevelt's speech following the Pearl Harbor attack. The fact that Johnson chose to elevate Selma and voting rights to that level was significant.

The problem then was producing a speech on one day's notice. One of Johnson's speechwriters, Horace Busby, had been at work for some time on a written message to the Congress that was to accompany reintroduction of the voting rights legislation. He had been assigned by top Johnson aide and sometime-speechwriter Jack Valenti,

▲ Reporters surrounding Alabama Governor George Wallace and President Lyndon B. Johnson as they leave the meeting in which Johnson persuaded Wallace to ask for federal help.

and had gone through five drafts. When Johnson discovered who was writing the speech, he hit the roof. He ordered that Richard Goodwin start work, "and now."

LBJ Taps Ex-JFK Speechwriter

Goodwin had been a speechwriter for John F. Kennedy until driven out of the White House following a clash with Kennedy's confidante Ted Sorensen. Goodwin had cooled his heels at the State Department until LBJ succeeded JFK, when he was recalled to the White House.

"Don't you know a liberal Jew has his finger on the pulse of America?" Johnson roared at Goodwin in typical crude but shrewd fashion. When Goodwin arrived for work that Monday morning, he had eight hours to complete the speech in time for it to be loaded onto the teleprompter before the evening address.

There was no time to account for the subtleties of political debate, or to concede merit to the views of the opposition, Goodwin recalled in a memoir. "There was no other side," he wrote. "Only justice—upheld or denied. While . . . a floor beneath my office, there waited a man ready to match my fervor with his own. And he was the President of the United States."

Goodwin locked himself in his office and for the rest of the day rifled through Busby's material, Johnson's past statements, and thought through his own knowledge of Johnson built up over a year of close contact.

Goodwin's Speech Was "Pure Johnson"

Despite the time pressure and his own personal belief in the justice of the civil rights issue, Goodwin later wrote that the speech was "pure Johnson." His job was to "heighten and polish" Johnson's beliefs and his natural way of expressing himself.

"I would not have written the same speech in the same way for Kennedy or any other politician, or for myself," he wrote. "It was by me, but it was for and of the Lyndon Johnson I had carefully studied and came to know."

As Goodwin finished each page, it was delivered to Johnson for review. Valenti, White House press secretary Bill Moyers, and other aides edited on the fly along with the president before the final product was sent to waiting stenographers. When Goodwin finished the final page, he realized it was 6:00 p.m., past the teleprompter deadline. Johnson would have to read the first few pages from his loose-leaf binder while Valenti sneaked across the floor of the House of Representatives to load the rest into the machine.

"I speak tonight for the dignity of man and the destiny of democracy," Johnson began. For once, his slow Southern drawl seemed entirely appropriate as he spoke in sadness rather than anger of the events of Selma and the civil rights struggle.

He noted the great issues the country had confronted, but noted that, "rarely in any time does an issue lay bare the secret heart of America itself." Economic issues or foreign threats are much different challenges from those pertaining to "the values and purposes and the meaning of our beloved nation." In other words, Johnson implied, discrimination is contrary to American ideals and prejudice is un-American. For a Texas president to characterize ostentatiously patriotic Southerners as "un-American" because of their bigotry was unprecedented.

Turning Selma into a Positive

Invoking the horrors of Selma, Johnson then cast them in a positive light. Selma, he noted, was a historical turning point on a par with Lexington, Concord, and Appomattox. The beatings and indignities suffered there had "summoned into convocation all the majesty of this great government." Those atrocities, therefore, would result in action to right historic wrongs.

While condemning the actions in Selma as barbaric and un-American, Johnson took care elsewhere in the speech to place some blame for discrimination on the North and to note the contributions of Southerners in building the country. The problem, he said, was an American problem. Discrimination had to be rooted out in every region of the country.

Johnson's specific aim was passage of voting rights legislation, and he used part of the speech to outline the legislation and its effects.

"But even if we pass this bill, the battle will not be over," he warned. "What happened in Selma is part of a far larger movement which reaches into every section and state of America. It is the effort of American Negroes to secure for themselves the full blessings of American life. Their cause must be our cause too. Because it is not just Negroes, but really it is all of us, who must overcome the crippling legacy of bigotry and injustice."

Then Johnson paused and slowly intoned, "And we shall overcome."

Key Phrase Flowed Naturally

Goodwin said that he did not deliberately insert the phrase in the speech, but that it just "flowed naturally" from the preceding paragraphs. But it had an immense impact. The audience of lawmakers sat in silence for a moment and then erupted in applause, realizing that a Southern president had adopted the civil rights anthem as his own. Watching at home, Dr. Martin Luther King shed tears.

While writing the speech, Richard Goodwin had been interrupted only once, by the president himself. Johnson wanted to remind Goodwin of his own background and experience, and Goodwin used Johnson's reminiscence to great effect near the end of the speech.

Johnson recalled that his first job after college was as a teacher in Cotulla, Texas, in a small Mexican-American school. Few of them spoke English, he said, and most came to class hungry. Though they did not speak of prejudice they knew it, and Johnson said he "saw it in their eyes."

"Somehow you never forget what poverty and hatred can do when you see its scars on the hopeful face of a young child.

"I never thought then, in 1928, that I would be standing here in 1965," Johnson continued. "It never even occurred to me in my fondest dreams that I might have the chance to help the sons and daughters of those students and to help people like them all over this country."

▼ A 1928 photograph of Lyndon B. Johnson (center) with his fifth, sixth, and seventh grade classes at the Welhausen School in Cotulla, Texas.

Johnson Seized the Moment

The President continued, "But now I do have that chance—and I'll let you in on a secret—I mean to use it. And I hope that you will use it with me."

The very personal story humanized the coarse and forceful Johnson. Doris Kearns Goodwin, who married Richard Goodwin in 1975 and later assisted Johnson with his memoirs and wrote a highly regarded biography of him, wrote, "it had been that rare thing in politics, rarer still for Lyndon Johnson—a speech that shaped the course of events. For once, Americans would honor him for a greatness of spirit as well as a mastery of technique. For on this issue he was more than a giver of gifts; he had become a moral leader."

Two weeks later, accompanied by federal troops, Dr. Martin Luther King led hundreds of marchers to Montgomery, the capital of Alabama. Within five months, Johnson signed the voting rights bill into law.

Not since Reconstruction had the federal government made such an intrusion into local government. Under its provisions, all jurisdictions were required to register at least half of the local population of voting age. Failure to do so would be considered evidence of discrimination by the Justice Department, at which point the federal government would take over the voter registration process.

The law worked. Most Southern states realized they were beaten and voluntarily opened voter rolls. When Mississippi failed to comply, the Justice Department took over. Within three years, enrollment of black voters in Mississippi jumped from six percent to forty-four percent. Many jurisdictions now had a majority of black voters, and began electing black mayors and public officials. Before long, even hard-core segregationists such as George Wallace of Alabama began campaigning for black votes.

The courting of black voters continues to this day. No Southern officials dare discount minority voters—and black and Latino voting blocs have made their presence felt at the national level, helping to elect Barack Obama as the nation's first black president.

The voting rights bill was not the only civil rights law passed during the era, but it was one of the most important. And much of the credit goes to those brave souls who endured beatings, jailing, and even the loss of their lives. Yet no small portion of the credit goes to the flawed man who failed often and left office unloved and underappreciated. In this instance, Lyndon Johnson was offered the chance to help the sons and daughters of those he once taught, and he took it.

- -

Presidential Address to Joint Session of Congress
March 15, 1965, United States Capitol, Washington, DC

- -

Mr. Speaker, Mr. President, Members of the Congress:

I speak tonight for the dignity of man and the destiny of democracy.

I urge every member of both parties, Americans of all religions and of all colors, from every section of this country, to join me in that cause.

At times history and fate meet at a single time in a single place to shape a turning point in man's unending search for freedom. So it was at Lexington and Concord. So it was a century ago at Appomattox. So it was last week in Selma, Alabama.

There, long-suffering men and women peacefully protested the denial of their rights as Americans. Many were brutally assaulted. One good man, a man of God, was killed.

There is no cause for pride in what has happened in Selma. There is no cause for self-satisfaction in the long denial of equal rights of millions of Americans. But there is cause for hope and for faith in our democracy in what is happening here tonight.

For the cries of pain and the hymns and protests of oppressed people have summoned into convocation all the majesty of this great Government—the Government of the greatest Nation on earth.

Our mission is at once the oldest and the most basic of this country: to right wrong, to do justice, to serve man.

In our time we have come to live with moments of great crisis. Our lives have been marked with debate about great issues; issues of war and peace, issues of prosperity and depression. But rarely in any time does an issue lay bare the secret heart of America itself. Rarely are we met with a challenge, not to our growth or abundance, our welfare or our security, but rather to the values and the purposes and the meaning of our beloved Nation.

The issue of equal rights for American Negroes is such an issue. And should we defeat every enemy, should we double our wealth and conquer the stars,

▲ The first page of an early draft of the speech with handwritten amendments by two different presidential aides, one in pencil and others in blue pen.

and still be unequal to this issue, then we will have failed as a people and as a nation.

For with a country as with a person, "What is a man profited, if he shall gain the whole world, and lose his own soul?"

There is no Negro problem. There is no Southern problem. There is no Northern problem. There is only an American problem. And we are met here tonight as Americans—not as Democrats or Republicans—we are met here as Americans to solve that problem.

This was the first nation in the history of the world to be founded with a purpose. The great phrases of that purpose still sound in every American heart, North and South: "All men are created equal"—"government by consent of the governed"—"give me liberty or give me death." Well, those are not just clever words, or those are not just empty theories. In their name Americans have fought and died for two centuries, and tonight around the world they stand there as guardians of our liberty, risking their lives.

Those words are a promise to every citizen that he shall share in the dignity of man. This dignity cannot be found in a man's possessions; it cannot be found in his power, or in his position. It really rests on his right to be treated as a man equal in opportunity to all others. It says that he shall share in freedom, he shall choose his leaders, educate his children, and provide for his family according to his ability and his merits as a human being.

To apply any other test—to deny a man his hopes because of his color or race, his religion or the place of his birth—is not only to do injustice, it is to deny America and to dishonor the dead who gave their lives for American freedom.

Our fathers believed that if this noble view of the rights of man was to flourish, it must be rooted in democracy. The most basic right of all was the right to choose your own leaders. The history of this country, in large measure, is the history of the expansion of that right to all of our people.

Many of the issues of civil rights are very complex and most difficult. But about this there can and should be no argument. Every American citizen must have an equal right to vote. There is no reason which can excuse the denial of that right. There is no duty which

weighs more heavily on us than the duty we have to ensure that right.

Yet the harsh fact is that in many places in this country men and women are kept from voting simply because they are Negroes.

Every device of which human ingenuity is capable has been used to deny this right. The Negro citizen may go to register only to be told that the day is wrong, or the hour is late, or the official in charge is absent. And if he persists, and if he manages to present himself to the registrar, he may be disqualified because he did not spell out his middle name or because he abbreviated a word on the application.

And if he manages to fill out an application he is given a test. The registrar is the sole judge of whether he passes this test. He may be asked to recite the entire Constitution, or explain the most complex provisions of State law. And even a college degree cannot be used to prove that he can read and write.

For the fact is that the only way to pass these barriers is to show a white skin.

Experience has clearly shown that the existing process of law cannot overcome systematic and ingenious discrimination. No law that we now have on the books-and I have helped to put three of them there—can ensure the right to vote when local officials are determined to deny it.

In such a case our duty must be clear to all of us. The Constitution says that no person shall be kept from voting because of his race or his color. We have all sworn an oath before God to support and to defend that Constitution. We must now act in obedience to that oath.

Wednesday I will send to Congress a law designed to eliminate illegal barriers to the right to vote.

The broad principles of that bill will be in the hands of the Democratic and Republican leaders tomorrow. After they have reviewed it, it will

Extend the rights of citizenship to every citizen.

~~And then this law shall never apply in your town and all Americans will be glad of it.~~

There is no constitutional issue here. The command of the Constitution is plain.

There is no moral issue. It is wrong to deny any American the right to vote.

There is no issue of states rights or ~~Federal~~ National rights. There is only the struggle for human rights.

~~The only issue is whether we will be true to the purpose of America, or whether we will fail in our duty and strike at the vitality of our country.~~

I have no doubt what will be your answer.

Last time a President sent a civil rights bill to Congress it contained a provision to protect voting rights. That bill was passed after eight long months of debate. And when that bill came to my desk for signature, the heart of the voting provision ~~was~~ had been eliminated.

This time, on this issue, there must be no delay, no hesitation, no compromise with our purpose.

We cannot ~~take the~~ refuse to protect the right of Americans to vote.

We cannot wait another eight months. We have already waited ~~for 95~~ a hundred years and more. The time for waiting is gone.

I ask you to work long hours, nights, and weekends to pass this bill. For outside this chamber is the outraged conscience of a nation, ~~and~~ the grave concern of many nations — ~~the demanding voice of our heritage, and the harsh judgment of history on our acts.~~ — and the harsh judgment of history on our acts.

◄ The first page of an early draft of the speech with handwritten amendments by two different presidential aides, one in pencil and others in blue pen.

This bill will strike down restrictions to voting in all elections—Federal, State, and local—which have been used to deny Negroes the right to vote.

This bill will establish a simple, uniform standard which cannot be used, however ingenious the effort, to flout our Constitution.

It will provide for citizens to be registered by officials of the United States Government if the State officials refuse to register them.

It will eliminate tedious, unnecessary lawsuits which delay the right to vote.

Finally, this legislation will ensure that properly registered individuals are not prohibited from voting.

come here formally as a bill. I am grateful for this opportunity to come here tonight at the invitation of the leadership to reason with my friends, to give them my views, and to visit with my former colleagues.

I have had prepared a more comprehensive analysis of the legislation which I had intended to transmit to the clerk tomorrow but which I will submit to the clerks tonight. But I want to really discuss with you now briefly the main proposals of this legislation,

I will welcome the suggestions from all of the Members of Congress—I have no doubt that I will get some—on ways and means to strengthen this law and to make it effective. But experience has plainly shown that this is the only path to carry out the command of the Constitution.

To those who seek to avoid action by their National Government in their own communities; who want to and who seek to maintain purely local control over elections, the answer is simple:

Open your polling places to all your people.

Allow men and women to register and vote whatever the color of their skin.

Extend the rights of citizenship to every citizen of this land.

There is no constitutional issue here. The command of the Constitution is plain.

There is no moral issue. It is wrong—deadly wrong—to deny any of your fellow Americans the right to vote in this country.

There is no issue of States rights or national rights. There is only the struggle for human rights.

I have not the slightest doubt what will be your answer.

The last time a President sent a civil rights bill to the Congress it contained a provision to protect voting rights in Federal elections. That civil rights bill was passed after 8 long months of debate. And when that bill came to my desk from the Congress for my signature, the heart of the voting provision had been eliminated.

This time, on this issue, there must be no delay, no hesitation and no compromise with our purpose.

We cannot, we must not, refuse to protect the right of every American to vote in every election that he may desire to participate in. And we ought not and we cannot and we must not wait another 8 months before we get a bill. We have already waited a hundred years and more, and the time for waiting is gone.

10.

from the Great Lakes down to the Gulf of Mexico, from the Golden Gate to the harbors along the Atlantic -- will rally now together in this cause to vindicate the freedom of us all. For all of us owe this duty; all of us will respond to it.

The real hero of this struggle is the American Negro. His actions and protests -- his courage to risk safety and even life -- have awakened the conscience of the nation. His demonstrations have been designed to call attention to injustice, to provoke change and stir reform. He has called upon us to make good the promise of America. And who among us can say we would have made the same progress were it not for his persistent bravery, and his faith in American democracy.

For at the heart of battle for equality is a belief in the democratic process. Equality depends not on the force of arms but the force of moral right -- not on recourse to violence but on respect for law.

We intend to fight this battle where it should be fought -- in the courts, in the Congress, and in the hearts of men.

We must preserve the right of free speech and the right of free assembly. But the right of free speech does not carry with it the right to holler fire in a crowded theatre.

So I ask you to join me in working long hours— nights and weekends, if necessary—to pass this bill. And I don't make that request lightly. For from the window where I sit with the problems of our country I recognize that outside this chamber is the outraged conscience of a nation, the grave concern of many nations, and the harsh judgment of history on our acts.

But even if we pass this bill, the battle will not be over. What happened in Selma is part of a far larger

◀▼ Handwritten edits and underlining by
Johnson on two pages of one of the later drafts
of the speech.

*We must preserve the right of free assembly but
we assembly does not clog ~~with it~~*

by blocking public thoroughfare

~~If~~ the right to endanger the safety of others ~~on a public highway.~~

We do have a right to protest -- and a right to march under conditions that do not infringe the Constitutional rights of our neighbors. I intend to protect all those rights as long as I am permitted to serve in this Office.

We will guard against violence, knowing it strikes from our hands the very weapons with which we seek progress -- obedience to law, and belief in American values.

In Selma as elsewhere we seek peace. We seek order. We seek unity.

But we will not accept the peace of stifled rights, the order imposed by fear, the unity that stifles protest. For peace cannot be purchased at the cost of liberty.

In Selma, as in every city, we are working for just and peaceful settlement. We must remember that after this speech -- *this and the* after the police and the marshalls have gone -- after this bill is passed, the people of Selma must still live and work together. When the attention of the nation has gone elsewhere they must try to heal the wounds and build a new community. This cannot easily be done on a battleground of violence as the history of the South itself shows. It is in recognition of this that men of both races have shown such impressive responsibility in recent days.

movement which reaches into every section and State of America. It is the effort of American Negroes to secure for themselves the full blessings of American life.

Their cause must be our cause too. Because it is not just Negroes, but really it is all of us, who must overcome the crippling legacy of bigotry and injustice.

And we shall overcome.

As a man whose roots go deeply into Southern soil I know how agonizing racial feelings are. I know how difficult it is to reshape the attitudes and the structure of our society.

But a century has passed, more than a hundred years, since the Negro was freed. And he is not fully free tonight.

It was more than a hundred years ago that Abraham Lincoln, a great President of another party, signed the Emancipation Proclamation, but emancipation is a proclamation and not a fact.

A century has passed, more than a hundred years, since equality was promised. And yet the Negro is not equal.

A century has passed since the day of promise. And the promise is unkept.

The time of justice has now come. I tell you that I believe sincerely that no force can hold it back. It is right in the eyes of man and God that it should come. And when it does, I think that day will brighten the lives of every American.

For Negroes are not the only victims. How many white children have gone uneducated, how many white families have lived in stark poverty, how many white lives have been scarred by fear, because we have wasted our energy and our substance to maintain the barriers of hatred and terror?

So I say to all of you here, and to all in the Nation tonight, that those who appeal to you to hold on to the past do so at the cost of denying you your future.

This great, rich, restless country can offer opportunity and education and hope to all: black and white, North and South, sharecropper and city dweller. These are the enemies: poverty, ignorance, disease.

They are the enemies and not our fellow man, not our neighbor. And these enemies too, poverty, disease and ignorance, we shall overcome.

Now let none of us in any sections look with prideful righteousness on the troubles in another section, or on the problems of our neighbors. There is really no part of America where the promise of equality has been fully kept. In Buffalo as well as in Birmingham, in Philadelphia as well as in Selma, Americans are struggling for the fruits of freedom.

This is one Nation. What happens in Selma or in Cincinnati is a matter of legitimate concern to every American. But let each of us look within our own hearts and our own communities, and let each of us put our shoulder to the wheel to root out injustice wherever it exists.

As we meet here in this peaceful, historic chamber tonight, men from the South, some of whom were at Iwo Jima, men from the North who have carried Old Glory to far corners of the world and brought it back without a stain on it, men from the East and from the West, are all fighting together without regard to religion, or color, or region, in Viet-Nam. Men from every region fought for us across the world 20 years ago.

And in these common dangers and these common sacrifices the South made its contribution of honor and gallantry no less than any other region of the great Republic—and in some instances, a great many of them, more.

And I have not the slightest doubt that good men from everywhere in this country, from the Great Lakes to the Gulf of Mexico, from the Golden Gate to the harbors along the Atlantic, will rally together now in this cause to vindicate the freedom of all Americans. For all of us owe this duty; and I believe that all of us will respond to it. Your President makes that request of every American.

The real hero of this struggle is the American Negro. His actions and protests, his courage to risk safety and even to risk his life, have awakened the conscience of this Nation. His demonstrations have been designed to call attention to injustice, designed to provoke change, designed to stir reform.

He has called upon us to make good the promise of America. And who among us can say that we would have made the same progress were it not for his persistent bravery, and his faith in American democracy.

For at the real heart of battle for equality is a deep-seated belief in the democratic process. Equality depends not on the force of arms or tear gas but upon the force of moral right; not on recourse to violence but on respect for law and order.

There have been many pressures upon your President and there will be others as the days come and go. But I pledge you tonight that we intend to fight this battle where it should be fought: in the courts, and in the Congress, and in the hearts of men.

We must preserve the right of free speech and the right of free assembly. But the right of free speech does not carry with it, as has been said, the right to holler fire in a crowded theater. We must preserve the right to free assembly, but free assembly does not carry with it the right to block public thoroughfares to traffic.

We do have a right to protest, and a right to march under conditions that do not infringe the constitutional rights of our neighbors. And I intend to protect all those rights as long as I am permitted to serve in this office.

We will guard against violence, knowing it strikes from our hands the very weapons which we seek—progress, obedience to law, and belief in American values.

In Selma as elsewhere we seek and pray for peace. We seek order. We seek unity. But we will not accept

▲ President Lyndon B. Johnson delivering remarks at the signing ceremony for the Voting Rights Act.

the peace of stifled rights, or the order imposed by fear, or the unity that stifles protest. For peace cannot be purchased at the cost of liberty.

In Selma tonight, as in every—and we had a good day there—as in every city, we are working for just and peaceful settlement. We must all remember that after this speech I am making tonight, after the police and the FBI and the Marshals have all gone, and after you have promptly passed this bill, the people of Selma and the other cities of the Nation must still live and work together. And when the attention of the Nation has gone elsewhere they must try to heal the wounds and to build a new community.

This cannot be easily done on a battleground of violence, as the history of the South itself shows. It is in recognition of this that men of both races have shown such an outstandingly impressive responsibility in recent days—last Tuesday, again today,

The bill that I am presenting to you will be known as a civil rights bill. But, in a larger sense, most of the program I am recommending is a civil rights program. Its object is to open the city of hope to all people of all races.

Because all Americans just must have the right to vote. And we are going to give them that right.

All Americans must have the privileges of citizenship regardless of race. And they are going to have those privileges of citizenship regardless of race.

But I would like to caution you and remind you that to exercise these privileges takes much more than just legal right. It requires a trained mind and a healthy body. It requires a decent home, and the chance to find a job, and the opportunity to escape from the clutches of poverty.

Of course, people cannot contribute to the Nation if they are never taught to read or write, if their bodies are stunted from hunger, if their sickness goes untended, if their life is spent in hopeless poverty just drawing a welfare check.

So we want to open the gates to opportunity. But we are also going to give all our people, black and white, the help that they need to walk through those gates.

My first job after college was as a teacher in Cotulla, Tex., in a small Mexican-American school. Few of them could speak English, and I couldn't speak much Spanish. My students were poor and they often came to class without breakfast, hungry. They knew even in their youth the pain of prejudice. They never seemed to know why people disliked them. But they knew it was so, because I saw it in their eyes. I often walked home late in the afternoon, after the classes were finished, wishing there was more that I could do. But all I knew was to teach them the little that I knew, hoping that it might help them against the hardships that lay ahead.

Somehow you never forget what poverty and hatred can do when you see its scars on the hopeful face of a young child.

I never thought then, in 1928, that I would be standing here in 1965. It never even occurred to me in my fondest dreams that I might have the chance to help the sons and daughters of those students and to help people like them all over this country.

But now I do have that chance—and I'll let you in on a secret—I mean to use it. And I hope that you will use it with me.

This is the richest and most powerful country which ever occupied the globe. The might of past empires is little compared to ours. But I do not want to be the President who built empires, or sought grandeur, or extended dominion.

I want to be the President who educated young children to the wonders of their world. I want to be the President who helped to feed the hungry and to prepare them to be taxpayers instead of taxeaters.

I want to be the President who helped the poor to find their own way and who protected the right of every citizen to vote in every election.

I want to be the President who helped to end hatred among his fellow men and who promoted love among the people of all races and all regions and all parties.

I want to be the President who helped to end war among the brothers of this earth.

And so at the request of your beloved Speaker and the Senator from Montana; the majority leader, the Senator from Illinois; the minority leader, Mr. McCulloch, and other Members of both parties, I came here tonight—not as President Roosevelt came down one time in person to veto a bonus bill, not as President Truman came down one time to urge the passage of a railroad bill—but I came down here to ask you to share this task with me and to share it with the people that we both work for. I want this to be the Congress, Republicans and Democrats alike, which did all these things for all these people.

Beyond this great chamber, out yonder in 50 States, are the people that we serve. Who can tell what deep and unspoken hopes are in their hearts tonight as they sit there and listen. We all can guess, from our own lives, how difficult they often find their own pursuit of happiness, how many problems each little family has. They look most of all to themselves for their futures. But I think that they also look to each of us.

Above the pyramid on the great seal of the United States it says—in Latin—"God has favored our undertaking."

God will not favor everything that we do. It is rather our duty to divine His will. But I cannot help believing that He truly understands and that He really favors the undertaking that we begin here tonight.

▼　American civil rights campaigner Martin Luther King and his wife Coretta Scott King leading the voting rights march from Selma, Alabama, to the state capital in Montgomery.

President Richard Milhous Nixon

> **And so tonight—to you, the great silent majority of my fellow Americans—I ask for your support.**

The speech was one of the greatest successes of Richard Nixon's presidency, and the phrase was his most memorable —aside from his not-so-flattering Watergate statements.

Nixon employed a number of talented speechwriters and media advisors in his White House, most notably William Safire, later a leading author, newspaper columnist, and language authority; and Patrick Buchanan, who became a conservative icon and ran his own credible campaign for the presidency in 1992. But this speech, Nixon wrote himself.

Strangely for a Republican, Nixon's political hero was Democrat Woodrow Wilson, one of the most capable writers and speakers ever to occupy the White House. "Like . . . Wilson," writes Richard Reeves in his Nixon biography, "Nixon believed writing—clarifying and transferring ideas into enlightening and persuasive rhetoric—was the most important part of the Presidency."

It was natural that Nixon would want to spend a lot of time on Vietnam, and to translate his beliefs into a speech. At the time, the Vietnam War was the most important issue Nixon faced—domestically and internationally. It colored every other issue—

▲ President Richard M. Nixon pictured during his televised address on the Vietnam War.

indeed, had driven Lyndon Johnson from office. Vietnam was largely responsible for Nixon's own election over Hubert Humphrey, who as Johnson's vice president had been saddled with the responsibility for the war's escalation.

Talking Peace and Making War

The Soviet Union was the major supplier of arms to the North Vietnamese, so the conflict was a point of Cold War contention between the superpowers. Domestically, anti-war sentiment had only grown since the election. Despite Nixon's campaign pledge to end the war, he had not done so, and had given mixed signals about Vietnam in his public statements.

During the month of October that Nixon devoted to writing his speech, a nationwide non-violent demonstration called "Moratorium Day" was held, and another was scheduled for the following month. Smaller demonstrations were occurring daily around the country, and even some Republicans were advising him to get out. Congressional "bug out" resolutions proposing that the United States end its involvement in Vietnam became a joke in the Nixon White House.

Democratic Senate leader Mike Mansfield and others suggested to Nixon that he could leave Vietnam immediately and gain political capital by blaming the war on Kennedy and Johnson. At times, Nixon seemed to be leaning in that direction. He nibbled around the edges of withdrawal by escalating peace talks in Paris and announcing the "Vietnamization" of the war, reducing air operations and beginning to reduce US troop levels. He generally talked peace and pledged complete withdrawal if North Vietnam would allow free elections. Behind the scenes, however, he was initiating secret plans for major escalations of the war—including "Operation Duck Hook," massive, punishing bombing attacks on North Vietnam designed to do as much damage as possible in a short time.

Throughout the year, Nixon purposely kept his intentions murky, and while he was preparing his address, shared his plans with no one. "Silence is power," he was fond of saying—a tactic he learned from French President Charles de Gaulle.

"Don't Get Rattled," Nixon Wrote

On the night 20,000 demonstrators held a candlelight vigil outside the White House, Nixon wrote at the top of his yellow legal pad, "Don't Get Rattled—Don't Waver —Don't React." At one point, he leaked word to reporters he had been watching a football game during the demonstration. Television commentators and politicians pronounced the moratorium a huge success and saw support for the war eroding every day.

Throughout the month, Nixon worked alone, saying nothing. Speculation escalated to a fever pitch about what he would say in his address. Newspapers reported almost daily, fueled by Republican congressional leaders' statements of hopes for such developments as a unilateral cease-fire by the Americans. House minority leader Gerald Ford speculated that all Americans could be out of Vietnam by July.

The *Washington Post* conjectured that, "The thirty-minute address to be carried nationwide via television and radio might be used to announce US troop withdrawals beyond the 60,000-man reduction already ordered."

Nixon and his aides worried about the building support among anti-war activists for Nixon's supposed peace efforts and for his coming speech. "The main result is a massive buildup of hopes for major breakthrough in November 3 speech," wrote Chief of Staff H. R. Haldeman in his diary. "Problem is there won't be one, and the letdown will be tremendous." The paranoid Nixon White House concluded that "liberals" were intentionally building the president up for the "biggest possible fall."

October 27, 1969

MEMORANDUM

TO: Henry Kissinger

FROM: The President

I would like one brief paragraph, 100 words or less, on the reason we intervened in Vietnam in the first place. I am not sure that I will cover this point but I want a paragraph or two submitted to me for my consideration.

Also, with regard to the casualties I want to make only one pointed reference to the reduction in casualties rather than pointing up the fact that they are one-third less this year than they were for last year, and one-half for September and October of what they were in September and October of last year. I would like to be able to say that our casualties for the month of September or for the month of October were the lowest in three years or something direct and simple like that if the facts bear it out.

With regard to the ratio of American to Vietnamese casualties, I would like to be able to point out very briefly that for the past two years American casualties have exceeded Vietnamese casualties (I think this is actually the case although as you know the Vietnamese casualty figures are always inflated). Then I would go on to say that now Vietnamese casualties are twice as great as American casualties. This makes the point far more effectively than simply to state the fact that Vietnamese casualties are greater than American casualties because most people are not aware of the fact that there has been a change in that respect.

◀ The memo that Nixon sent to Kissinger requesting a "brief paragraph…on the reason we intervened in Vietnam in the first place."

he needed to get to work. In the days that followed, he sent only two brief memos to Kissinger, one asking for a brief paragraph for the speech on "the reasons we intervened in Vietnam in the first place." The second asked simply, "is it possible we were wrong from the start in Vietnam?"

Nixon returned to Camp David on October 31 and worked through the night. Around 4:00 a.m., he recounted in his memoirs, he wrote a sentence asking that "the great silent majority of Americans" support him.

The phrase was by no means new. It had been in use for thousands of years, going back to Homer, as a euphemism for the dead. John F. Kennedy wrote in his book

Nixon Ignored Major Events

Meanwhile, Nixon was working twelve- to fourteen-hour days alone at Camp David, ignoring major events around him such as the Supreme Court decision that overturned a delay in busing of minority students that Nixon had personally ordered. It was a stinging setback for Nixon, but he did not react.

He also dealt curtly with his national security advisor, Henry Kissinger, at one point walking out of his regular morning briefing on grounds that

Profiles in Courage, "Some of them may have been representing the actual sentiments of the silent majority of their constituents in opposition to the screams of a vocal minority." Senator Kennedy gave then-Vice President Nixon an autographed copy and Nixon promised that he would read it. Presumably he did. Nixon himself had talked about "the quiet majority" in the 1968 campaign. And months before Nixon's speech, Vice President Spiro Agnew had used the phrase, without exciting any notice.

"The Baby's Been Born"

Neither Nixon himself, Safire, or any of his other aides thought much of the line. It was more or less a throwaway. On the morning of November 1, Nixon called H.R. "Bob" Haldeman with the news that "The baby's been born."

Nixon showed the speech to Safire half an hour before airtime. Safire, a student of presidential history, quickly found a major gaffe. Nixon said that half a century earlier Woodrow Wilson wrote the words "war to end wars." Safire knew that Wilson never wrote those words—they came from H. G. Wells. Nixon grudgingly changed "wrote" to "said" in his text—even though there was no record of Wilson having spoken them. Nixon also said that he sat at the very desk Wilson used—another error that no one caught. The desk that Nixon treasured as belonging to his hero actually came from a different Wilson, Ulysses S. Grant's vice president, Henry Wilson.

The speech ran more than 4,000 words—which the veteran Nixon knew would fill a half-hour of airtime. Facing the cameras of three networks, Nixon quickly made it clear he was not going to offer any revelations of imminent withdrawal from Vietnam.

He used his familiar technique—going back to his earliest days in politics and presaging his style during his Watergate addresses—of a kind of internal dialogue, asking and then

answering questions. The people, he began, "cannot and should not be asked to support a policy which involves the overriding issues of war and peace unless they know the truth about that policy." This speech would answer their questions.

▶ A page from the reading copy of the speech with handwritten changes by Safire, including the correction of the word "wrote" to "spoke" in reference to Woodrow Wilson's "war to end wars" quote.

War Had Taken 31,000 Lives

He first reviewed the situation he faced when he took office—the war had been going on for four years, 31,000 Americans had been killed, 540,000 troops were in Vietnam with no plan to reduce the number, and no progress had been made to bring them home.

He had been urged, he said, to get out immediately, lest "Johnson's war becomes Nixon's war." Nixon said immediate withdrawal would have been "a popular and easy course" but that he had considered the effect of such withdrawal on America and the world. He had decided to follow the harder route of staying in Vietnam and adopting a strategy that would not lose the war but would "Win America's peace."

Nixon then went into a short review of how we had gotten into the war in the first place, noting that he, among others, had been strongly critical of the Johnson escalation. "The question facing us today is: Now that we are in the war, what is the best way to end it?"

"Precipitate withdrawal" is not the answer, he said, and repeatedly used that phrase throughout the rest of the speech. He went into significant detail about the atrocities that could be expected if the United States pulled out right away, and followed with a list of American settlement initiatives. He concluded that if there was no peace, it was because Hanoi did not want peace.

(2) If a vocal minority, however fervent its cause, prevails over reason and the will of the majority this nation has no future as a free society.

But even more disturbing than the message on the placards was the message I saw on the faces of those young Americans who were demonstrating.

1. It was a message of hate -- bitter, deep, implacable for the President of the United States.

I would like to address a word to the young people of this nation who feel that way, ~~and to others who oppose my policy for peace.~~

~~1. I do not hate those who oppose me.~~ *2 roll: resent our idealism -*

(1) I share your concern for peace. I commend those who in demonstrating for peace recognized that the use of violence would be indefensible.

2. I know that the hatred I saw on those young faces reflected a deep idealism which makes our young people such a potential force for good in America and in the world.

▲ A page from the fourth draft of the speech, the two crossed out paragraphs demonstrating Nixon's dislike of the peace activists.

The Nixon Doctrines

Then Nixon turned to the section he probably thought would be the most memorable part of the speech, outlining what he called "The Nixon Doctrine." In fact, these were principles he had first stated earlier in the year in a speech on Guam, and that had been called "The Guam Doctrine."

The gist of the Nixon Doctrine was that the United States would honor its treaty commitments, use its nuclear shield to protect any threatened allies, and provide military and economic assistance to countries whose freedom was threatened but not fight their wars for them. He would follow that doctrine in Vietnam, gradually turning the war over to the South Vietnamese forces as they became stronger. But he would not leave until they could defend themselves, and would not set a date or give details of withdrawal. Otherwise, he said, the North Vietnamese would just play a waiting game until the American departure, then take over and savage the South Vietnamese people.

The Nixon Doctrine excited no interest, but what he said later made the speech historically significant. After completing his detailed, lawyerly case for staying the course in Vietnam, he got to a section that he had revised over and over. He began by addressing young people, saying that he respected their idealism and desire for peace. (The infamous White House tapes later made clear Nixon's contempt for peace activists, and in fact one point of the speech was to drive a wedge between the activists and the general populace.)

He said, "So tonight, to you, the great silent majority of my fellow Americans—I ask for your support . . . Let us be united for peace. Let us also be united against defeat. Because let us understand: North Vietnam cannot defeat or humiliate the United States. Only Americans can do that."

Gratuitous Shot at Anti-War Movement

Even in making his appeal to the "silent majority" Nixon, typically, could not resist a shot against the anti-war movement. Yet the appeal worked better than he could have imagined. Safire later wrote that Americans who supported the war were afflicted with "pluralistic ignorance"—unawareness that they were in the majority.

Television commentators were disappointed that the speech lacked a bombshell from Nixon; they seemed to agree that the president had said nothing new. Anticipating trouble, the White House prepared a detailed defense of the speech that included hostile responses to the liberal media.

But something very interesting happened. A Gallup poll showed seventy-seven percent approval. The more than 50,000 telegrams and 30,000 letters sent to the White House were overwhelmingly supportive. Nixon told Safire, "If I thought it would be picked up, I would have capitalized it [the phrase] in the press."

Nixon wrote in his memoirs, "Very few speeches actually influence the course of history. The November 3 speech was one of them. Its impact came as a surprise to me; it was one thing to make a rhetorical appeal to the Silent Majority—it was another actually to hear from them."

Nixon believed that his appeal to the "silent majority" had blunted the momentum of the anti-war demonstrators. The Vietnam War dragged on for more than three years with thousands of additional lives lost before Nixon announced he had negotiated "peace with honor." Two years later, the North Vietnamese swept across the country and the last Americans were evacuated from Saigon by helicopter.

Despite the failure in Vietnam, Nixon had identified a political force, and the "Silent Majority" has remained on the minds of politicians in the decades since.

Address to the Nation on the War in Vietnam
November 3, 1969, White House, Washington DC

Good evening, my fellow Americans:

Tonight I want to talk to you on a subject of deep concern to all Americans and to many people in all parts of the world—the war in Vietnam.

I believe that one of the reasons for the deep division about Vietnam is that many Americans have lost confidence in what their Government has told them about our policy. The American people cannot and should not be asked to support a policy which involves the overriding issues of war and peace unless they know the truth about that policy.

Tonight, therefore, I would like to answer some of the questions that I know are on the minds of many of you listening to me.

How and why did America get involved in Vietnam in the first place?

How has this administration changed the policy of the previous administration?

What has really happened in the negotiations in Paris and on the battlefront in Vietnam?

What choices do we have if we are to end the war?

What are the prospects for peace?

Now, let me begin by describing the situation I found when I was inaugurated on January 20.

—The war had been going on for 4 years.

—31,000 Americans had been killed in action.

—The training program for the South Vietnamese was behind schedule.

—540,000 Americans were in Vietnam with no plans to reduce the number.

—No progress had been made at the negotiations in Paris and the United States had not put forth a comprehensive peace proposal.

—The war was causing deep division at home and criticism from many of our friends as well as our enemies abroad.

In view of these circumstances there were some who urged that I end the war at once by ordering the immediate withdrawal of all American forces.

From a political standpoint this would have been a popular and easy course to follow. After all, we became involved in the war while my predecessor was in office. I could blame the defeat which would be the result of my action on him and come out as the Peacemaker. Some put it to me quite bluntly: This was the only way to avoid allowing Johnson's war to become Nixon's war.

But I had a greater obligation than to think only of the years of my administration and of the next election. I had to think of the effect of my decision on the next generation and on the future of peace and freedom in America and in the world.

Let us all understand that the question before us is not whether some Americans are for peace and some Americans are against peace. The question at issue is not whether Johnson's war becomes Nixon's war.

The great question is: How can we win America's peace?

Well, let us turn now to the fundamental issue. Why and how did the United States become involved in Vietnam in the first place?

Fifteen years ago North Vietnam, with the logistical support of Communist China and the Soviet Union, launched a campaign to impose a Communist government on South Vietnam by instigating and supporting a revolution.

▶ The first page of Nixon's fifth draft of the speech with handwritten amendments by the president.

In response to the request of the Government of South Vietnam, President Eisenhower sent economic aid and military equipment to assist the people of South Vietnam in their efforts to prevent a Communist takeover. Seven years ago, President Kennedy sent 16,000 military personnel to Vietnam as combat advisers. Four years ago, President Johnson sent American combat forces to South Vietnam.

Now, many believe that President Johnson's decision to send American combat forces to South Vietnam was wrong. And many others—I among them have been strongly critical of the way the war has been conducted.

But the question facing us today is: Now that we are in the war, what is the best way to end it?

In January I could only conclude that the precipitate withdrawal of American forces from Vietnam would be a disaster not only for South Vietnam but for the United States and for the cause of peace.

For the South Vietnamese, our precipitate withdrawal would inevitably allow the Communists to repeat the massacres which followed their takeover in the North 15 years before.

RN - DRAFT NUMBER 5

Tonight I want to talk to you on a subject that deeply concerns every American and other people throughout the world - the war in Vietnam.

1. I believe that one of the reasons for the deep division in this nation about Vietnam is that many Americans have lost confidence in what their government has told them about Vietnam.

(1) The American people cannot and should not be asked to support a policy which involves the over-riding issues of war and peace unless they know the truth about that policy.

Tonight I would like to answer some of the questions that I know that are on the minds of many of those listening to me.

1. How and why did America get involved in Vietnam in the first place?

2. How has this Administration changed the policy of the previous Administration?

3. What has really happened in the negotiations in Paris and on the battlefront in Vietnam?

—They then murdered more than 50,000 people and hundreds of thousands more died in slave labor camps.

—We saw a prelude of what would happen in South Vietnam when the Communists entered the city of Hue last year. During their brief rule there, there was a bloody reign of terror in which 3,000 civilians were clubbed, shot to death, and buried in mass graves.

—With the sudden collapse of our support, these atrocities of Hue would become the nightmare of the entire nation—and particularly for the million and a half Catholic refugees who fled to South Vietnam when the Communists took over in the North.

For the United States, this first defeat in our Nation's history would result in a collapse of confidence in American leadership, not only in Asia but throughout the world.

Three American Presidents have recognized the great stakes involved in Vietnam and understood what had to be done.

In 1963, President Kennedy, with his characteristic eloquence and clarity, said: ". . . we want to see a stable government there, carrying on a struggle to maintain its national independence.

"We believe strongly in that. We are not going to withdraw from that effort. In my opinion, for us to withdraw from that effort would mean a collapse not only of South Viet-Nam, but Southeast Asia. So we are going to stay there."

President Eisenhower and President Johnson expressed the same conclusion during their terms of office.

For the future of peace, precipitate withdrawal would thus be a disaster of immense magnitude.

—A nation cannot remain great if it betrays its allies and lets down its friends.

—Our defeat and humiliation in South Vietnam without question would promote recklessness in the councils of those great powers who have not yet abandoned their goals of world conquest.

—This would spark violence wherever our commitments help maintain the peace—in the Middle East, in Berlin, eventually even in the Western Hemisphere.

Ultimately, this would cost more lives.

It would not bring peace; it would bring more war.

For these reasons, I rejected the recommendation that I should end the war by immediately withdrawing all of our forces. I chose instead to change American policy on both the negotiating front and battlefront.

In order to end a war fought on many fronts, I initiated a pursuit for peace on many fronts.

In a television speech on May 14, in a speech before the United Nations, and on a number of other occasions I set forth our peace proposals in great detail.

—We have offered the complete withdrawal of all outside forces within 1 year.

—We have proposed a cease-fire under international supervision.

—We have offered free elections under international supervision with the Communists participating in the organization and conduct of the elections as an organized political force. And the Saigon Government has pledged to accept the result of the elections.

We have not put forth our proposals on a take-it-or-leave-it basis. We have indicated that we are willing to discuss the proposals that have been put forth by the other side. We have declared that anything is negotiable except the right of the people of South Vietnam to determine their own future. At the Paris peace conference, Ambassador Lodge has demonstrated our flexibility and good faith in 40 public meetings.

Hanoi has refused even to discuss our proposals. They demand our unconditional acceptance of their terms, which are that we withdraw all American forces immediately and unconditionally and that we overthrow the Government of South Vietnam as we leave.

We have not limited our peace initiatives to public forums and public statements. I recognized, in January, that a long and bitter war like this usually cannot be settled in a public forum. That is why in addition to the

October 27, 1969

◄ A memo from Nixon to Kissinger regarding the section of the speech that refers to his letter to Ho Chi Minh.

MEMORANDUM

TO: Henry Kissinger

FROM: The President

I think the portion of the speech dealing with the Ho Chi Minh letter would be strengthened if I could indicate how it was delivered. Everyone knows, for example, that we have no diplomatic relations with North Vietnam. See if you can prepare a sentence which would cover this point in a subtle way. It adds to the whole quality of mystery which people will be interested to hear.

On another subject, I recall some press speculation about another troop withdrawal announcement in December since the one we have previously announced will run out then. Will you check with Laird to see what has been speculated publicly on this score. My guess is that we will, in any event, be getting enormous pressure to make an announcement in December and that it might be well to indicate without fanfare that the next troop replacement announcement scheduled for the middle of December will take into account the three criteria.

public statements and negotiations I have explored every possible private avenue that might lead to a settlement.

Tonight I am taking the unprecedented step of disclosing to you some of our other initiatives for peace—initiatives we undertook privately and secretly because we thought we thereby might open a door which publicly would be closed.

I did not wait for my inauguration to begin my quest for peace.

—Soon after my election, through an individual who is directly in contact on a personal basis with the leaders of North Vietnam, I made two private offers for a rapid, comprehensive settlement. Hanoi's replies called in effect for our surrender before negotiations.

—Since the Soviet Union furnishes most of the military equipment for North Vietnam, Secretary of State Rogers, my Assistant for National Security Affairs, Dr. Kissinger, Ambassador Lodge, and I, personally, have met on a number of occasions with representatives of the Soviet Government to enlist their assistance in getting meaningful negotiations started. In addition, we have had extended discussions directed toward that same end with representatives of other governments which have diplomatic relations with North Vietnam. None of these initiatives have to date produced results.

—In mid-July, I became convinced that it was necessary to make a major move to break the deadlock in the Paris talks. I spoke directly in this office, where I am now sitting, with an individual who had known Ho Chi Minh [President, Democratic Republic of Vietnam] on a personal basis for 25 years. Through him I sent a letter to Ho Chi Minh.

I did this outside of the usual diplomatic channels with the hope that with the necessity of making statements for propaganda removed, there might be constructive progress toward bringing the war to an end. Let me read from that letter to you now.

"Dear Mr. President:

"I realize that it is difficult to communicate meaningfully across the gulf of four years of war. But

▲ White House adviser and speechwriter Patrick Buchanan, pictured in 1974.

precisely because of this gulf, I wanted to take this opportunity to reaffirm in all solemnity my desire to work for a just peace. I deeply believe that the war in Vietnam has gone on too long and delay in bringing it to an end can benefit no one—least of all the people of Vietnam. . . .

"The time has come to move forward at the conference table toward an early resolution of this tragic war. You will find us forthcoming and open-minded in a common effort to bring the blessings of peace to the brave people of Vietnam. Let history record that at this critical juncture, both sides turned their face toward peace rather than toward conflict and war."

I received Ho Chi Minh's reply on August 30, 3 days before his death. It simply reiterated the public position North Vietnam had taken at Paris and flatly rejected my initiative.

The full text of both letters is being released to the press.

—In addition to the public meetings that I have referred to, Ambassador Lodge has met with Vietnam's chief negotiator in Paris in II private sessions. We have taken other significant initiatives which must remain secret to keep open some channels of communication which may still prove to be productive.

But the effect of all the public, private, and secret negotiations which have been undertaken since the bombing halt a year ago and since this administration came into office on January 20, can be summed up in one sentence: No progress whatever has been made except agreement on the shape of the bargaining table.

Well now, who is at fault?

It has become clear that the obstacle in negotiating an end to the war is not the President of the United States. It is not the South Vietnamese Government.

The obstacle is the other side's absolute refusal to show the least willingness to join us in seeking a just peace. And it will not do so while it is convinced that all it has to do is to wait for our next concession, and our next concession after that one, until it gets everything it wants.

There can now be no longer any question that progress in negotiation depends only on Hanoi's deciding to negotiate, to negotiate seriously.

I realize that this report on our efforts on the diplomatic front is discouraging to the American people, but the American people are entitled to know the truth—the bad news as well as the good news where the lives of our young men are involved.

Now let me turn, however, to a more encouraging report on another front.

At the time we launched our search for peace I recognized we might not succeed in bringing an end to the war through negotiation. I, therefore, put into effect another plan to bring peace—a plan which will bring the war to an end regardless of what happens on the negotiating front.

It is in line with a major shift in U.S. foreign policy which I described in my press conference at Guam on July, 25. Let me briefly explain what has been described as the Nixon Doctrine—a policy which not only will help end the war in Vietnam, but which is an essential element of our program to prevent future Vietnams.

We Americans are a do-it-yourself people. We are an impatient people. Instead of teaching someone else to do a job, we like to do it ourselves. And this trait has been carried over into our foreign policy.

In Korea and again in Vietnam, the United States furnished most of the money, most of the arms, and most of the men to help the people of those countries defend their freedom against Communist aggression.

Before any American troops were committed to Vietnam, a leader of another Asian country expressed this opinion to me when I was traveling in Asia as a private citizen. He said: "When you are trying to assist another nation defend its freedom, U.S. policy should be to help them fight the war but not to fight the war for them."

Well, in accordance with this wise counsel, I laid down in Guam three principles as guidelines for future American policy toward Asia:

—First, the United States will keep all of its treaty commitments.

—Second, we shall provide a shield if a nuclear power threatens the freedom of a nation allied with us or of a nation whose survival we consider vital to our security.

—Third, in cases involving other types of aggression, we shall furnish military and economic assistance when requested in accordance with our treaty commitments. But we shall look to the nation directly threatened to assume the primary responsibility of providing the manpower for its defense.

After I announced this policy, I found that the leaders of the Philippines, Thailand, Vietnam, South Korea, and other nations which might be threatened by Communist aggression, welcomed this new direction in American foreign policy.

The defense of freedom is everybody's business— not just America's business. And it is particularly the responsibility of the people whose freedom is threatened. In the previous administration, we Americanized the war in Vietnam. In this administration, we are Vietnamizing the search for peace.

The policy of the previous administration not only resulted in our assuming the primary responsibility for fighting the war, but even more significantly did not adequately stress the goal of strengthening the South Vietnamese so that they could defend themselves when we left.

The Vietnamization plan was launched following Secretary Laird's visit to Vietnam in March. Under the plan, I ordered first a substantial increase in the training and equipment of South Vietnamese forces.

In July, on my visit to Vietnam, I changed General Abrams' orders so that they were consistent with the objectives of our new policies. Under the new orders, the primary mission of our troops is to enable the South Vietnamese forces to assume the full responsibility for the security of South Vietnam.

Our air operations have been reduced by over 20 percent.

And now we have begun to see the results of this long overdue change in American policy in Vietnam.

—After 5 years of Americans going into Vietnam, we are finally bringing American men home. By December 15, over 60,000 men will have been

withdrawn from South Vietnam—including 20 percent of all of our combat forces.

—The South Vietnamese have continued to gain in strength. As a result they have been able to take over combat responsibilities from our American troops.

Two other significant developments have occurred since this administration took office.

—Enemy infiltration, infiltration which is essential if they are to launch a major attack, over the last 3 months is less than 20 percent of what it was over the same period last year.

—Most important—United States casualties have declined during the last 2 months to the lowest point in 3 years.

Let me now turn to our program for the future.

We have adopted a plan which we have worked out in cooperation with the South Vietnamese for the complete withdrawal of all U.S. combat ground forces, and their replacement by South Vietnamese forces on an orderly scheduled timetable. This withdrawal will be made from strength and not from weakness. As South Vietnamese forces become stronger, the rate of American withdrawal can become greater.

I have not and do not intend to announce the timetable for our program. And there are obvious reasons for this decision which I am sure you will

▲   A candlelight march past the White House in October 1969 protesting about the Vietnam War.

understand. As I have indicated on several occasions, the rate of withdrawal will depend on developments on three fronts.

One of these is the progress which can be or might be made in the Paris talks. An announcement of a fixed timetable for our withdrawal would completely remove any incentive for the enemy to negotiate an agreement. They would simply wait until our forces had withdrawn and then move in.

The other two factors on which we will base our withdrawal decisions are the level of enemy activity and the progress of the training programs of the South Vietnamese forces. And I am glad to be able to report tonight progress on both of these fronts has been greater than we anticipated when we started the program in June for withdrawal. As a result, our timetable for withdrawal is more optimistic now than when we made our first estimates in June. Now, this clearly demonstrates why it is not wise to be frozen in on a fixed timetable.

We must retain the flexibility to base each withdrawal decision on the situation as it is at that time rather than on estimates that are no longer valid.

Along with this optimistic estimate, I must—in all candor—leave one note of caution.

If the level of enemy activity significantly increases we might have to adjust our timetable accordingly.

However, I want the record to be completely clear on one point.

At the time of the bombing halt just a year ago, there was some confusion as to whether there was an understanding on the part of the enemy that if we stopped the bombing of North Vietnam they would stop the shelling of cities in South Vietnam. I want to be sure that there is no misunderstanding on the part of the enemy with regard to our withdrawal Program.

We have noted the reduced level of infiltration, the reduction of our casualties, and are basing our withdrawal decisions partially on those factors.

If the level of infiltration or our casualties increase while we are trying to scale down the fighting, it will be the result of a conscious decision by the enemy.

Hanoi could make no greater mistake than to assume that an increase in violence will be to its advantage. If I conclude that increased enemy action jeopardizes our remaining forces in Vietnam, I shall not hesitate to take strong and effective measures to deal with that situation.

This is not a threat. This is a statement of policy, which as Commander in Chief of our Armed Forces, I am making in meeting my responsibility for the protection of American fighting men wherever they may be.

My fellow Americans, I am sure you can recognize from what I have said that we really only have two choices open to us if we want to end this war.

—I can order an immediate, precipitate withdrawal of all Americans from Vietnam without regard to the effects of that action.

—Or we can persist in our search for a just peace through a negotiated settlement if possible, or through continued implementation of our plan for Vietnamization if necessary—a plan in which we will withdraw all of our forces from Vietnam on a schedule in accordance with our program, as the South Vietnamese become strong enough to defend their own freedom.

I have chosen this second course.

It is not the easy way.

It is the right way.

It is a plan which will end the war and serve the cause of peace—not just in Vietnam but in the Pacific and in the world.

In speaking of the consequences of a precipitate withdrawal, I mentioned that our allies would lose confidence in America.

Far more dangerous, we would lose confidence in ourselves. Oh, the immediate reaction would be a sense of relief that our men were coming home. But as we saw the consequences of what we had done, inevitable remorse

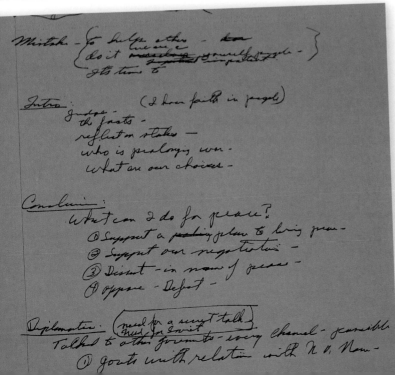

◀ A page of handwritten notes by Nixon outlining of topics to cover in the speech.

▲ President Richard M. Nixon, visiting US troops in Vietnam, March 1970.

and divisive recrimination would scar our spirit as a people.

We have faced other crisis in our history and have become stronger by rejecting the easy way out and taking the right way in meeting our challenges. Our greatness as a nation has been our capacity to do what had to be done when we knew our course was right.

I recognize that some of my fellow citizens disagree with the plan for peace I have chosen. Honest and patriotic Americans have reached different conclusions as to how peace should be achieved.

In San Francisco a few weeks ago, I saw demonstrators carrying signs reading: "Lose in Vietnam, bring the boys home."

Well, one of the strengths of our free society is that any American has a right to reach that conclusion and to advocate that point of view. But as President of the United States, I would be untrue to my oath of office if I allowed the policy of this Nation to be dictated by the minority who hold that point of view and who try to impose it on the Nation by mounting demonstrations in the street.

For almost 200 years, the policy of this Nation has been made under our Constitution by those leaders in the Congress and the White House elected by all of the people. If a vocal minority, however fervent its cause, prevails over reason and the will of the majority, this Nation has no future as a free society.

And now I would like to address a word, if I may, to the young people of this Nation who are particularly concerned, and I understand why they are concerned, about this war.

I respect your idealism.

I share your concern for peace.

I want peace as much as you do.

There are powerful personal reasons I want to end this war. This week I will have to sign 83 letters to mothers, fathers, wives, and loved ones of men who have given their lives for America in Vietnam. It is very little satisfaction to me that this is only one-third as many letters as I signed the first week in office. There is nothing I want more than to see the day come when I do not have to write any of those letters.

—I want to end the war to save the lives of those brave young men in Vietnam.

—But I want to end it in a way which will increase the chance that their younger brothers and their sons will not have to fight in some future Vietnam someplace in the world.

—And I want to end the war for another reason. I want to end it so that the energy and dedication of you, our young people, now too often directed into bitter hatred against those responsible for the war, can be turned to the great challenges of peace, a better life for all Americans, a better life for all people on this earth.

I have chosen a plan for peace. I believe it will succeed.

If it does succeed, what the critics say now won't matter. If it does not succeed, anything I say then won't matter.

I know it may not be fashionable to speak of patriotism or national destiny these days. But I feel it is appropriate to do so on this occasion

Two hundred years ago this Nation was weak and poor. But even then, America was the hope of millions in the world. Today we have become the strongest and richest nation in the world. And the wheel of destiny has turned so that any hope the world has for the survival of peace and freedom will be determined by whether the American people have the moral stamina and the courage to meet the challenge of free world leadership.

Let historians not record that when America was the most powerful nation in the world we passed on the other side of the road and allowed the last hopes for peace and freedom of millions of people to be suffocated by the forces of totalitarianism.

And so tonight—to you, the great silent majority of my fellow Americans—I ask for your support.

I pledged in my campaign for the Presidency to end the war in a way that we could win the peace. I have initiated a plan of action which will enable me to keep that pledge.

The more support I can have from the American people, the sooner that pledge can be redeemed; for the more divided we are at home, the less likey, the enemy is to negotiate at Paris.

Let us be united for peace. Let us also be united against defeat. Because let us understand: North Vietnam cannot defeat or humiliate the United States. Only Americans can do that.

Fifty years ago, in this room and at this very desk, President Woodrow Wilson spoke words which caught the imagination of a war-weary world. He said: "This is the war to end war." His dream for peace after World War I was shattered on the hard realities of great power politics and Woodrow Wilson died a broken man.

▲ President Richard M. Nixon conferring with National Security Adviser Henry Kissinger, General Counsel John Erlichman, and Chief of Staff H. R. Haldeman.

Tonight I do not tell you that the war in Vietnam is the war to end wars. But I do say this: I have initiated a plan which Will end this war in a way that will bring us closer to that great goal to which Woodrow Wilson and every American President in our history has been dedicated—the goal of a just and lasting peace.

As President I hold the responsibility for choosing the best path to that goal and then leading the Nation along it.

I pledge to you tonight that I shall meet this responsibility with all of the strength and wisdom I can command in accordance with your hopes, mindful of your concerns, sustained by your prayers.

Thank you and goodnight.

President Ronald Wilson Reagan

"These are the boys of Pointe du Hoc. These are the men who took the cliffs. These are the champions who helped free a continent. These are the heroes who helped end a war.

Ronald Reagan delivered many successful speeches during his time as president, but arguably the three highlights were his "Mr. Gorbachev, tear down this wall" remark in Berlin, his moving tribute to "The Boys

President Ronald W. Reagan commemorating the fortieth Anniversary of the D-Day Invasion of 1944 at the site of the US Ranger Monument on June 6, 1984, at Pointe du Hoc, France.

of Pointe du Hoc" on the fortieth anniversary of the D-Day invasion, and his elegy to the seven astronauts killed in the Challenger disaster.

The "tear down this wall" phrase was essentially one memorable turn of phrase in a very ordinary and somewhat disorganized speech. The Pointe du Hoc and Challenger remarks were beautifully crafted and inspirational from beginning to end. It is no accident that one person, Peggy Noonan, wrote the latter two.

Noonan penned a very interesting memoir about her experiences in the Reagan White House called *What I Saw at the Revolution*. Historian Douglas Brinkley wrote an account both of the speech and the heroic exploits of the 2nd Ranger Battalion that inspired it, called, appropriately, *The Boys of Pointe du Hoc*. Both books tell the story of the rangers' unparalleled valor that day, and the often frustrating attempt to produce the speech that paid them tribute.

Peggy Noonan has become one of the most famous speechwriters ever to come out of the White House. Others—the playwright Robert Sherwood and poet Archibald MacLeish—were celebrities before they began writing for Franklin Delano Roosevelt. Some, notably conservative commentators like writers Pat Buchanan and William Safire, became prominent after their White House days. Many others have used their White House connections to land high-level media jobs. Few have achieved anything approaching the celebrity of Peggy Noonan.

Noonan a Conservative Heroine

Noonan left the Reagan White House in exasperation after two years, but was recalled by George H. W. Bush. She was responsible for his "thousand points of light" analogy. An unabashed conservative, she has become practically a

▲ An early 1990s photograph of Peggy Noonan in her office.

heroine to those of similar political opinion through her books, newspaper columns, and electronic media commentaries.

In March 1984, however, she was an unknown quantity. A New Jersey native, she came from a working class family and worked her way through college. She landed a small-time radio job writing news and editorials for on-air personalities and swiftly worked her way up through the ranks. CBS eventually came calling and she went to work for Dan Rather, writing his radio commentaries.

The quality of the commentaries drew notice, and so did the fact that Rather seemed to be growing more conservative, or at least more balanced. The turnover among White House speechwriters was high, and staffers were always on the lookout for fresh writing talent. An admirer recommended her to Reagan's head speechwriter Ben Elliott, and she was summoned to a meeting with him. Writing for Reagan was her dream job, she later said, and when offered a speechwriting slot she quickly accepted.

Noonan, and others, have written that the White House was, if not exactly sexist, at least male-dominated. She was not used to working at a place where "the men were in charge," having come from the news business where there were roughly as many women as men and they were treated as equals.

Big Assignment for New Writer

When she was given the Pointe du Hoc assignment, Noonan had been at work in the White House only a few weeks, and had written nothing but a couple of puff pieces. Some male White House veterans were upset that she was given the task on two counts: first, that a new writer was handed such an important speech, and second, that a woman with no combat experience would be writing about a military topic. But with the backing of Elliott and his boss, Chief of Staff Richard Darman, the assignment stayed with her. They knew she was the kind of "impressionistic" writer who could craft stirring lines, and Elliott told her "I hired you to write this speech."

Noonan writes at length about being "paralyzed" by the assignment, particularly since her bosses were asking her to make the speech another Gettysburg Address, that it should "make people cry." She also learned that Darman and others wanted to use material from the speech at the upcoming Republican Convention where Reagan would be nominated for a second term.

Noonan faced a number of problems when she started. She had never met Reagan face to face, and would not meet him until well after he gave the speech. As a student of both Reagan and presidential speaking styles, though, she realized that Reagan had, consciously or unconsciously, patterned his style after FDR, whom he admired and often quoted.

Noonan also had no idea of the impressive physical setting for the speech, or that a number of rangers who scaled those cliffs would be there. So she started out by reading a D-Day speech Reagan had given two years earlier, which she recalled was full of facts and statistics, but failed to evoke the human drama. She read a number of books about D-Day that gave her a sense of the dramatic landings.

But Don't Offend the Germans

The National Security Council (NSC) sent over a briefing paper indicating that the speech should be emotional and stirring, but should talk about the reconciliation of former adversaries and the strength of American commitment to Europe. They wanted an announcement of a US-Soviet summit on arms control as the central theme. Above all, they wanted to avoid specific mention of Nazi aggression or defeat, to avoid offending West German chancellor Helmut Kohl. Kohl had already been prohibited from attending the ceremony, but presumably no one thought *that* had offended him.

The speech did not come easy for Noonan. She drank many cups of coffee, smoked many cigarettes, and paced her office floor late into the night in the course of producing fifteen drafts before she had something she felt was worthy of showing to Elliott. He made minimal changes. Then began the infamous White House "staffing" process.

Begun during the Ford Administration and carried on by every White House since, the "staffing" or "staffing up" process involved sending out a speech draft to anyone on the staff, or in other agencies of government, who had interest and expertise in the subject.

A minor speech might be seen, and marked up, by twenty people. A major one would be reviewed by fifty or more. The Pointe du Hoc speech was a major one.

The speech-making process was "like sending a beautiful newborn fawn out into the jagged wilderness where the grosser animals would pierce its tender flesh and render mortal wounds," Noonan wrote in her memoir. "But perhaps I understate." She was still so new that she had trouble deciding which changes she could ignore and which were mandatory.

Noonan Fights for Her Words

"It was really awful for me because rhetoric is a form of communication between a leader and his people," she said. "Anything that is art or part art is delicate. And anything that is delicate can't survive the tinkering hands and mauling of twenty-five people."

When it came to the survival of her words and phrases, she won some and she lost some. Many of the same people who had objected to her writing the speech in the first place tore the draft to shreds with their comments. Many replaced her elegant language with clunky wonk-speak. With the backing of Elliott and Darman, she stood firm on most points. The NSC wanted a paragraph paying tribute to the Russians who had died in the war. Noonan

THE WHITE HOUSE
WASHINGTON

May 30, 1984

MEMORANDUM FOR BEN ELLIOTT

FROM: PEGGY NOONAN

SUBJECT: Pointe du Hoc changes

Here is the final version of the Pointe du Hoc address. Most of the changes suggested by State and NSC had to do with points of style (such as changing "millions cried out for liberation" to "millions sought liberation"). I incorporated those suggestions I judged to be an improvement and rejected the rest. In all, I'd say I accepted 50 percent.

Bob Kimmit, who seems to speak for both State and NSC on these matters, suggested two changes dealing with substance. He suggested we add a graph at the end of page six, saying: "It is fitting here to remember also the great sacrifices made by the Russian people during World War II. Their terrible loss of 20 million lives testifies to all the world the necessity of avoiding another war."

I have not incorporated this suggestion because it is irrelevant (the subject here is Normandy, and the Russians weren't at that party), unneeded (brings up the whole new topic of what losses each nation suffered in the war when we don't talk about the millions of French, British, German and American dead), and . . . it has that egregious sort of special pleading ring that just stops the flow; it sounds like we stopped the speech dead to throw a fish to the bear.

Kimmitt also asks that we add a line at the end of full paragraph two, page 6: "D-Day marked the beginning of an enduring American commitment to European security." I did not incorporate this because of time considerations and also because I feel the passage already makes that point.

Finally, Bud McFarlane suggested a number of stylistic changes. I accepted four of them (things like changing the "boom" of the cannon to the "roar" of the cannon) and rejected one. Bud wants us to change the last sentence of the speech from "borne by their memory" to "sustained by their sacrifice". I prefer "borne . . ." because it is more personal, more lyrical and more positive. Better to be borne that sustained, I always say.

That's it.

▲ A memo from Peggy Noonan to Ben Elliot in which she outlines her reasons for the changes that she did and didn't implement in the speech.

▲ **US soldiers from the 2nd Ranger Battalion surrounding German prisoners at the Pointe du Hoc, France on June 6, 1944.**

objected both on grounds of irrelevance and flow—a digression in what was essentially a tone poem meant for heart-tugging delivery by a superb speaker.

She had a protracted row with national security advisor Bud McFarlane, who wanted to change the words in the last sentence from "borne by their memory" to "sustained by their sacrifice." He would change it in each succeeding draft, and she would

change it back. She explained that "borne is more personal, more lyrical and more positive." In the final speech, the nod to the Russian dead stayed in, but she won "borne."

Members of the advance team working on the event still complained that the speech was not stirring enough—there were no tears in it. But Noonan had not been given some very vital information. She had never visited the site of the speech, had never seen the dramatic promontory of Pointe du Hoc, a sheer cliff rising a hundred feet and jabbing out into the Atlantic "like a cursed dagger," in Brinkley's description. She also had not been told that more than sixty of the members of the 2nd Battalion would be in attendance—not scattered through the audience, but sitting up front in a group.

Honoring the Boys

Forty years earlier, 225 of them—known as Rudder's Rangers—had landed on the rocky beach below Pointe du Hoc. The promontory divided Utah Beach from Omaha Beach, the two key landing points for the Allied forces. The rangers' objective was to take out the heavy German gun emplacements that fired down on the invading soldiers.

The rangers shot grappling hooks from rocket launchers to secure ropes and ladders to scale the cliffs. Braving withering fire from the Germans on the cliff above, those that completed the ascent thrust their daggers into the cliff top to pull themselves the last few feet. They drove the Germans back, and then fought off several counterattacks the following day to hold Pointe du Hoc. By the time they were relieved, only ninety of the 225 were able to go on fighting.

Finally, Noonan now had all the facts she needed to paint a vivid word picture. Despite the bureaucratic interference, Noonan strung together a series of strong paragraphs. They were perfectly suited to Reagan's earnest demeanor and his extraordinary sense of drama.

One last piece fell into place when Noonan, a baseball fan, read sportswriter Roger Kahn's book on the 1955 Brooklyn Dodger team that won the World Series, *The Boys of Summer.* Noonan thought about the group of senior citizens who would be facing Reagan as he gave the speech. They were only boys when they scaled those cliffs and took that vital piece of land. The key words came to her: the boys of Pointe du Hoc.

Reagan Tells Story of Heroism

On June 6, 1984, Reagan told their story. He set the scene, contrasting the "soft" air of the peaceful day with the deadly chaos of forty years earlier, punctuated by shells and bullets and the cries of the wounded and dying. He described the assault of the rangers on the cliffs, then dramatically turned to the ranks of graying men before him.

"Behind me," intoned Reagan, "is a memorial that symbolizes the Ranger daggers that were thrust into the top of these cliffs. And before me are the men who put them there. These are the boys of Pointe du Hoc. These are the men who took the cliffs. These are the champions who helped free a continent. These are the heroes who helped end a war."

There was not, as the saying goes, a dry eye in the house. Reagan went on for another ten minutes in the same inspirational vein, along the way making the points that his national security advisors wanted him to make about strength, defense, and solidarity with Europe. He later delivered a speech at Omaha Beach, another stirring paean to sacrifice and strength. Tony Dolan, another young speechwriter on the staff, wrote that one, and if not for the majestic imagery of the Noonan speech, that would be the one remembered.

Peggy Noonan met Ronald Reagan for the first time six weeks after the Pointe du Hoc speech. He had to be reminded who she was, and that she had written the speech. "That was wonderful," he said, "It was like 'Flanders Field'." She was struck, she later said, by his frailty and apparent confusion. He was still her hero, but was like a "Lion in Winter," she recalled. Nevertheless, Reagan was re-elected by a landslide several months later. True to Darman's vision, the Pointe du Hoc footage figured prominently in his campaign advertisements.

Address on the 40th Anniversary of D-Day
June 6, 1984, US Rangers Monument, Pointe du Hoc, Normandy, France

The President has seen_____

(NOONAN)

WEDNESDAY, JUNE 6, 1984

215 027 SS
SP 891

POINTE DU HOC

WE ARE HERE TO MARK THAT DAY IN HISTORY WHEN THE ALLIED ARMIES JOINED IN BATTLE TO RECLAIM THIS CONTINENT TO LIBERTY. FOR 4 LONG YEARS, MUCH OF EUROPE HAD BEEN UNDER A TERRIBLE SHADOW. FREE NATIONS HAD FALLEN, JEWS CRIED OUT IN THE CAMPS, MILLIONS CRIED OUT FOR LIBERATION. EUROPE WAS ENSLAVED, AND THE WORLD PRAYED FOR ITS RESCUE. HERE, IN NORMANDY, THE RESCUE BEGAN. HERE THE ALLIES STOOD, AND FOUGHT AGAINST TYRANNY IN A GIANT UNDERTAKING UNPARALLELED IN HUMAN HISTORY.

WE STAND ON A LONELY, WINDSWEPT POINT ON THE NORTHERN SHORE OF FRANCE. THE AIR IS SOFT, BUT, 40 YEARS AGO AT THIS MOMENT, THE AIR WAS DENSE WITH SMOKE AND THE CRIES OF MEN; THE AIR WAS FILLED WITH THE CRACK OF RIFLE FIRE AND THE ROAR OF CANNON.

We're here to mark that day in history when the Allied armies joined in battle to reclaim this continent to liberty. For 4 long years, much of Europe had been under a terrible shadow. Free nations had fallen, Jews cried out in the camps, millions cried out for liberation. Europe was enslaved, and the world prayed for its rescue. Here in Normandy the rescue began. Here the Allies stood and fought against tyranny in a giant undertaking unparalleled in human history.

We stand on a lonely, windswept point on the northern shore of France. The air is soft, but 40 years ago at this moment, the air was dense with smoke and the cries of men, and the air was filled with the crack of rifle fire and the roar of cannon. At dawn, on the morning of the 6th of June, 1944, 225 Rangers jumped off the British landing craft and ran to the bottom of these cliffs. Their mission was one of the most difficult and daring of the invasion: to climb these sheer and desolate cliffs and take out the enemy guns. The Allies

◄ The first page of the President's reading copy of the speech.

had been told that some of the mightiest of these guns were here and they would be trained on the beaches to stop the Allied advance.

The Rangers looked up and saw the enemy soldiers — the edge of the cliffs shooting down at them with machineguns and throwing grenades. And the American Rangers began to climb. They shot rope ladders over the face of these cliffs and began to pull themselves up. When one Ranger fell, another would take his place. When one rope was cut, a Ranger would grab another and begin his climb again. They climbed, shot back, and held their footing. Soon, one by one, the Rangers pulled themselves over the top, and in seizing the firm land at the top of these cliffs, they began to seize back the continent of Europe. Two hundred and twenty-five came here. After 2 days of fighting, only 90 could still bear arms.

Behind me is a memorial that symbolizes the Ranger daggers that were thrust into the top of these cliffs. And before me are the men who put them there.

These are the boys of Pointe du Hoc. These are the men who took the cliffs. These are the champions who helped free a continent. These are the heroes who helped end a war.

Gentlemen, I look at you and I think of the words of Stephen Spender's poem. You are men who in your ``lives fought for life . . . and left the vivid air signed with your honor.''

I think I know what you may be thinking right now—thinking ``we were just part of a bigger effort; everyone was brave that day.'' Well, everyone was. Do you remember the story of Bill Millin of the 51st Highlanders? Forty years ago today, British troops were pinned down near a bridge, waiting desperately for help. Suddenly, they heard the sound of bagpipes, and some thought they were dreaming. Well, they weren't. They looked up and saw Bill Millin with his bagpipes, leading the reinforcements and ignoring the smack of the bullets into the ground around him.

Lord Lovat was with him—Lord Lovat of Scotland, who calmly announced when he got to the bridge, ``Sorry I'm a few minutes late,'' as if he'd been delayed by a traffic jam, when in truth he'd just come from the bloody fighting on Sword Beach, which he and his men had just taken.

There was the impossible valor of the Poles who threw themselves between the enemy and the rest of Europe as the invasion took hold, and the unsurpassed courage of the Canadians who had already seen the horrors of war on this coast. They knew what awaited them there, but they would not be deterred. And once they hit Juno Beach, they never looked back.

All of these men were part of a rollcall of honor with names that spoke of a pride as bright as the colors they bore: the Royal Winnipeg Rifles, Poland's 24th Lancers, the Royal Scots Fusiliers, the Screaming Eagles, the Yeomen of England's armored divisions, the forces of Free France, the Coast Guard's ``Matchbox Fleet'' and you, the American Rangers.

Forty summers have passed since the battle that you fought here. You were young the day you took these cliffs; some of you were hardly more than boys, with the deepest joys of life before you. Yet, you risked everything here. Why? Why did you do it? What impelled you to put aside the instinct for self-preservation and risk your lives to take these cliffs? What inspired all the men of the armies that met here? We look at you, and somehow we know the answer. It was faith and belief; it was loyalty and love.

The men of Normandy had faith that what they were doing was right, faith that they fought for all humanity, faith that a just God would grant them mercy on this beachhead or on the next. It was the deep knowledge—and pray God we have not lost it—that there is a profound, moral difference between the use of force for liberation and the use of force for conquest. You were here to liberate, not to conquer, and so you and those others did not doubt your cause.

And you were right not to doubt.

You all knew that some things are worth dying for. One's country is worth dying for, and democracy is worth dying for, because it's the most deeply honorable form of government ever devised by man. All of you loved liberty. All of you were willing to fight tyranny, and you knew the people of your countries were behind you.

The Americans who fought here that morning knew word of the invasion was spreading through the darkness back home. They fought—or felt in their hearts, though they couldn't know in fact, that in Georgia they were filling the churches at 4 a.m., in Kansas they were kneeling on their porches and praying, and in Philadelphia they were ringing the Liberty Bell.

Something else helped the men of D-day: their rockhard belief that Providence would have a great hand in the events that would unfold here; that God was an ally in this great cause. And so, the night before the invasion, when Colonel Wolverton asked his parachute troops to kneel with him in prayer he told them: Do not bow your heads, but look up so you can see God and ask His blessing in what we're about

MEMORANDUM

NATIONAL SECURITY COUNCIL

4118
Add-On

May 30, 1984

ACTION

MEMORANDUM FOR ROBERT M. KIMMITT

FROM: TYRUS W. COBB

SUBJECT: Pointe du Hoc Speech

Speechwriters provided me with a copy of the latest (final??) version of the Pointe du Hoc speech, which incorporated most of historical corrections, and some of our stylistic suggestions. This version does not reflect Bud's suggested changes made on May 28 in a version forwarded to Darman by you.

It has two other problems that I would have raised had I seen it again Monday. A reference to the Canadian slaughter at Dieppe is still in -- the Army historians tell me this is especially sensitive with the Canadians since they believe that it was the fault of the British that they suffered such extensive casualties. The other point -- the reference to the Soviet losses, a paragraph that NSC (Jack feels especially strongly) and State wanted, still is not in the speech.

Ben told us yesterday that speechwriters felt that this smacked of "detentism" and didn't want it in; I explained why we thought it necessary. I don't think that we should go to the mat, but I also don't believe that this is the speechwriters call. Could you please check with Bud on his preference.

If Bud agrees, I have drafted a note from you to Darman, forwarding a revised manuscript suggesting the elimination of the reference to Dieppe, incorporating Bud's style changes and the addition of the reference to the Soviet sacrifices.

Jack Matlock, Peter Sommer and Jim Rentschler concur.

RECOMMENDATION

After checking with Bud, that you sign the memo to Darman at Tab I.

Approve _____   Disapprove _____

Attachment
     Tab A - Pointe du Hoc Speech (May 25 Version)

▲ An NSC memo from Tyrus W. Cobb to Robert M. Kimmitt outlining some of the NSC's problems with the speech, including their desire that the reference to the "Canadian slaughter at Dieppe" be removed.

to do. Also that night, General Matthew Ridgway on his cot, listening in the darkness for the promise God made to Joshua: ``I will not fail thee nor forsake thee.''

These are the things that impelled them; these are the things that shaped the unity of the Allies.

When the war was over, there were lives to be rebuilt and governments to be returned to the people. There were nations to be reborn. Above all, there was a new peace to be assured. These were huge and daunting tasks. But the Allies summoned strength from the faith, belief, loyalty, and love of those who fell here. They rebuilt a new Europe together.

There was first a great reconciliation among those who had been enemies, all of whom had suffered so greatly. The United States did its part, creating the Marshall plan to help rebuild our allies and our former enemies. The Marshall plan led to the Atlantic alliance—a great alliance that serves to this day as our shield for freedom, for prosperity, and for peace.

In spite of our great efforts and successes, not all that followed the end of the war was happy or planned. Some liberated countries were lost. The great sadness of this loss echoes down to our own time in the streets of Warsaw, Prague, and East Berlin. Soviet troops that came to the center of this continent did not leave when peace came. They're still there, uninvited, unwanted, unyielding, almost 40 years after the war. Because of this, allied forces still stand on this continent. Today, as 40 years ago, our armies are here for only one purpose—to protect and defend democracy. The only territories we hold are memorials like this one and graveyards where our heroes rest.

◄ A page from a May 23 draft of the speech containing a longer reference to the Canadian slaughter at Dieppe; in the final version the phrase was removed, although the reference to the events remained.

Page 4

There was the impossible valor of the Poles, who threw themselves between the enemy and the rest of Europe as the Invasion took hold. And the unsurpassed courage of the Canadians, the only troops who knew exactly what they would face when they hit the beaches. Two years before, their countrymen had been slaughtered at Dieppe. They knew what awaited them here, but they would not be deterred, and once they hit Juno Beach they never ~~let go.~~ looked back.

~~All of these men~~ The men of Normandy were part of a roll call of honor, with names that ~~speak~~ spoke of a pride as bright as the colors they ~~wore:~~ bore: the Royal Winnipeg Rifles, ~~the Manitoba Grenadiers,~~ Poland's 24th Lancers, the Royal Scots Fusiliers, the Yeomen of England's armoured divisions, the forces of Free France, the Regiment de Chars de Combat, the ~~101st~~ 82nd Airborne. These names are written forever on this sand and on this wind, for truly these are men who "in their lives fought for life . . . and left the vivid air signed with their honor."

What inspired the men of the armies that met here? What impelled them to put all thought of self-preservation behind, and risk their lives to take these beaches and hold these cliffs?

It was faith and belief; it was loyalty and love. It was faith that what they were doing was right, faith that they fought for all humanity, faith that a just God would grant them mercy on this beachhead -- or the next. It was the deep knowledge (and pray God we have not lost it) that there is a profound, moral difference between the use of force for liberation and the use of force for conquest. They were here to liberate, not to conquer,

PRESIDENTIAL ADDRESS: POINTE DU HOC
WEDNESDAY, JUNE 6, 1984

We are here to mark that day in history when the Allied armies joined in battle to reclaim this continent to liberty. For 4 long years, much of Europe had been under a terrible shadow. Free nations had fallen, Jews cried out in the camps, millions cried out for liberation. Europe was enslaved, and the world prayed for its rescue. Here, in Normandy, the rescue began. Here the West stood, and fought against tyranny in a giant undertaking unparalleled in human history.

We stand on a lonely, windswept point on the northern shore of France. As I speak, the air is soft and full of sunlight. But 40 years ago at this moment, the air was dense with smoke and the cries of men, the air was filled with the crack of rifle fire and the roar of cannon. At dawn on the morning of the 6th of June, 1944, 225 American Rangers jumped off a British landing craft and ran to the bottom of these cliffs. Their mission was one of the most difficult and daring of the Invasion: to climb these sheer and desolate cliffs and take out the enemy guns. The Allies had been told that the mightiest of those guns were here, and they would be trained on the beaches to stop the Allied advance.

The Rangers looked up and saw the enemy soldiers at the edge of the cliffs shooting down at them with machine guns and throwing grenades. And the American Rangers began to climb. They shot rope ladders over the face of these cliffs and they began to pull themselves up. And when one Ranger would fall another would take his place, and when one rope was cut a Ranger

* * *

◀ The first page of a May 31 draft of the speech showing the huge number of changes that were suggested by numerous people.

We in America have learned bitter lessons from two World Wars: It is better to be here ready to protect the peace, than to take blind shelter across the sea, rushing to respond only after freedom is lost. We've learned that isolationism never was and never will be an acceptable response to tyrannical governments with an expansionist intent.

But we try always to be prepared for peace; prepared to deter aggression; prepared to negotiate the reduction of arms; and, yes, prepared to reach out again in the spirit of reconciliation. In truth, there is no reconciliation we would welcome more than a reconciliation with the Soviet Union, so, together, we can lessen the risks of war, now and forever.

It's fitting to remember here the great losses also suffered by the Russian people during World War II: 20 million perished, a terrible price that testifies to all the world the necessity of ending war. I tell you from my heart that we in the United States do not want war. We want to wipe from the face of the Earth the terrible weapons that man now has in his hands. And I tell you, we are ready to seize that beachhead. We look for some sign from the Soviet Union that they are willing to move forward, that they share our desire and love for peace, and that they will give up the ways of conquest. There must be a changing there that will allow us to turn our hope into action.

▶ President Ronald W. Reagan and First Lady Nancy Reagan peering out of a German bunker at Pointe du Hoc, France on June 6, 1984.

We will pray forever that some day that changing will come. But for now, particularly today, it is good and fitting to renew our commitment to each other, to our freedom, and to the alliance that protects it.

We are bound today by what bound us 40 years ago, the same loyalties, traditions, and beliefs. We're bound by reality. The strength of America's allies is vital to the United States, and the American security guarantee is essential to the continued freedom of Europe's democracies. We were with you then; we are with you now. Your hopes are our hopes, and your destiny is our destiny.

Here, in this place where the West held together, let us make a vow to our dead. Let us show them by our actions that we understand what they died for. Let our actions say to them the words for which Matthew Ridgway listened: ``I will not fail thee nor forsake thee.''

Strengthened by their courage, heartened by their value [valor], and borne by their memory, let us continue to stand for the ideals for which they lived and died.

Thank you very much, and God bless you all.

President Ronald Wilson Reagan

"The crew of the space shuttle *Challenger* honored us by the manner in which they lived their lives. We will never forget them, nor the last time we saw them, this morning, as they prepared for their journey and waved goodbye and 'slipped the surly bonds of earth' to 'touch the face of God.'"

On January 28, 1986, Ronald Reagan was scheduled to deliver his annual State of the Union Address. He wound up giving quite a different speech.

That same day, shortly after its launch, the space shuttle *Challenger* exploded mid-air before a televised world audience. Reagan's brief, heartfelt elegy to the crew is now remembered as one of the ten best American political speeches of the twentieth century.

In addition to the immediate deadline of crafting the speech, the *Challenger* disaster presented some extra dimensions that made it even more of a test for Reagan, the "Great Communicator." The majority of American adults were at work at 11:39 a.m. when the blast occurred, blunting the horror somewhat. However, many children saw the horrific event as it happened. Classrooms across the country were tuned in to the launch via special NASA hookups, because one of the astronauts was Christa McAuliffe, the first teacher to venture into space.

▲ President Ronald Reagan making his address to the nation on the explosion of the space shuttle *Challenger* from the Oval Office of the White House.

As word quickly spread, Americans turned to TV news. It is estimated that eighty-five percent of the population saw footage of the disaster within an hour after it happened. Initial reports called it an explosion, but investigations later determined that the shuttle and rocket actually broke up because of failure of some of its "O-ring" seals, and that the crew was probably still alive when they plunged into the ocean.

In more than twenty-five years of manned space flight, no astronaut had ever been killed in such a dreadful and public manner. Three astronauts had perished in a launchpad fire, and several more died in training accidents, but out of public view. The wide publicity given to McAuliffe's participation after she had won a national contest to join the crew intensified the public shock and grief.

White House Preoccupied with State of the Union

On the morning of the 28th, the White House was preoccupied with the coming State of the Union speech. Chief of Staff Donald Regan gave a briefing to television anchormen and commentators on what they would be hearing that night. They were scheduled to meet the President for lunch and further discussion of the speech.

Tensions ran high over the State of the Union address. During Reagan's first term, a group of ideologically committed conservative speechwriters enjoyed free access to the President, and grew adept at molding his ideas into rhetoric that captured the public's imagination. Reagan won reelection by a landslide. At the start of his second term, his easygoing Chief of Staff, James Baker, swapped jobs with Treasury Secretary Donald Regan.

Regan was a short-tempered martinet who effectively cut off the speechwriters' channels to Reagan. Worse, he surrounded himself with his own group of loyalists who began to edit speech drafts heavily—and badly. The speechwriters dubbed Regan's staffers "the Mice." Battles began

to break out between the speechwriters, Regan and his staff, and turf-conscious senior officials at the State and Defense departments.

The staff conflicts continued to build, boiling over during the preparation of the State of the Union speech. Rewrite followed rewrite, and news of the infighting and name-calling eventually reached the media. The *New York Times* reported that conservative icon Pat Buchanan, a recent addition as Reagan's communications director, had criticized Regan and "the Mice" for lack of political courage. Regan's aides responded that Buchanan's speechwriters were "politically naive hard-liners."

Sir, the *Challenger* Just Blew Up

The State of the Union speech went through many drafts before settling into final form, not because anyone was happy with it, but because everyone was exhausted by the struggle. That was the situation as Reagan prepared for his press luncheon and Vice President Bush and Buchanan burst into the Oval Office where Buchanan blurted, "Sir, the *Challenger* just blew up."

Reagan and the others rushed into his small private office adjacent to the Oval Office and watched what the rest of America was watching—trails of steam from the rocket fuel shooting in all directions and debris falling from ten miles up. Afterwards, Reagan answered questions from the reporters assembled in the White House for the luncheon.

National Security Council spokesperson Karna Small took notes while Reagan responded to the reporters. He could not stop thinking about the families of the crew, he said.

What can we tell the children, a reporter asked? "Pioneers have always given their lives on the frontier," Reagan responded. "The problem is that

THE PRESIDENT: We were all sitting in there, and I was preparing myself for your questions on the State of the Union Address when the Vice President and John Poindexter came into the room. And all they could say at the time was that they had received a flash that the space shuttle had exploded. And we immediately went into the adjoining room where I have a TV set to get on this, because there was no direct word and -- except that word that had -- being made public also. And there we saw the replaying and saw the thing actually happen. And it just was -- I say -- a very traumatic experience.

Q   But how does that effect your State of the Union speech tonight? I mean, we were told you were going to give an upbeat -- "the State of the Union is good," you know, optimistic speech. This has got to cast a pall on it, doesn't it?

THE PRESIDENT: Yes, it sure does. And, certainly, there could be no speech without mentioning this. But you can't stop governing the nation because of a tragedy of this kind. So, yes, one will continue.

Q   Mr. President --

Q   -- philosophically, do you take some solace in the fact that over the years the American space program has been remarkably safe, that we've not lost as many people as we've been led to believe have been lost in the Soviet Union?

THE PRESIDENT: Well, I think we've all had a great pride in that. And it is a kind of -- well, it'd be something to cling to right now, although it doesn't lessen our grief at what has just taken place.

Q   Mr. President, sending civilians in space is based on the assumption that it was routine to go into space, that it was now safe, even a teacher we could send up. Do you think that notion has now -- is now gone?

THE PRESIDENT: Well, what would you -- what could you say, other than that here was a program that had a 100-percent safety record? The only other fatality did not take place in a space shuttle. It took place in an old-type of capsule --

Q   Mr. President --

MR. BUCHANAN: One question. One more question.

Q   -- so many children have -- you know -- been a part of this particular space shuttle because of the teacher. And they're doing classrooms. Can you do something to help help them -- say something that would help them to understand --

THE PRESIDENT: I think people closer to them have got to be doing that. As I say, the world is a hazardous place, always has been, in pioneering. And we've always known that there are pioneers that give their lives out there on the frontier. And now this has happened. It probably is more of a shock to -- to all of us because of the fact that we see it happen now and -- thanks to the media -- not just hearing about it as if something that happened miles away. But I think -- I think those that have to do with them and -- must, at the same time, make it plain to them that life does go on and -- and you don't back up and quit some worthwhile endeavor because of tragedy.

▲ A page from the White House press release of President Reagan's question and answer session with reporters immediately after he had heard news of the tragedy.

it's more of a shock to all as we see it happening . . . but we must make it clear that life goes on."

Karna Small rushed her notes to Peggy Noonan, who had already begun work on his remarks. Her reporter's training had taken over and she began to "handle the horror by writing the show" even before she had any input from the President.

Only Buchanan Liked Noonan Draft

She finished a draft and took it to Donald Regan's office, where it would be reviewed by Regan, Buchanan, "the Mice," and presidential spokesman Larry Speakes. No one liked it except Buchanan, she said later. "The Mice" were especially unhappy.

"Did you see how he held it," Buchanan said later of one of "the Mice." "Like a dog had relieved itself on it."

Former White House speechwriter Robert Schlesinger pinpoints the untenable situation faced by Noonan and other speechwriters of the Reagan White House in his book *White House Ghosts*. Noonan had concluded the remarks by quoting the last line of John Gillespie Magee's stirring poem, "High Flight," saying that the *Challenger* crew had "slipped the surly bonds of earth" to "touch the face of God."

"One pudgy young NSC staffer," writes Schlesinger, "apparently inspired by the old telephone jingle, tried to rework the line to read that the astronauts had slipped the surly bonds to "reach out and touch someone—touch the face of God." Noonan thought it was the worst edit she encountered at the White House.

Fortunately for Noonan—and for the legacy of the Reagan Presidency—neither Regan nor his cohorts had time to destroy the speech. Noonan's draft went to Reagan much as she had written it, and conveying much of the President's language in his initial remarks to the press.

Reagan Spoke as Friend and Neighbor

As usual when she was left free from the interference of editors, Noonan adeptly captured Reagan's speaking style—deceptively simple and plain, but delivered with perfect emotional pitch. Reagan rarely spoke as the "imperial" President, and emphatically rejected any rhetoric that tried to make him sound pompous or imposing. He presented himself as a friend and neighbor, and that was exactly what was called for as he led the nation in mourning the fallen heroes. He signaled his intent as he had so many times by invoking his wife's name as the joint deliverer of the message: "Nancy and I are pained to the core . . ."

Reagan, with Noonan's perceptive assistance, took care to frame his remarks so that the schoolchildren who had witnessed the disaster

▲ An early, 1.00 pm, draft of the speech, with annotations clearly visible.

The typescript draft reads:

(Noonan)
January 28, 1986
1:00 p.m.

PRESIDENTIAL REMARKS: DEATH OF SPACE SHUTTLE CHALLENGER CREW
TUESDAY, JANUARY 28, 1986

Ladies and gentlemen, we have a brief statement. Nancy and I are pained by this tragedy -- as you are, as all of the people of our country are. This is a national loss.

We forget what courage it takes to go into space and explore the heavens, we forget what it takes. In more than a quarter of a century of the United States space program we have never lost an astronaut in flight -- we have never had a tragedy like this. And so we have forgotten the courage it takes, and the courage it took for the crew of the shuttle. But they -- the Magnificent Seven -- were, by necessity, always aware of the dangers, and they overcame whatever fears they had to do their jobs brilliantly.

Here are seven heroes -- Michael Smith, Francis Scobee, Judith Resnik, Ronald McNair, Ellison Onizuka, Gregory Jarvis, and Christa McAuliffe. We mourn them, we mourn them as a Nation, together.

To the families of the Seven: We cannot bear, as you do, the full impact of this tragedy -- but we feel the loss, and we are thinking about you so very much. Your daughters and sons, your husbands, wives and parents -- they were daring and brave and they had that special grace, that special spirit that said: give me a challenge and I'll meet it with joy. They had a hunger to explore the universe and discover its truths. They wished to serve and they did, and brilliantly.

They honored us by the manner in which they lived their lives. We will never forget them nor the last time we saw them -- this morning, as they prepared for their journey, and waved goodbye, and "slipped the surly bonds of earth" to "touch the face of God".

in their classrooms could understand. Simple sentences, words of one syllable, sincerely delivered; that was the Reagan style and it had rarely worked better than in this instance.

Reagan said all the right things, paying tribute to all the dead astronauts by name, and then speaking directly to their families while praising them. Noonan had included all the points of his initial reaction in responding to the reporters—that they were pioneers, we had never lost an astronaut in flight, the *Challenger* crew died striving to pull us into the future, and the future belongs to the brave. The fact that the speech clearly reflected his thoughts as expressed on first hearing the news earlier only added to the genuineness and conviction he brought to his public statement.

Solemn Tone, Hopeful Words

The tone of the speech was solemn, but the words were hopeful. Nowhere does Reagan entertain the possibility of quitting space. Interestingly, at the beginning he makes the same argument that President Kennedy had made twenty-five years earlier, saying "We don't hide our space program. We don't keep secrets and cover things up. We do it all up front and in public." That statement was as clearly aimed at the Soviets as was Kennedy's, and is indicative that in Reagan's mind space remained political, as it had in Kennedy's.

Noonan did a fine job on a very tight deadline—a little over five hours from the disaster to the speech—but the hurry showed in one or two places. The penultimate paragraph is a clunky comparison of the *Challenger* crew to British explorer Sir Francis Drake, who "lived by the sea, died on it and was buried in it." It is highly unlikely that section would have survived the first rewrite—but there wasn't time for a rewrite.

The Drake reference could have been omitted entirely, since the final paragraph expressed the same sentiment, but better. That closing ranks among the finest ever uttered by any president, particularly in such agonizing circumstances.

Reagan's final words were highlighted by the ending lines of the poem "High Flight." Its author, John Gillespie Magee Jr., was an Anglo-American pilot who was killed at age nineteen early in World War II, shortly after writing the poem. The *Challenger* astronauts, Reagan said in conclusion, had "slipped the surly bonds of earth," to "touch the face of God." That was the line that the young NSC staffer had wanted to squash flat.

The line itself is poetic and poignant. Noonan had learned the poem as a schoolgirl, but there is both a deeper and a broader connection. Reagan himself had heard the poem decades earlier. His old friend, Hollywood star Tyrone Power, had carried the poem on a slip of paper with him as he flew missions as a Marine pilot during the war. He recited it to Reagan after returning from the service, and Reagan himself read it at Power's funeral when he died of a heart attack in 1958 at age forty-four.

Poem Appealed on Many Levels

Beyond the familiarity of speechwriter and President with the poem, the reference illustrates how completely Reagan and Noonan were culturally attuned to the American people. "High Flight" had become widely known in many parts of the US in the 1950s, when local television stations across the country were still signing off the air overnight. For many Americans—including children and adolescents enjoying the secret thrill of staying up until stations went off the air—the inspiring film and recitation of "High Flight" was the last thing shown before the signal went dead and the snow appeared on the old black and white set. As a result, many Americans hearing Reagan's final words were doubly consoled, by the words themselves and, subliminally, by a cherished old memory from decades past.

Reagan's address provided exactly what was needed to get the country past one of the most horrendous days in its history. There was no public outcry or demand for the end of the shuttle program. The investigation of the causes of the accident, and steps to address the culture of complacency at NASA that led to it proceeded calmly. Three years later, the shuttle flew again.

Reagan delivered his delayed State of the Union speech the following week. He made no mention of the *Challenger* tragedy, and the speech was basically a jumbled hash, bearing the fingerprints and footprints of the many factions at work in the White House and agencies. The disgusted Noonan left the White House soon after, returning only to write Reagan's farewell address as he left office and George H.W. Bush's inaugural speech. During this period, other talented speechwriters were either fired or forced out. Except for the Noonan-penned farewell and one other notable exception—the "Mr. Gorbachev, tear down this wall" line from Reagan's 1987 Berlin speech—Reagan's public addresses never again reached the high level of his first years in office.

Address to the Nation on the Explosion of the Space Shuttle *Challenger*
January 28, 1986, White House, Washington DC

Ladies and gentlemen, I'd planned to speak to you tonight to report on the state of the Union, but the events of earlier today have led me to change those plans. Today is a day for mourning and remembering. Nancy and I are pained to the core by the tragedy of the shuttle *Challenger*. We know we share this pain with all of the people of our country. This is truly a national loss.

Nineteen years ago, almost to the day, we lost three astronauts in a terrible accident on the ground. But we've never lost an astronaut in flight; we've never had a tragedy like this. And perhaps we've forgotten

▼ The "seven heroes" who lost their lives in the *Challenger* disaster: Front row from left, Mike Smith, Dick Scobee, Ron McNair. Back row from left, Ellison Onizuka, Christa McAuliffe, Greg Jarvis, Judith Resnik.

(NOONAN)

JANUARY 28, 1986
36756055

PRESIDENT's BACKUP COPY
ADDRESS TO THE NATION:
DEATH OF SPACE SHUTTLE CHALLENGER CREW

LADIES AND GENTLEMEN, I HAD PLANNED TO SPEAK TO YOU TONIGHT TO REPORT ON THE STATE OF THE UNION, BUT THE EVENTS OF EARLIER TODAY HAVE LED ME TO CHANGE THOSE PLANS. TODAY IS A DAY FOR MOURNING, AND REMEMBERING.

NANCY AND I ARE PAINED TO THE CORE BY THE TRAGEDY OF THE SHUTTLE CHALLENGER. WE KNOW WE SHARE THIS PAIN WITH ALL OF THE PEOPLE OF OUR COUNTRY. THIS IS TRULY A NATIONAL LOSS.

NINETEEN YEARS AGO ALMOST TO THE DAY, WE LOST THREE ASTRONAUTS IN A TERRIBLE ACCIDENT ON THE GROUND. BUT WE HAVE NEVER LOST AN ASTRONAUT IN FLIGHT. WE HAVE NEVER HAD A TRAGEDY LIKE THIS. AND PERHAPS WE HAVE FORGOTTEN THE COURAGE IT TOOK FOR THE CREW OF THE SHUTTLE. BUT THEY, THE CHALLENGER SEVEN, WERE AWARE OF THE DANGERS -- AND OVERCAME THEM AND DID THEIR JOBS BRILLIANTLY.

WE MOURN SEVEN HEROES -- MICHAEL SMITH, DICK SCOBEE, JUDITH RESNIK, RONALD McNAIR, ELLISON (OH-NIH-ZOO-KUH), GREGORY JARVIS, AND CHRISTA McAULIFFE. WE MOURN THEIR LOSS AS A NATION, TOGETHER.

◄ The first page of the president's backup copy of the speech.

loss as a nation together. For the families of the seven, we cannot bear, as you do, the full impact of this tragedy. But we feel the loss, and we're thinking about you so very much. Your loved ones were daring and brave, and they had that special grace, that special spirit that says, ``Give me a challenge, and I'll meet it with joy.'' They had a hunger to explore the universe and discover its truths. They wished to serve, and they did. They served all of us. We've grown used to wonders in this century. It's hard to dazzle us. But for 25 years the United States space program has been doing just that. We've grown used to the idea of space, and perhaps we forget that we've only just begun. We're still pioneers. They, the members of the *Challenger* crew, were pioneers.

the courage it took for the crew of the shuttle. But they, the *Challenger* Seven, were aware of the dangers, but overcame them and did their jobs brilliantly. We mourn seven heroes: Michael Smith, Dick Scobee, Judith Resnik, Ronald McNair, Ellison Onizuka, Gregory Jarvis, and Christa McAuliffe. We mourn their

And I want to say something to the schoolchildren of America who were watching the live coverage of the shuttle's takeoff. I know it is hard to understand, but sometimes painful things like this happen. It's all part of the process of exploration and discovery. It's all part of taking a chance and expanding man's horizons. The future doesn't belong to the fainthearted; it belongs to the brave. The *Challenger* crew was pulling us into the future, and we'll continue to follow them.

I've always had great faith in and respect for our space program, and what happened today does nothing to diminish it. We don't hide our space program. We don't keep secrets and cover things up. We do it all up front and in public. That's the way freedom is, and we wouldn't change it for a minute. We'll continue our quest in space. There will be more shuttle flights and more shuttle crews and, yes, more volunteers, more civilians, more teachers in space. Nothing ends here; our hopes and our journeys continue. I want to add that I wish I could talk to every man and woman who works for NASA or who worked on this mission and tell them: ``Your dedication and professionalism have moved and impressed us for decades. And we know of your anguish. We share it."

There's a coincidence today. On this day 390 years ago, the great explorer Sir Francis Drake died aboard ship off the coast of Panama. In his lifetime the great frontiers were the oceans, and an historian later said, ``He lived by the sea, died on it, and was buried in it." Well, today we can say of the *Challenger* crew: Their dedication was, like Drake's, complete.

The crew of the space shuttle *Challenger* honored us by the manner in which they lived their lives. We will never forget them, nor the last time we saw them, this morning, as they prepared for their journey and waved goodbye and "slipped the surly bonds of earth" to "touch the face of God."

▼ The space shuttle *Challenger* (STS-51L) taking off from the Kennedy Space Centre, Florida.

President Ronald Wilson Reagan

> " Mr. Gorbachev, tear down this wall! "

▲ President Ronald W. Reagan with the West German Chancellor, Helmut Kohl, at the Brandenburg Gate on June 12, 1987.

An indelible image of Ronald Reagan is him standing near the Brandenburg Gate within sight of the infamous Berlin Wall and almost shouting, "Mr. Gorbachev, tear down this wall!" It is great theater, but ironically, the immortal words almost did not make it into the speech at all. Only Reagan's rhetorical instincts, and the arguments of his speechwriter, preserved them for history.

Berlin, a Western enclave deep within East Germany, was a constant point of contention between the superpowers from the moment World War II ended. The famed Berlin Airlift kept West Berlin supplied with food and fuel after the Soviets cut off access in 1948, and West Berlin's situation remained precarious during the ensuing two decades.

When President Kennedy visited Berlin in 1963, Cold War tensions were high. Berliners lived in constant fear that their enclave of democracy, located well within East Germany, would be invaded and subsumed into that communist state. The East German communists built the Berlin Wall, surrounding West Berlin, in 1961. Kennedy's strong support of West Berlin as articulated in his "Ich bin ein Berliner" speech caused the Soviets and their East German vassals to back off.

By the 1970s, the era of détente was beginning and tensions over Berlin had eased. The four wartime powers that had divided Berlin and Germany at the end of World War II (the United States, the United Kingdom, France, and the Soviet Union) signed a new agreement on the status of Berlin. It was not a formal treaty, and was purposely vague. Berlin was not even mentioned by name. But the treaty reestablished ties between the two parts of Berlin and improved travel and communications.

German Relations Thawed, but Wall Stood

The agreement also recognized the existence of two German states and established diplomatic ties. West Berlin was informally recognized as part of West Germany. With uncertainties about its status resolved, West Berlin prospered along with the rest of West Germany. East Berlin stayed as bleak and backward as the rest of the Soviet bloc. Despite the thaw in relations, the Berlin Wall still stood and those who tried to flee over the wall could be, and were, shot.

▶ Commandos of the National People's Army of the German Democratic Republic starting the erection of the Berlin Wall on August 13, 1961.

The Reagan presidency, however, brought back heightened tensions, as Reagan initiated a record peacetime defense buildup. Though the USSR bristled at the escalation, during this time Mikhail Gorbachev came to power and began a series of economic and social reforms known as "perestroika."

Reagan saw some hope for increased freedom within the Soviet bloc, including Berlin, and decided to visit West Berlin after an economic summit meeting in Italy. He set his speech at the historic Brandenburg Gate, which had been kept closed since the city was divided. He wanted a speech that would be as memorable as Kennedy's.

Speechwriter Peter Robinson was assigned to produce a draft. He was told only that the president would speak at the Berlin Wall, there

Page 2 *Which*

14. Question: In which aspects can we accept normalization? In which can Berlin never be normal?

15. Lack of enthusiasm, compared to J.F.K., shows, in a way, normalcy, success.

~~Leickner:~~ *Lechner*

16. Difference between J.F.K. and now: No immediate danger. This gone, compared to ultimatum of Khruschev. Talk instead about the long-term march of liberty -- and the patience it requires. *Americans gave to Berlin.*
   The copy of the Liberty Bell. RIAS(?) ~~quotes Jefferson.~~
~~This repeated solemnly.~~ *Bell has on it quotation from Jefferson.*

Fr. Elz: *au*

17. Must reaffirm the basic values.

Strauch(?): *yes*

18. If the Russians are willing to open up, then the wall must go. Open the Brandenburg Gate.

19. Larry/Leichner. 750 years. This an opportunity to stress long-term developments. Could remark on the worldwide basis.

20. Brandenburg Gate. *yes* Always served as a place of victory, display of power. Now the wall goes nearly through it. Unter den Linden(?) -- a tree-lined strasse, 1788-1791. Used to be considered a boundary of Berlin.

21. Strauch. 750 years a long time in German history. 45 years of separation is almost nothing. The division is one we do not recognize.

22. The existence of a totalitarian state depends on your division.

23. Leichner: Must include greeting to the people of East Berlin and East Germany (Pope has done this).

24. Address Berliners as a whole. *East and West alike*

25. But: Not just the sadness of the *East*, but a splendid city in its own right.

26. Strauch. Well-known state level of culture -- opera, symphony. Also the subculture -- *one* huge Greenwich Village. The most interesting cultural city in Germany.

** **

would be a large crowd, and he "probably ought to talk about foreign policy." Not content to sift through State Department white papers and country briefings, Robinson left for Berlin.

Speechwriter Told What Not to Say

In his book *How Ronald Reagan Changed My Life*, Robinson recalls that the ranking diplomat mainly advised him on what *not* to say—particularly warning him against bashing the Soviets, or mentioning the Wall. Germans had gotten used to it, he said, and any statement about the Wall would be in bad taste. The diplomat instead broached several pedestrian ideas such as increasing air routes to Berlin and turning Berlin into a conference center.

That night, Robinson says, he broke away from his unhelpful official guides to accept a dinner invitation among ordinary Germans. When he asked if fellow guests had "gotten used to" the Wall, one said he would never get used to it because he hadn't seen his sister, who lived on the other side of the wall, for twenty years. His hostess erupted that if Gorbachev was serious about peace he would "tear down this wall." When Robinson returned

◀ The second page of Peter Robinson's typed record of the forty-five notes he made during his dinner at the Elz's. Point eighteen specifically mentions the need for the wall to come down.

THE WHITE HOUSE
WASHINGTON

May 5, 1987

Dear Mr. and Mrs. Elz:

In my nearly 2 weeks in Germany and Italy, dinner at your home represented the high point. I learned an enormous amount; in turning to my journal today, I found that during our discussion I had taken no fewer than 45 notes. But what came across most powerfully was the depth of feeling -- the love -- that the Berliners in your home had for their city.

I cannot thank you enough. When you come to Washington this autumn, please do get in touch. And then, of course, there is always the possibility that we will meet again in Germany. After all, "Ich hab noch einen koffer in Berlin."

Sincerely,

Peter M. Robinson
Speechwriter to the President

P.S. I am assuming that by now the U.S. Mission in Berlin has invited you and those I met at your home to hear the President's speech. If not, please let me know, and I'll straighten it out.

Herr and Frau Dieter Elz
Limonenstrasse 11
Berlin
West Germany

▲ A letter from speechwriter Peter Robinson to the Elz's who hosted the dinner he attended in Berlin.

to Washington, and after many revisions, he put the phrase in the speech.

While Robinson claims that he originated the line, others have different recollections. Richard Allen, a White House national security advisor, remembers a 1978 trip to Berlin when he was an aide to then-Governor Reagan. Standing near the Wall, Reagan said, "We've got to find a way to knock this thing down." Aides recall him occasionally mentioning that he would like to see the wall come down during staff meetings years before the Berlin speech. Reagan himself does little to clarify the origin. In his autobiography, he quotes the "tear down" passages, but merely says that he "felt strongly" about them, not that he or anyone else originated them.

Experts Try to Stop the Saber-Rattling

Regardless of who thought of it or wrote it first, the line almost didn't make it into the speech. White House and State Department foreign policy experts were determined to take every opportunity to further improve relations with the Soviets. They would never agree to high-profile saber-rattling by the president within sight of the Berlin Wall. Robinson and his fellow speechwriters knew this, and pulled a fast one to keep the phrase in the speech.

Reagan was to give nine speeches on his European trip, and they bundled the Berlin draft among them, delivering them to the foreign policy reviewers late in the week. The writers knew the policy wonks would not have time to read the whole stack, and remove the offending language, before their regular Monday morning speechwriting meeting with Reagan.

At the meeting, Reagan remarked that he liked the phrase, and the speechwriters were exultant. With his backing, "tear down this wall" stood a good chance of staying in. The opposition continued, though. Colin Powell, then on the National Security Council, repeatedly tried to have it excised because it might insult the Soviets and cool relations. Chief of Staff Howard Baker thought it should be dropped because it was "unpresidential." The attempts to remove it continued even after the President left on the European trip. The speechwriters stood firm, pointing out that Reagan wanted the line in.

They were not so lucky with the rest of the president's remarks on that day. The speech went through several rounds of the process the White House came to call "staffing up," circulating through the offices of dozens of officials within the White House and many government agencies. All speechwriters who have worked at the White House (including this writer) know that when they put their deathless prose into the mill of multiple reviewers, it will come back with hoofprints all over it. The staffing up process has been the standard at the White House since the Ford Administration, and is the reason that so much presidential prose in recent years is flat and sometimes downright incoherent. That's what happened to the Berlin Wall speech.

Logically, "tear down this wall" should have been a powerful conclusion to the speech, but it was not. The immortal line wound up buried about halfway through the speech and was followed by about ten minutes worth of anticlimactic detail.

Reagan and his advisers hoped that speaking at the site would highlight his belief that encouraging democracy would eventually bring the Wall down. He offered several initiatives in the speech to that end, and the "tear down this wall" line was to be the logical conclusion. But during "staffing up," the immortal line wound up buried and the speech became far less coherent.

Too Much German

Early in the speech Reagan follows Kennedy's lead by making not one but three attempts at speaking in German. In the first, he invokes the name of Paul Lincke, known as the "Father of German Musical Comedy," and the composer of "Berliner Luft," the Berlin Air, which is otherwise known as the hymn of Berlin. If Americans recognize Lincke's name at

PRESIDENTIAL ADDRESS: BRANDENBURG GATE
BERLIN, GERMANY
FRIDAY, JUNE 12, 1987

[Check on attendance of Pres. von Weiszaecker at event.]

Chancellor Kohl, Governing Mayor Diepgen, ladies and gentlemen: Twenty-four years ago, President John F. Kennedy visited Berlin, speaking to the people of this city and the world at the City Hall. Since then, two other Presidents have come, each in his turn, to Berlin. Today I myself make my second visit to your city.

We come to Berlin, we American Presidents, because it is our duty to speak, in this place, of freedom. But I must confess, we are drawn here by other things as well: By the feeling of history in this city, more than 500 years older than our own Nation. By the beauty of the Grunewald and the Tiergarten. Most of all, by your courage and determination.

Perhaps the composer Paul Lincke understood something about American Presidents. You see, like so many Presidents before me, I come here today because wherever I go, whatever I do:
(Ish hob knack Inen coffer in Ber.leen)
"Ich hab noch einen koffer in Berlin." ["I still have a suitcase in Berlin" -- words from a much-loved song.]

Our gathering today is being broadcast throughout Western Europe and North America. I understand that it is being seen and heard as well in the East.

To those listening throughout Eastern Europe, I extend my warmest greetings and the goodwill of the American people. To

all, they know him as the composer of "Glow, Little Glowworm," a 1930s hit. But he was well known to Reagan's Berlin audience.

The line written for Reagan was "Ich hab noch einen koffer in Berlin," which means "I still have a suitcase in Berlin"—the title of a very popular tune by Lincke. It was a good local touch and doubtless well received, but it was a frivolous and lightweight

▲ A page from a June 8 draft of the speech with the German words spelled out phonetically.

phrase compared to Kennedy's legendary "Ich bin ein Berliner."

The second and third German phrases add little to the speech. "There is only one Berlin"

does not seem particularly inventive, and the final German phrase is a laugh-line reference to "Berliner schnauze," a Berlin dialect that would be equivalent of Cockney rhyming slang in England or Brooklynese in America. It seems as if either Reagan or his speechwriter were showing off. One German phrase would have been enough.

Reagan precedes the "tear down this wall" phrase by complimenting the Soviets in a backhanded way on their efforts toward reform and openness, but then afterwards goes on to delineate his policy of resistance to Soviet expansionism and peace through strength, citing the Strategic Defense Initiative (Star Wars) and other defense programs. Reagan ends the speech with another allusion to the Berlin Wall, quoting from graffiti on the wall, "This wall will fall. Beliefs become reality," and ending with "For it cannot withstand faith; it cannot withstand truth. The wall cannot withstand freedom." It was a nice ending, but nowhere as powerful as "tear down this wall" would have been.

Reagan's Delivery Helped the Speech Live On

The old professional actor knew good lines when he heard them, and had no need to ask a director what his motivation was. His voice started strong and built to a crescendo as he spoke the key sentences, "General Secretary Gorbachev, if you seek peace, if you seek prosperity for the Soviet Union and Eastern Europe, if you seek liberalization: Come here to this gate! Mr. Gorbachev, open this gate! Mr. Gorbachev,

▲ West Berliners crowding in front of the Berlin Wall on November 11, 1989, to watch East German border guards demolishing a section of the wall in order to open a new crossing point between East and West Berlin near the Potsdamer Platz.

tear down this wall!" Reagan wrote in his autobiography, and other writers also have noted, that he was angry when he delivered the key line. He had been told that a crowd had gathered on the East Berlin side of the wall to hear him speak, and had been roughly dispersed by the police.

The speech received little Western media coverage at the time, and Soviet news agencies dismissed it as war-mongering and "provocative," despite the intermittently conciliatory tone. Gorbachev did not respond.

Two years later, the East German communist government fell, along with those of other Eastern European countries, and the Soviet Union collapsed. Gorbachev did not tear down the wall; the people of East and West Berlin started the job, and bulldozers finished it. Berlin, and the rest of Germany, were reunified. It was only then that

Reagan's phrase came into prominence, as former West German chancellor Helmut Kohl, among others, pointed to Reagan's speech as a historic moment and the beginning of the end of the division of Germany it symbolized.

In retrospect the speech as a whole is a rather ordinary, disorganized recitation of many things Reagan said before or after. It serves as a classic example of the fate of so many presidential speeches—the victim of a mixture of overzealous editing and overcautious policymaking by a staff anxious to prove its value. It lives on because it contains what are arguably the most famous six words of the Reagan presidency, "Mr. Gorbachev, tear down this wall!"

Address on East-West Relations
June 12, 1987, Brandenburg Gate, Berlin

Chancellor Kohl, Governing Mayor Diepgen, ladies and gentlemen: Twenty-four years ago, President John F. Kennedy visited Berlin, speaking to the people of this city and the world at the City Hall. Well, since then two other presidents have come, each in his turn, to Berlin. And today I, myself, make my second visit to your city.

We come to Berlin, we American presidents, because it's our duty to speak, in this place, of freedom. But I must confess, we're drawn here by other things as well: by the feeling of history in this city, more than 500 years older than our own nation; by the beauty of the Grunewald and the Tiergarten; most of all, by your courage and determination. Perhaps the composer Paul Lincke understood something about American presidents. You see, like so many presidents before me, I come here today because wherever I go, whatever I do: Ich hab noch einen Koffer in Berlin. [I still have a suitcase in Berlin.]

Our gathering today is being broadcast throughout Western Europe and North America. I understand that it is being seen and heard as well in the East. To those listening throughout Eastern Europe, a special word: Although I cannot be with you, I address my remarks to you just as surely as to those standing here before me. For I join you, as I join your fellow countrymen in the West, in this firm, this unalterable belief: Es gibt nur ein Berlin. [There is only one Berlin.]

Behind me stands a wall that encircles the free sectors of this city, part of a vast system of barriers that divides the entire continent of Europe. From the Baltic, south, those barriers cut across Germany in a gash of barbed wire, concrete, dog runs, and guard towers. Farther south, there may be no visible, no

▲ President Ronald W. Reagan delivering his address at the Brandenburg Gate, Berlin, on June 12, 1987.

obvious wall. But there remain armed guards and checkpoints all the same—still a restriction on the right to travel, still an instrument to impose upon ordinary men and women the will of a totalitarian state. Yet it is here in Berlin where the wall emerges most clearly; here, cutting across your city, where the news photo and the television screen have imprinted this brutal division of a continent upon the mind of the world. Standing before the Brandenburg Gate, every man is a German, separated from his fellow men. Every man is a Berliner, forced to look upon a scar.

President von Weizsacker has said, "The German question is open as long as the Brandenburg Gate is closed." Today I say: As long as the gate is closed, as long as this scar of a wall is permitted to stand, it is not the German question alone that remains open, but the question of freedom for all mankind. Yet I do not come here to lament. For I find in Berlin a message of hope, even in the shadow of this wall, a message of triumph.

In this season of spring in 1945, the people of Berlin emerged from their air-raid shelters to find devastation. Thousands of miles away, the people of the United States reached out to help. And in 1947 Secretary of State—as you've been told—George Marshall announced the creation of what would become known as the Marshall Plan. Speaking precisely 40 years ago this month, he said: "Our policy is directed not against any country or doctrine, but against hunger, poverty, desperation, and chaos."

In the Reichstag a few moments ago, I saw a display commemorating this 40th anniversary of the Marshall Plan. I was struck by the sign on a burnt-out, gutted structure that was being rebuilt. I understand that Berliners of my own generation can remember seeing signs like it dotted throughout the western sectors of the city. The sign read simply: "The Marshall Plan is helping here to strengthen the free world." A strong, free world in the West, that dream became real. Japan rose from ruin to become an economic giant. Italy, France, Belgium—virtually every nation in Western Europe saw political and economic rebirth; the European Community was founded.

In West Germany and here in Berlin, there took place an economic miracle, the Wirtschaftswunder. Adenauer, Erhard, Reuter, and other leaders understood the practical importance of liberty—that just as truth can flourish only when the journalist is given freedom of speech, so prosperity can come about only when the farmer and businessman enjoy economic freedom. The German leaders reduced tariffs, expanded free trade, lowered taxes. From 1950 to 1960 alone, the standard of living in West Germany and Berlin doubled.

Where four decades ago there was rubble, today in West Berlin there is the greatest industrial output of any city in Germany—busy office blocks, fine homes and apartments, proud avenues, and the spreading lawns of parkland. Where a city's culture seemed to have been destroyed, today there are two great universities, orchestras and an opera, countless theaters, and museums. Where there was want, today there's abundance—food, clothing, automobiles—the wonderful goods of the Ku'damm. From devastation, from utter ruin, you Berliners have, in freedom, rebuilt a city that once again ranks as one of the greatest on earth. The Soviets may have had other plans. But my friends, there were a few things the Soviets didn't count on—Berliner Herz, Berliner Humor, ja, und Berliner Schnauze. [Berliner heart, Berliner humor, yes, and a Berliner Schnauze.]

In the 1950s, Khrushchev predicted: "We will bury you." But in the West today, we see a free world that has achieved a level of prosperity and well-being unprecedented in all human history. In the Communist world, we see failure, technological backwardness, declining standards of health, even want of the most basic kind—too little food. Even today, the Soviet Union still cannot feed itself. After these four decades, then, there stands before the entire world one great and inescapable conclusion: Freedom leads to prosperity. Freedom replaces the ancient hatreds among the nations with comity and peace. Freedom is the victor.

And now the Soviets themselves may, in a limited way, be coming to understand the importance of freedom. We hear much from Moscow about a new policy of reform and openness. Some political prisoners have been released. Certain foreign news broadcasts are no longer being jammed. Some economic enterprises have been permitted to operate with greater freedom from state control.

Are these the beginnings of profound changes in the Soviet state? Or are they token gestures, intended to raise false hopes in the West, or to strengthen the Soviet system without changing it? We welcome

PRESIDENT REAGAN'S BERLIN SPEECH
GENERAL CONSIDERATIONS AND
COMMENTS ON DRAFT -- 5/27 1:30 p.m.

Kornblum Comments on Brandenburg Address (furnished by Rodman)

GENERAL CONSIDERATIONS

-- The President will speak in Berlin at a time of change and uncertainty in Germany and Europe. Gorbachev's new look has intrigued many in Germany. There is hope that he is a Soviet leader with whom one finally can deal. He utilizes the rhetoric of peace and compromise.

-- The desire for stability is so strong in Germany that many are overlooking the continued totalitarianism of the Soviet state. Germans are impatient for movement. They hope Gorbachev can make it possible.

' -- This does not mean a weakening of the ties to the United States or that there is less dedication to democracy.

-- What it does mean is that the Germans want from America a sign that we understand their desire for movement while at the same time maintaining the firm basis of defense necessary for the continued freedom of their country.

The result is a contradictory approach which is often hard to predict. For example:

--A considerable segment of Kohl's Christian Democratic Party opposes the zero-zero option.

-- At the same time, the Secretary General of this party calls on Germans to "take Gorbachev at his word," and to make detente the main goal of German foreign policy.

German officials expect the President's Berlin speech to be a major policy statement on East-West relations. It will come two weeks after Gorbachev's appearance at the East Berlin party summit. To be successful, this speech should do the following:

-- Make a firm statement of American principles, our dedication to freedom in Europe and of the strength of open societies.

-- Give proof of our understanding of the special German needs in Europe and the world.

-- Present a concrete strategy for dealing with the Gorbachev phenomenon.

◀ The first page of a memo outlining the situation in Berlin at the time of the speech as well as addressing the areas that the speech should cover.

I understand the fear of war and the pain of division that afflict this continent— and I pledge to you my country's efforts to help overcome these burdens. To be sure, we in the West must resist Soviet expansion. So we must maintain defenses of unassailable strength. Yet we seek peace; so we must strive to reduce arms on both sides.

Beginning 10 years ago, the Soviets challenged the Western alliance with a grave new threat, hundreds of new and more deadly SS-20 nuclear missiles, capable of striking every capital in Europe. The Western alliance responded by committing itself to a counter-deployment unless the Soviets agreed to negotiate a better solution; namely, the elimination of such weapons on both sides. For many months, the Soviets refused to bargain in earnestness. As the alliance, in turn, prepared to go forward with its counter-deployment, there were difficult days—days of protests like those during my 1982 visit to this city—and the Soviets later walked away from the table.

But through it all, the alliance held firm. And I invite those who protested then— I invite those who protest today—to mark this fact: Because we remained strong, the Soviets came back to the table. And because we remained strong, today we have within reach the possibility, not merely of limiting the growth of arms, but of eliminating, for the first time, an entire class of

change and openness; for we believe that freedom and security go together, that the advance of human liberty can only strengthen the cause of world peace. There is one sign the Soviets can make that would be unmistakable, that would advance dramatically the cause of freedom and peace.

General Secretary Gorbachev, if you seek peace, if you seek prosperity for the Soviet Union and Eastern Europe, if you seek liberalization: Come here to this gate! Mr. Gorbachev, open this gate! Mr. Gorbachev, tear down this wall!

nuclear weapons from the face of the earth.

As I speak, NATO ministers are meeting in Iceland to review the progress of our proposals for eliminating these weapons. At the talks in Geneva, we have also proposed deep cuts in strategic offensive weapons. And the Western allies have likewise made far-reaching proposals to reduce the danger of conventional war and to place a total ban on chemical weapons.

While we pursue these arms reductions, I pledge to you that we will maintain the capacity to deter Soviet aggression at any level at which it might occur. And in cooperation with many of our allies, the United States is pursuing the Strategic Defense Initiative—research to base deterrence not on the threat of offensive retaliation, but on defenses that truly defend; on systems, in short, that will not target populations, but shield them. By these means we seek to increase the safety of Europe and all the world.

But we must remember a crucial fact: East and West do not mistrust each other because we are armed; we are armed because we mistrust each other. And our differences are not about weapons but about liberty. When President Kennedy spoke at the City Hall those 24 years ago, freedom was encircled, Berlin was under siege. And today, despite all the pressures upon this city, Berlin stands secure in its liberty. And freedom itself is transforming the globe.

Page 6

policy of openness and liberalization -- to use the Russian term, "glasnost." Some political prisoners have been released. B.B.C. broadcasts are no longer jammed. Certain small enterprises have been permitted to operate with greater freedom from state control.

Are these the beginnings of profound changes in the Soviet state? Or are they token gestures, intended only to raise false hopes in the West? It is impossible to tell.

But there is one sign the Soviets can make that would be unmistakable.

General Secretary Gorbachev, if you seek peace, come to Berlin. If you seek prosperity for the Soviet Union and Eastern Europe, come to Berlin. If you seek liberalization -- if you seek "glasnost" -- come to Berlin.

Come here, to this wall.

Herr Gorbachev, machen Sie dieses Tor auf.

[Mr. Gorbachev, open this gate.] *tear down this wall*

While we watch and wait, we in the West must force the Soviets to deal with their internal problems, not attempt to flee them by expanding their empire still more. For make no mistake: The Soviet Union today represents the only remaining expansionist -- the only remaining imperialist -- power on Earth. So we must maintain defenses of unassailable strength. And yet it is our nature as free peoples to make manifest our goodwill. So we must strive to reduce arms on both sides.

Only 10 years ago, the Soviets challenged the Western Alliance with a grave new threat: the deployment of hundreds of

▲ A page from a May 20 draft of the speech with the "tear down this wall" line added in in red pen.

In the Philippines, in South and Central America, democracy has been given a rebirth. Throughout the Pacific, free markets are working miracle after miracle of economic growth. In the industrialized nations, a technological revolution is taking place—a revolution marked by rapid, dramatic advances in computers and telecommunications.

In Europe, only one nation and those it controls refuse to join the community of freedom. Yet in this age of redoubled economic growth, of information and innovation, the Soviet Union faces a choice: It must make fundamental changes, or it will become obsolete.

Today thus represents a moment of hope. We in the West stand ready to cooperate with the East to promote true openness, to break down barriers that separate people, to create a safe, freer world. And surely there is no better place than Berlin, the meeting place of East and West, to make a start. Free people of Berlin: Today, as in the past, the United States stands for the strict observance and full implementation of all parts of the Four Power Agreement of 1971. Let us use this occasion, the 750th anniversary of this city, to usher in a new era, to seek a still fuller, richer life for the Berlin of the future. Together, let us maintain and develop the ties between the Federal Republic and the Western sectors of Berlin, which is permitted by the 1971 agreement.

And I invite Mr. Gorbachev: Let us work to bring the Eastern and Western parts of the city closer together, so that all the inhabitants of all Berlin can enjoy the benefits that come with life in one of the great cities of the world.

To open Berlin still further to all Europe, East and West, let us expand the vital air access to this city, finding ways of making commercial air service to Berlin more convenient, more comfortable, and more economical. We look to the day when West Berlin can become one of the chief aviation hubs in all central Europe.

With our French and British partners, the United States is prepared to help bring international meetings to Berlin. It would be only fitting for Berlin to serve as the site of United Nations meetings, or world conferences on human rights and arms control or other issues that call for international cooperation.

There is no better way to establish hope for the future than to enlighten young minds, and we would be honored to sponsor summer youth exchanges, cultural events, and other programs for young Berliners from the East. Our French and British friends, I'm certain, will do the same. And it's my hope that an authority can be found in East Berlin to sponsor visits from young people of the Western sectors.

◄ President Ronald W. Reagan reviewing the honor guard of the Royal Regiment of Scotland on June 12, 1987, after his landing at Berlin Tempelhof Airport prior to delivering his speech.

One final proposal, one close to my heart: Sport represents a source of enjoyment and ennoblement, and you may have noted that the Republic of Korea—South Korea—has offered to permit certain events of the 1988 Olympics to take place in the North. International sports competitions of all kinds could take place in both parts of this city. And what better way to demonstrate to the world the openness of this city than to offer in some future year to hold the Olympic games here in Berlin, East and West? In these four decades, as I have said, you Berliners have built a great city. You've done so in spite of threats—the Soviet attempts to impose the East-mark, the blockade. Today the city thrives in spite of the challenges implicit in the very presence of this wall. What keeps you here? Certainly there's a great deal to be said for your fortitude, for your defiant courage. But I believe there's something deeper, something that involves Berlin's whole look and feel and way of life— not mere sentiment. No one could live long in Berlin without being completely disabused of illusions. Something instead, that has seen the difficulties of life in Berlin but chose to accept them, that continues to build this good and proud city in contrast to a surrounding totalitarian presence that refuses to release human energies or aspirations. Something that speaks with a powerful voice of affirmation, that says yes to this city, yes to the future, yes to freedom. In a word, I would submit that what keeps you in Berlin is love—love both profound and abiding.

Perhaps this gets to the root of the matter, to the most fundamental distinction of all between East and West. The totalitarian world produces backwardness because it does such violence to the spirit, thwarting the human impulse to create, to enjoy, to worship. The totalitarian world finds even symbols of love and of worship an affront. Years ago, before the East Germans began rebuilding their churches, they erected a secular structure: the television tower at Alexander

▲ Former President Ronald W. Reagan and former Soviet Premier Mikhail Gorbachev meeting in 1992, three years after the fall of the Berlin Wall.

Platz. Virtually ever since, the authorities have been working to correct what they view as the tower's one major flaw, treating the glass sphere at the top with paints and chemicals of every kind. Yet even today when the sun strikes that sphere—that sphere that towers over all Berlin—the light makes the sign of the cross. There in Berlin, like the city itself, symbols of love, symbols of worship, cannot be suppressed.

As I looked out a moment ago from the Reichstag, that embodiment of German unity, I noticed words crudely spray-painted upon the wall, perhaps by a young Berliner: "This wall will fall. Beliefs become reality." Yes, across Europe, this wall will fall. For it cannot withstand faith; it cannot withstand truth. The wall cannot withstand freedom.

And I would like, before I close, to say one word. I have read, and I have been questioned since I've been here about certain demonstrations against my coming. And I would like to say just one thing, and to those who demonstrate so. I wonder if they have ever asked themselves that if they should have the kind of government they apparently seek, no one would ever be able to do what they're doing again.

Thank you and God bless you all.

President George Herbert Walker Bush

> " The new breeze blows, a page turns, the story unfolds. And so today a chapter begins, a small and stately story of unity, diversity, and generosity — shared, and written, together. "

On January 20, 1989, George Herbert Walker Bush took the oath of office as America's forty-first president. The speech he held in his hands was a good one, full of uplifting sentiments and drafted for him by Ronald Reagan's favorite speechwriter, Peggy Noonan. There was just one problem—one that would dog him throughout his single term. He was not Ronald Reagan.

Bush did not particularly like to give speeches, despite all the speaking he had done in decades of public life as a congressman, agency head, and Reagan's vice president. His voice, in contrast to Reagan's rounded tones, was high and reedy, with a peculiar staccato cadence in conversation and on the platform. He sounded, as political opponents charged, "wimpy," vocally resembling famed children's TV host Fred Rogers. Both the odd tempo of speech and the voice were fodder for comedians throughout his term.

The president compounded his basic disadvantage by a careless attitude toward preparation. Most presidents through the mid-twentieth century wrote or co-wrote most of their speeches. Even more recent presidents devoted time and effort to rehearsal. Richard Nixon, for all his other faults, not only wrote but also memorized his major speeches, and delivered some notable

▲ George H.W. Bush taking the Oath of Office as the forty-first President of the United States on Inaugural Day, January 20, 1989.

addresses before his downfall. Reagan rehearsed his speeches as he had his movie roles—reading them aloud repeatedly and marking up passages for pauses and emphasis. Bush told aides that he never read his speeches out loud ahead of time. Nor, he said, did he give any thought to how he wanted the words to sound. He just didn't want to take the time.

I Am Not President Reagan

"I am not President Reagan," Bush told his speechwriters. Reagan, the "Great Communicator," organized his administration around carefully staged events and images, including polished and persuasive speeches and memorable phrases. Bush and his advisors attached little importance to speeches. He believed that persuasiveness would flow from his actions and policies, not his words.

Robert Schlesinger notes in his book about presidential speaking, *White House Ghosts*, that although Bush personally admired and respected Reagan and his oratory, he did not care for speeches that favored "style over substance" and showed a disdain for oratory. Schlesinger quotes Bush speechwriter Curt Smith as noting that he would sometimes get speech drafts back with the notation "sounds like Reagan," or "too much like Reagan. Take it out."

Bush prided himself on being a plain-spoken man of action. Once he reached the White House, said Noonan, his speechwriters ranked only slightly higher in the pecking order than his dog, Millie. He wanted speeches that were not too emotional. "If you give me a ten, I'm going to send it back and say, 'Give me an eight,'" he instructed his speechwriters. He also wanted his speechwriters to use as many Yogi Berra quotes as possible. The old Yankee catcher epitomized simple, if sometimes twisted and humorous, wisdom. Bush said he would rather quote Yogi than Thomas Jefferson.

There were two major exceptions to his contemptuous attitude toward the podium. One was in his campaign—highlighted by his speech accepting the Republican nomination. The second was in his inaugural speech. Noonan drafted both. The acceptance speech contained the three phrases most associated with Bush, all written by Noonan. One was the "thousand points of light" theme of volunteerism. A second was the "kinder, gentler nation" for which he wished. Third was "read my lips, no new taxes," an attempt to counter the "wimp factor" by paraphrasing a line from movie tough guy Clint Eastwood.

Convention Speech Hailed as Best of Career

The Republican convention speech was hailed as the best of his career, and he used variations of it during his successful campaign. Noonan had left the Reagan White House in 1986 because of lack of access to the president and clashes with senior staff. She joined the Bush campaign because as a true-believing Conservative, she wanted to see the Reagan Revolution continue.

The campaign, aided by Reagan's popularity and in no small part due to Noonan's speeches and the "read my lips" pledge, ended with a Bush victory. By then, Noonan had decided she did not want to return to the White House under the rhetorically challenged Bush. She stayed home with her new baby and began writing books and newspaper commentary.

She had, however, one more assignment to complete for her hero, Reagan. He asked her to write his farewell speech to the nation. She quickly accepted, and embarked on a series of meetings with the fading president—already showing the first signs of Alzheimer's disease.

She was given an office at the White House, and while she was drafting the Reagan speech, Bush came to visit and asked her to draft his inaugural address. "When I agreed to work with Reagan," she recalls in her book *What I Saw at the Revolution*, "I knew I could not work with Bush. There would be no time; you cannot hear two such different voices and do them [both] justice."

Bush Wouldn't Take No for an Answer

Noonan turned Bush down, with the excuse that she had promised chief of staff Ken Duberstein that she would devote all her energies to the Reagan speech. Bush "would not take no" for an answer, and went right to the Oval Office to ask Reagan directly if he minded if she worked on his inaugural speech. "Why no, George, not at all," replied Reagan, and Noonan was on the hook to produce the speech.

She was still fully involved with the Reagan speech, which was going through many drafts and changes. Nevertheless, she met with Bush and gathered notes on the speech. Finally, she finished Reagan's speech and he delivered it on January 11. The next day, she gathered her notes on her meetings with Bush and met with him and the staff. Compared to the process of writing the Reagan speech, this one was easy.

She writes, "Bush knew what he wanted: Begin with a prayer, maintain a gentle tone, a section on bipartisanship, a plea for unity. . . Quick work, [a first draft] in to Bush on the fifteenth. No dramatic or portentous statements, neither John Kennedy or John Wayne. . . He will be low-key,

MEMO TO   MARY LUKENS
FROM   PEGGY NOONAN
DATE   WED JANangst 1989

Mary, there are four items from the inaugural address to be checked by a researcher(s).

1. The Salutation. The Vice President wants to open his speech with these words noting these dignitaries:
   "Mr. Chief Justice, Mr. President, Vice President Quayle, Senator Mitchell, Speaker Wright, Senator Dole, Congressman Michel, fellow citizens, neighbors, and friends."
   Q: Is there any mistake of protocal in this? I think not from the salutations I've read in the past 20 years. There seems flexibility here. But the Vice President does not want to make a mistake.

2. An Assertion. The Vice President will say,
   "I have just repeated word for word the oath taken by George Washington 200 years ago, and the bible on which I placed my hand is the bible on which he placed his."

3. The researcher Bob Simon some time back passed on to me a quote that had caught his eye from, I believe, St. Augustine. The sentiment communicated was: "In crucial things, unity — in important things, diversity — in all things, generosity."
   I need the exact quote, who said it, where it's from.

4. The Vice President may use the following quote, which he believes is from a liberal or moderate former Justice of the Supreme Court (perhaps Hugo Black, he's not sure.) The quote is: "Great nations like great men must keep their word."

I want the researcher(s) to be assigned to work directly with me; no middle man, no confusion. Please give them my # at home, 759-0440. And, naturally, I do not want them sharing the above with anyone.

Thanks Mary, as always.

▲ A memo from Peggy Noonan requesting that a researcher check four items for the upcoming speech.

TO: Peggy Noonan
FR: Bob Simon

Answers: 1/18/89

1.   I checked the salutation with Judy McClennan, chief of
      protocol at the Inaugural Committee. She said it was OK. I
      also checked with Susan Porter Rose, Mrs. Bush's chief of
      staff, and she said it was OK and that she did not think
      anyone had been overlooked and needed to be added. (Note:
      Rev. Billy Graham is giving the invocation and benediction.
      Both Reagan and Kennedy mentioned clergy present. Just a
      thought.)

2.   As we discussed, the oath of office is prescribed in Article
      II of the Constitution and has been repeated exactly by
      every president since George Washington in 1789. As we
      discussed, George Washington added the phrase "so help me
      God" to the end of the official oath, and every president
      since then has used that phrase except Theodore Roosevelt,
      who said, "and so I swear."

      The King James bible used by Washington in 1789 will brought
      to the platform by Mrs. Bush for the President-Elect's use.
      FYI: George Washington kissed the Bible after taking the
      oath.

3.   Here is the exact quote: "In essential things, unity; in
      doubtful things, liberty; in all things, charity."

      Three quote dictionaries repeated this quotation. One
      attributed it as the personal motto of Richard Baxter (1615-
      1691), an English Puritan who was a chaplain Cromwell's
      army. The quote is also attributed to Philip Melanchthon,
      an associate of Martin Luther who lived a century before
      Baxter. A classics professor at Catholic University told me
      the quotation is used often and that it appeared in an
      encyclical by Pope John XXIII.

      The definitive source on this quote was Dr. Fred VanFutterin
      of LaSalle University, who is a noted St. Augustine scholar.
      He said Augustine is "without question" the originator of
      the quotation and wrote it in a letter in the year 417 or
      418. He said he could find a copy of it if we need it.

4.   The quote is correct. "Great nations, like great men, must
      keep their word."

      The source: Justice Hugo Black in his 1960 dissenting
      opinion in the case FPC vs. Tuscarora Indian Nation (392
      U.S. 99, 142). This quotation has been used by other
      justices since then, including a case involving the CIA,
      which might be where GB picked it up.

◀ A memo from researcher Bob Simon answering Peggy Noonan's queries.

noise, laughter, and bustle.

"It felt like a new breeze," she recalled. "There was a literal movement of air. A new history beginning today."

New Breeze Became Inaugural Theme

That became the inaugural message. "A new breeze is blowing, and a nation refreshed by freedom stands ready to push on," he said in the speech, and several other variations of the "new breeze" line appeared in the speech.

Because of the time pressure, Noonan worked several late nights, getting input from Bush staffers, to complete the final draft. "I am," she writes, "the kind of tired that makes you feel brittle as a stick. And I am not a speechwriter any more."

Just nine days separated Reagan's farewell from the Bush inaugural, and the juxtaposition was striking. Reagan delivered Noonan's speech with exactly the proper wistful tone. He was his charming self, closing with the metaphor of America as the shining city on a hill that he had repeated so many times. The city is "more prosperous, more secure and happier than it was eight years ago . . . and she's still a beacon . . . for

direct, domestic." Bush gave her a line he wanted in the speech: The people did not send us here to bicker.

She found an overall theme for the speech in the contrast between the Reagan and Bush offices. Her office was in the West Wing, with the Oval Office forty feet down the corridor in one direction and the vice president's office twenty feet down the other way.

There was a stillness coming from the direction of Reagan's office, she said in a *New York Times* interview, but in the other direction there was all the pilgrims from all the lost places." Then he looked into the camera and simply closed with, "And so, good-bye, God bless you, and God bless the United States of America."

When it was his turn little more than a week later, the new president expressed many of the same sentiments. He began by thanking President Reagan "for all the wonderful things you have done for America" but then did not mention him again, or specifically praise his accomplishments. That was an omission that rankled many Reagan loyalists, and reportedly infuriated Nancy Reagan.

Bush then delivered a prayer of his own composition, and launched into the speech that one writer called "Jeffersonian in its call for reconciliation." All of the familiar Bush words were there: references to a nation that could be "kinder" and "gentler," the thousand points of light analogy, goodness and courage, self-sacrifice, and so on.

The Reaganites Bristle

"We are not the sum of our possessions," he said. "They are not the measure of our lives." Some recalled similar sentiments in the inaugural addresses of FDR and JFK, while others took the statement as a swipe at the Reagan-era atmosphere of no-holds-barred capitalism. Reagan conservatives also did not like his call for a return to the "old bi-partisanship" in government. He seemed to be saying that the Reagan era was one of divisiveness between parties—which of course it was, though not in comparison to the partisan squabbles of today.

Perhaps the most biting comment on the inaugural speech came from TRB, the Washington column of the *New Republic* magazine—a liberal, if irreverent publication of political commentary. The initials TRB have masked the identity of many commentators who have written the column over

the decades since the 1940s. "That was a very nice inaugural address George Bush gave," wrote the TRB of the time, "as nice as nice could be. It was nice to the Democrats, nice to the Russians, nice to the homeless, nice to kids and old folks, it was just incredibly nice. The new president's new breeze blew in off the West Front of the Capitol in the form of a great howling gale of niceness."

Waiting for Applause That Didn't Come

Another journalist wrote that the speech's words "could have been spoken with equal impact in the seventeenth century about the restorative powers of faith and prayer and good deeds and the balm of living in a community." Another thought Bush's delivery was "labored," and that he paused often for applause, only to be greeted with silence.

Peggy Noonan had given Bush the speech he wanted, and she was given a place of honor on the inaugural platform. She had little to say about the speech in her book other than that Bush gave the speech "in a forceful voice." She quoted the last part, which repeated the unifying theme, "The new breeze blows, a page turns, the story unfolds. And so, today a chapter begins, a small and stately story of unity, diversity, and generosity—shared, and written, together."

"It was a quiet speech," she writes, "and we left quietly, a big silent throng of us wafting from the Capitol and taking the broad avenues." In an article about Bush's speaking style, professor of speech communication Craig Smith called the speech "appropriate and often moving." It was "a simple speech that sets out goals in clear, plain English." Smith praised the theme of the "new breeze" as an excellent unifying metaphor, but unlike "thousand points of light," "kinder, gentler nation," and especially the "read my lips" line, it has not been remembered by history.

Smith also notes that it was one of the best speeches—along with his speech accepting the nomination—that Bush ever gave. He never matched it during his term as president, and certainly not during his campaign for re-election against Bill Clinton. That is partly because he did not try to match it—he valued substance over style, and after eight years of Reagan, the country was accustomed to style. When Bill Clinton came along, the country opted once again for style.

George H.W. Bush was a kind, gentle, decent man who tried to live up to the sentiments expressed in his first speech as president. His main problem, and the thing that more than anything else denied him re-election, was that he was not Ronald Reagan.

Inaugural Address
January 20, 1989, United States Capitol, Washington, DC

Mr. Chief Justice, Mr. President, Vice President Quayle, Senator Mitchell, Speaker Wright, Senator Dole, Congressman Michel, and fellow citizens, neighbors, and friends:

There is a man here who has earned a lasting place in our hearts and in our history. President Reagan, on behalf of our nation, I thank you for the wonderful things that you have done for America.

I've just repeated word for word the oath taken by George Washington 200 years ago, and the Bible on which I placed my hand is the Bible on which he placed his. It is right that the memory of Washington be with us today not only because this is our bicentennial inauguration but because Washington remains the Father of our Country. And he would, I think, be gladdened by this day; for today is the concrete expression of a stunning fact: our continuity, these 200 years, since our government began.

We meet on democracy's front porch. A good place to talk as neighbors and as friends. For this is a day when our nation is made whole, when our differences, for a moment, are suspended. And my first act as President is a prayer. I ask you to bow your heads.

Heavenly Father, we bow our heads and thank You for Your love. Accept our thanks for the peace that

▲ The inauguration ceremony of George H. W. Bush.

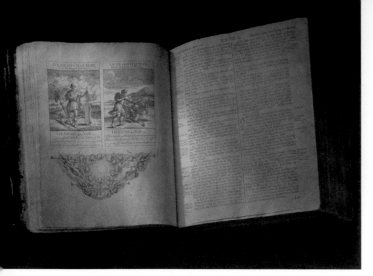

▲ The Inaugural Bible, opened to Genesis chapters forty-nine and fifty, as it was when used for swearing in of the first US President, George Washington, and again for George H. W. Bush.

yields this day and the shared faith that makes its continuance likely. Make us strong to do Your work, willing to heed and hear Your will, and write on our hearts these words: "Use power to help people." For we are given power not to advance our own purposes, nor to make a great show in the world, nor a name. There is but one just use of power, and it is to serve people. Help us remember, Lord. Amen.

I come before you and assume the Presidency at a moment rich with promise. We live in a peaceful, prosperous time, but we can make it better. For a new breeze is blowing, and a world refreshed by freedom seems reborn. For in man's heart, if not in fact, the day of the dictator is over. The totalitarian era is passing, its old ideas blown away like leaves from an ancient, lifeless tree. A new breeze is blowing, and a nation refreshed by freedom stands ready to push on. There is new ground to be broken and new action to be taken. There are times when the future seems thick as a fog; you sit and wait, hoping the mists will lift and reveal the right path. But this is a time when the future seems a door you can walk right through into a room called tomorrow.

Great nations of the world are moving toward democracy through the door to freedom. Men and women of the world move toward free markets through the door to prosperity. The people of the world agitate for free expression and free thought through the door to the moral and intellectual satisfactions that only liberty allows.

We know what works: Freedom works. We know what's right: Freedom is right. We know how to secure a more just and prosperous life for man on Earth: through free markets, free speech, free elections, and the exercise of free will unhampered by the state.

For the first time in this century, for the first time in perhaps all history, man does not have to invent a system by which to live. We don't have to talk late into the night about which form of government is better. We don't have to wrest justice from the kings. We only have to summon it from within ourselves. We must act on what we know. I take as my guide the hope of a saint: In crucial things, unity; in important things, diversity; in all things, generosity.

America today is a proud, free nation, decent and civil, a place we cannot help but love. We know in our hearts, not loudly and proudly but as a simple fact, that this country has meaning beyond what we see, and that our strength is a force for good. But have we changed as a nation even in our time? Are we enthralled with material things, less appreciative of the nobility of work and sacrifice?

My friends, we are not the sum of our possessions. They are not the measure of our lives. In our hearts we know what matters. We cannot hope only to leave our children a bigger car, a bigger bank account. We must hope to give them a sense of what it means to be a loyal friend; a loving parent; a citizen who leaves his home, his neighborhood, and town better than he found it. And what do we want the men and women who work with us to say when we're no longer there? That we were more driven to succeed than anyone

▶ The first page of the press copy of the speech issued by the Office of the Press Secretary.

around us? Or that we stopped to ask if a sick child had gotten better and stayed a moment there to trade a word of friendship?

No President, no government can teach us to remember what is best in what we are. But if the man you have chosen to lead this government can help make a difference; if he can celebrate the quieter, deeper successes that are made not of gold and silk but of better hearts and finer souls; if he can do these things, then he must.

America is never wholly herself unless she is engaged in high moral principle. We as a people have such a purpose today. It is to make kinder the face of the Nation and gentler the face of the world. My friends, we have work to do. There are the homeless, lost and roaming. There are the children who have nothing, no love and no normalcy. There are those who cannot free themselves of enslavement to whatever addiction—drugs, welfare, the demoralization that rules the slums. There is crime to be conquered, the rough crime of the streets. There are young women to be helped who are about to become mothers of children they can't care for and might not love. They need our care, our guidance, and our education, though we bless them for choosing life.

The old solution, the old way, was to think that public money alone could end these problems. But

we have learned that that is not so. And in any case, our funds are low. We have a deficit to bring down. We have more will than wallet, but will is what we need. We will make the hard choices, looking at what we have and perhaps allocating it differently, making our decisions based on honest need and prudent safety. And then we will do the wisest thing of all. We will turn to the only resource we have that in times of need always grows: the

INAUGURAL ADDRESS
OF THE PRESIDENT

The Capitol

12:05 P.M. EST

THE PRESIDENT: Mr. Chief Justice, Mr. President, Vice President Quayle, Senator Mitchell, Speaker Wright, Senator Dole, Congressman Michel, and fellow citizens, neighbors and friends.

There is a man here who has earned a lasting place in our hearts, and in our history. President Reagan, on behalf of our nation I thank you for the wonderful things that you have done for America. (Applause.)

I've just repeated word-for-word the oath taken by George Washington 200 years ago; and the Bible on which I placed my hand is the Bible on which he placed his.

It is right that the memory of Washington be with us today, not only because this is our Bicentennial Inauguration, but because Washington remains the father of our country. And he would, I think, be gladdened by this day. For today is the concrete expression of a stunning fact: Our continuity these 200 years since our government began.

We meet on democracy's front porch. A good place to talk as neighbors, and as friends. For this is a day when our nation is made whole, when our differences, for a moment, are suspended.

And my first act as President is a prayer. I ask you to bow your heads.

'Heavenly Father, we bow our heads and thank you for your love. Accept our thanks for the peace that yields this day and the shared faith that makes its continuance likely. Make us strong to do your work, willing to heed and hear your will, and write on our hearts these words: "Use power to help people." For we are given power not to advance our own purposes, nor to make a great show in the world, nor a name. There is but one just use of power, and it is to serve people. Help us remember, Lord. Amen.'

I come before you and assume the presidency at a moment rich with promise. We live in a peaceful, prosperous time, but we can make it better.

For a new breeze is blowing, and a world refreshed by freedom seems reborn; for in man's heart, if not in fact, the day of the dictator is over. (Applause.) The totalitarian era is passing, its old ideas blown away like leaves from an ancient lifeless tree.

A new breeze is blowing, and a nation refreshed by freedom stands ready to push on. There is new ground to be broken, and new action to be taken.

There are times when the future seems thick as a fog; you sit and wait, hoping the mists will lift and reveal the right path.

But this is a time when the future seems a door you can walk right through -- into a room called Tomorrow.

MORE

goodness and the courage of the American people.

And I am speaking of a new engagement in the lives of others, a new activism, hands-on and involved, that gets the job done. We must bring in the generations, harnessing the unused talent of the elderly and the unfocused energy of the young. For not only leadership is passed from generation to generation but so is stewardship. And the generation born after the Second World War has come of age.

I have spoken of a Thousand Points of Light, of all the community organizations that are spread like stars throughout the Nation, doing good. We will work hand in hand, encouraging, sometimes leading, sometimes being led, rewarding. We will work on this in the White House, in the Cabinet agencies. I will go to the people and the programs that are the brighter points of light, and I'll ask every member of my government to become involved. The old ideas are new again because they're not old, they are timeless: duty, sacrifice, commitment, and a patriotism that finds its expression in taking part and pitching in.

We need a new engagement, too, between the Executive and the Congress. The challenges before us will be thrashed out with the House and the Senate. And we must bring the Federal budget into balance.

And we must ensure that America stands before the world united, strong, at peace, and fiscally sound. But of course things may be difficult. We need to compromise; we've had dissension. We need harmony; we've had a chorus of discordant voices.

For Congress, too, has changed in our time. There has grown a certain divisiveness. We have seen the hard looks and heard the statements in which not each other's ideas are challenged but each other's motives. And our great parties have too often been far apart and untrusting of each other. It's been this way since Vietnam. That war cleaves us still. But, friends, that war began in earnest a quarter of a century ago, and surely the statute of limitation has been reached. This is a fact: The final lesson of Vietnam is that no great nation can long afford to be sundered by a memory. A new breeze is blowing, and the old bipartisanship must be made new again.

To my friends, and, yes, I do mean friends—in the loyal opposition and, yes, I mean loyal—I put out my hand. I am putting out my hand to you, Mr. Speaker. I am putting out my hand to you, Mr. Majority Leader. For this is the thing: This is the age of the offered hand. And we can't turn back clocks, and I don't want to. But when our fathers were young, Mr. Speaker, our differences ended at the water's edge. And we don't wish to turn back time, but when our mothers were young, Mr. Majority Leader, the Congress and the Executive were capable of working together to produce a budget on which this nation could live. Let us negotiate soon and hard. But in the end, let us produce. The American people await action. They didn't send us here to bicker. They ask us to rise above the merely partisan. "In crucial things, unity"— and this, my friends, is crucial.

To the world, too, we offer new engagement and a renewed vow: We will stay strong to protect the peace. The offered hand is a reluctant fist; once made— strong, and can be used with great effect. There are today Americans who are held against their will in foreign lands and Americans who are unaccounted for. Assistance can be shown here and will be long remembered. Good will begets good will. Good faith can be a spiral that endlessly moves on.

Great nations like great men must keep their word. When America says something, America means it, whether a treaty or an agreement or a vow made on marble steps. We will always try to speak clearly, for candor is a compliment; but subtlety, too, is good and has its place. While keeping our alliances and friendships around the world strong, ever strong, we will continue the new closeness with the Soviet Union, consistent both with our security and with progress. One might say that our new relationship in part reflects the triumph of hope and strength over experience. But hope is good, and so is strength and vigilance.

Here today are tens of thousands of our citizens who feel the understandable satisfaction of those who have taken part in democracy and seen their hopes fulfilled. But my thoughts have been turning the past few days to those who would be watching at home, to an older fellow who will throw a salute by himself when the flag goes by and the woman who will tell her sons the words of the battle hymns. I don't mean this to be sentimental. I mean that on days like this we remember that we are all part of a continuum, inescapably connected by the ties that bind.

Our children are watching in schools throughout our great land. And to them I say, Thank you for watching democracy's big day. For democracy belongs to us all, and freedom is like a beautiful kite that can go higher and higher with the breeze. And to all I say, No matter what your circumstances or where you are, you are part of this day, you are part of the life of our great nation.

A President is neither prince nor pope, and I don't seek a window on men's souls. In fact, I yearn for a greater tolerance, and easygoingness about each other's attitudes and way of life.

There are few clear areas in which we as a society must rise up united and express our intolerance. The most obvious now is drugs. And when that first cocaine was smuggled in on a ship, it may as well have been a deadly bacteria, so much has it hurt the body, the soul of our country. And there is much to be done and to be said, but take my word for it: This scourge will stop!

And so, there is much to do. And tomorrow the work begins. And I do not mistrust the future. I do not fear what is ahead. For our problems are large, but our heart is larger. Our challenges are great, but our will is greater. And if our flaws are endless, God's love is truly boundless.

Some see leadership as high drama and the sound of trumpets calling, and sometimes it is that. But I see history as a book with many pages, and each day we fill a page with acts of hopefulness and meaning. The new breeze blows, a page turns, the story unfolds. And so, today a chapter begins, a small and stately story of unity, diversity, and generosity—shared, and written, together.

Thank you. God bless you. And God bless the United States of America.

Index

Bibliography

A Century of Lawmaking for a New Nation: US Congressional Documents and Debates, 1774–1875. Library of Congress.

Adams, John Quincy. *The Diaries of John Quincy Adams: A Digital Collection.* Boston, Mass.: Massachusetts Historical Society, 2011.

Bernstein, Irving. *Guns or Butter: the Presidency of Lyndon Johnson.* Oxford University Ptress, 1996.

Boller, Paul F., Jr. *Presidential Anecdotes.* New York: Penguin Books, 1981.

Bradlee, Benjamin C. *Conversations with Kennedy.* New York: W.W. Norton & Co., 1975.

Brinkley, Douglas C. *The Boys of Pointe du Hoc.* New York: HarperCollins, 2005.

Bush, George H.W. *Speaking of Freedom.* New York: Scribner, 2009.

Bush, George W. *Decision Points.* New York: Crown, 2010.

Califano, Joseph A. *The Triumph and Tragedy of Lyndon Johnson: the White House years.* New York: Simon & Schuster, 1991.

Clarke, Thurston. *Ask Not: The Inauguration of John F. Kennedy and the Speech that Changed America.* New York: Penguin Books, 2005.

Dallek, Robert. *Harry S. Truman.* New York: Times Books, 2008.

Eisenhower, Dwight D., Drafts and background papers on Farewell Address, Dwight D. Eisenhower Presidential Library and Museum, Abilene KS.

Ferrell, Robert H. *Woodrow Wilson and World War I 1917–1921.* New York: Harper & Row, 1985.

Ford, Worthington Chauncey. *John Quincy Adams and the Monroe Doctrine. The American Historical Review, Vol. 8, No. 1 (Oct. 1902)* pp 28–52.

Frum, David. *The Right Man: the Surprise Presidency of George W. Bush.* New York: Random House, 2003.

Gilbert, Felix. *To the Farewell Address: Ideas of Early American Foreign Policy.* Princeton: Princeton University Press, 1961.

Heyse, Amy L. *Theodore Roosevelt Address (The Man with the Muck Rake), Voices of Democracy 5 (2010)* pp 1–17.

Holzer, Harold, Shenk, Joshua, Lincoln, Abraham. *In Lincoln's Hand: His Original Manuscripts with Commentary by Distinguished Americans.* New York: BantamDell, 2009.

Jefferson, Thomas. Papers. Drafts and Analysis of First Inaugural Address. Princeton University.

Kaufman, Burton Ira, ed. *Washington's Farewell Address: The View from the 20th Century.* Chicago: Quadrangle Books, 1969.

Kennedy, John F. *Drafts of Rice University Speech.* John F. Kennedy Presidential Library and Museum, Boston, MA.

Lincoln, Abraham. Drafts of First and Second Inaugural Addresses, Abraham Lincoln Presidential Library and Museum, Springfield IL; Library of Congress.

McCullough, David G. *Truman.* New York: Simon & Schuster, 1992.

Morris, Edmund. *Theodore Rex.* New York: Random House, 2001.

Morris, Edmund. *Dutch: A Memoir of Ronald Reagan.* New York: Random House, 1999.

Noonan, Peggy. *What I Saw at the Revolution: A Political Life in the Reagan Era.* New York, Random House, 1990.

Noonan, Peggy. *When Character Was King: A Story of Ronald Reagan.* New York: Viking Press, 2001.

Nixon, Richard M. *RN: The Memoirs of Richard Nixon.* New York: Simon & Schuster, 1978.

Paltsits, Victor Hugo, ed. *Washington's Farewell Address in Facsimile, with Transliterations of all the Drafts of Washington, Madison, & Hamilton; Together with Their Correspondence and Other Supporting Documents.* New York: The New York Public Library, 1935.

Perkins, Dexter. *A History of the Monroe Doctrine.* Boston: Little, Brown & Company, 1941.

Perret, Geoffrey. *Eisenhower.* New York: Random House, 1999.

Reagan, Ronald. *The Reagan Diaries.* New York: HarperCollins, 2007.

Reagan, Ronald. *An American Life.* New York: Simon & Schuster, 1990.

Reeves, Richard. *President Reagan: The Triuumph of Imagination.* New York: Simon & Schuster, 2005.

Reeves, Richard. *President Nixon: Alone in the White House.* New York: Simon & Schuster, 2001.

Robinson, Peter. *How Ronald Reagan Changed My Life.* New York: Regan Books, 2003.

Roosevelt, Franklin D., drafts and background documents, Franklin D. Roosevelt Presidential Library and Museum, Hyde Park NY.

Rosenman, Samuel I. *Working with Roosevelt.* New York: Harper & Brothers, 1952.

Schlesinger, Robert. *White House Ghosts: Presidents and Their Speechwriters.* New York: Simon and Schuster, 2008.

Sorensen, Ted. *Counselor: A Life at the Edge of History.* New York: HarperCollins, 2008.

Sorensen, Theodore. *The Kennedy Legacy.* New York: MacMillan, 1969.

Sorensen, Theodore (Compiler). *Let the Word Go Forth: The Speeches, Statements and Writings of John F. Kennedy 1945-1963.* New York: Delacorte Press, 1988.

Spalding, Matthew, and Patrick J. Garrity. *A Sacred Union of Citizens: George Washington's Farewell Address and the American Character.* Lanham, Md.: Rowman & Littlefield, 1996.

Tofel, Richard J. *Sounding the Trumpet: The Making of John F. Kennedy's Inaugural Address.* Chicago: Ivan R. Dee, 2005.

Truman, Harry S. Drafts and background papers on Truman Doctrine speech. Harry S. Truman Presidential Library and Museum, Independence MO.

Tulis, Jeffrey K. *The Rhetorical Presidency.* Princeton, NJ: Princeton University Press, 1987.

Waldman, Michael. *My Fellow Americans: The Most Important Speeches of America's Presidents, from George Washington to George W. Bush.* New York: SourceBooks-Media Fusion, 2003.

Wilson, Woodrow. Shorthand and Drafts of 14 Points Speech. American Treasures of the Library of Congress. U.S. Library of Congress.

Woodward, Bob. *Plan of Attack.* New York: Simon & Schuster, 2004.

Photo Credits

Getty Images:
1: George Skadding/Time Life Pictures,
2: George Silk/Time Life Pictures, 7: Time
Life Pictures/Mansell, 9: Diana Walker/
Time & Life Pictures, 10: Stock Montage,
20: Time Life Pictures/Mansell, 22: Stock
Montage, 25: Stock Montage, 26: Francis
Miller/Time Life Pictures, 27: MPI, 30: Stock
Montage, 32: Universal History Archive,
40: Stock Montage, 41: Hulton Archive, 43:
MPI, 45: Stock Montage, 51: MPI, 58: Stock
Montage, 70: Stock Montage, 71: MPI, 75:
Mathew B. Brady/Time & Life Pictures,
78: William Dinwiddie, 80: Underwood
& Underwood/Transcendental Graphics,
90: Stock Montage, 92: Hulton Archive, 95:
Eileen Darby/Time Life Pictures, 96: MPI,
102: Keystone, 104: NY Daily News Archive,
109: Keystone, 112: Keystone-France/
Gamma-Keystone, 114: Bob Landry/Time
Life Pictures, 118: Hank Walker/Time Life
Pictures, 121: Keystone-France/Gamma-
Keystone, 125: Topical Press Agency, 126:
Fotosearch, 127: Archive Holdings Inc.,
128: Underwood Archives, 131: Time Life
Pictures/National Park Service, 134: Al Fenn/
Time Life Pictures, 135: Hulton Archive, 139:
MPI, 144: Yale Joel/Time Life Pictures, 145:
Hulton Archive, 146: PhotoQuest, 152: Ed
Clark/Time Life Pictures, 155: Ed Clark/
Time Life Pictures, 156: George Silk/Time
Life Pictures, 163: FPG, 174: Bob Gomel/
Time Life Pictures, 176: Keystone, 177: Gene
Forte/Consolidated News Pictures, 189:
William Lovelace/Express, 190: Keystone-
France/Gamma-Keystone, 200: Walter
Bennett/Time & Life Pictures, 202: Keystone/
Consolidated News Pictures, 204: AFP, 205:
Fotosearch, 206: David Hume Kennerly,
207: Evelyn Floret//Time Life Pictures, 210:
AFP, 217: David Hume Kennerly, 218: Diana
Walker/Time & Life Pictures, 225: MPI,
226: Pool MAITRE/PIEL/Gamma-Rapho,
227: Keystone-France/Gamma-Keystone,
232/233: Gerard Malie/AFP, 234: MIKE
SARGENT/AFP, 238: MIKE SARGENT/AFP,
239: Time Life Pictures/DMI, 240: National
Archive/Newsmakers, 246: Martha Stanitz/
Time Life Pictures, 248: Dirck Halstead/Time
Life Pictures.

Library of Congress:
11: Series 1, Reel 5, James Madison Papers,
Manuscript Division, Library of Congress,
Washington, DC
12: Series 1, Reel 53, Thomas Jefferson
Papers, Manuscript Division, Library of
Congress, Washington, DC
28 T. Bensley, London, Broadside Collection
271, Box 23a, Courtesy of the Rare Book and
Special Collections Division, The Library of
Congress

31: Series 1, Reel 6, James Madison to
Thomas Jefferson, May 20, 1798, James
Madison Papers, Manuscript Division,
Library of Congress, Washington, DC
34: Series 1. Reel 23, Thomas Jefferson
Papers, Manuscript Division, Library of
Congress, Washington, DC
35: Series 1, Reel 23, Thomas Jefferson
Papers, Manuscript Division, Library of
Congress, Washington, DC
37: Series 1. Reel 23, Thomas Jefferson
Papers, Manuscript Division, Library of
Congress, Washington, DC
38: Series 1, Reel 23, Thomas Jefferson
Papers, Manuscript Division, Library of
Congress, Washington, DC
48: Series 1, Reel 54, Thomas Jefferson
Papers, Manuscript Division, Library of
Congress, Washington, DC
52, 53, 55: Series 1, Reel 8, James Monroe
Papers, Manuscript Division, Library of
Congress, Washington, DC
59: Series 1, Reel 17 Abraham Lincoln
Papers, Manuscript Division, Library of
Congress, Washington, DC
61: Benjamin Brown French Album (USZ62-
48090), Prints and Photographs Division,
Library of Congress, Washington, DC
62: Series 1, Reel 17. Abraham Lincoln
Papers, Manuscript Division, Library of
Congress, Washington, DC
63, 64, 66, 69: Series 1, Reel 18. Abraham
Lincoln Papers, Manuscript Division, Library
of Congress, Washington, DC
72: Photograph by Alexander Gardner
(LC-USA7-16837), Prints and Photographs
Division, Library of Congress, Washington,
DC
77: Series 3, Reel 97, Abraham Lincoln
Papers, Manuscript Division, Library of
Congress, Washington, DC
79: George Grantham Bain Collection
(LC-B2- 1129-9), Prints and Photographs
Division, Library of Congress, Washington,
DC
81, 83: Series 5A, Reel 419, Theodore
Roosevelt Papers, Manuscript Division,
Library of Congress, Washington, DC
85, 88: Series 5A, Reel 419, Theodore
Roosevelt Papers, Manuscript Division,
Library of Congress, Washington, DC
87: Series 5A, Reel 419, Theodore Roosevelt
Papers, Manuscript Division, Library of
Congress, Washington, DC
91: Series 5A, Reel 419, Theodore Roosevelt
Papers, Manuscript Division, Library of
Congress, Washington, DC
94: Series 7B, Reel 479, Woodrow Wilson
Papers, Manuscript Division, Library of
Congress, Washington, DC
P99: Series 7B, Reel 479, Woodrow Wilson
Papers, Manuscript Division, Library of

Congress, Washington, DC
100: Series 2, Reel 90, Woodrow Wilson
Papers, Manuscript Division, Library of
Congress, Washington, DC

Franklin D. Roosevelt Presidential Library:
103, 106, 107, 110: Speech, Franklin D.
Roosevelt, First Inaugural Address, March
1933, Master Speech File, Franklin D.
Roosevelt Library, Hyde Park, New York
115: Significant Documents Collection,
Franklin D. Roosevelt Significant Documents,
Box 1, Folder - Fdr-28: Rosenman's Draft Of
Peroration To Annual Message To Congress
(four Freedoms Speech), January 6, 1941
117: Speech, Franklin D. Roosevelt, Annual
Message to Congress, January 1941, Master
Speech File, Franklin D. Roosevelt Library,
Hyde Park, New York
122: Significant Documents Collection,
Franklin D. Roosevelt Significant Documents,
Box 1, Folder - Fdr-67: Fourth Draft, Fdr's
Speech To The Teamster's Union (fala
Speech), September 23, 1944
123: Significant Documents Collection,
Franklin D. Roosevelt Significant Documents,
Box 1, Folder - Fdr-29: Sixth Draft Of Annual
Message To Congress (four Freedoms
Speech)(pg. 18 Only), January 6, 1941
133: Significant Documents
Collection, Franklin D. Roosevelt Significant
Documents, Box 1, Folder - Fdr-36: Draft
No. 1 Of Message To Congress Requesting
Declaration Of War (day Of Infamy Speech),
December 7, 1941

Harry S. Truman Presidential Library:
136: Memo for the file re: drafting of
President's message to Congress, March
12, 1947; Truman Doctrine-Speech Drafts;
Subject File; Joseph M. Jones Papers
138: C. H. Humelsine to George Elsey, March
10, 1947; March 12, "Truman Doctrine"
Speech; 1947; Speech File; Harry S. Truman
Administration; George M. Elsey Papers
140: Draft suggestions for President's
Message to Congress on Greek Situation,
March 3, 1947; Truman Doctrine-Speech
Drafts; Subject File; Joseph M. Jones Papers
142: Draft of speech, March 10, 1947;
January-March, 1947; 1945-1953 Presidential
Speeches-Longhand Notes; Speech File;
President's Secretary's Files; Harry S.
Truman Papers

**Dwight D. Eisenhower Presidential
Library:**
147: Arthur Larson and Malcolm Moos
Records, Box 16, Farewell Address (1)
148: Ralph E. Williams Papers, Box 1,
Chronological (1)
150: Arthur Larson and Malcolm Moos

Records, Box 16, Farewell Address (2)
153: DDE's Papers as President, Speech Series, Box 38, Final TV Talk (3)

John F. Kennedy Presidential Library:
158 (both), 164: Theodore C. Sorensen Papers, JFK Speech Files 1961-1963, Box 62, File Inaugural Address 1/20/61 Memoranda, Speech materials & correspondence
All below downloaded from http://www.jfklibrary.org
161, 165: Inaugural address, 20 January 1961, Speech Files, President's Office Files, Digital Identifier: JFKPOF-034-002
168, 171, 172, 175: Address at Rice University, Houston, Texas, 12 September 1962, Speech Files, President's Office Files, Digital Identifier: JFKPOF-040-001

Lyndon B. Johnson Presidential Library:
181, 183, 184, 185: Courtesy of the Lyndon Baines Johnson Library, Austin, Texas
179: LBJ Library photo by unknown (serial number 28-13-4)
187: LBJ Library photo by Frank Wolfe (serial number 34958-1), 188: LBJ Library photo by Yoichi Okamoto (serial number W425-34)

Richard Nixon Presidential Library:
All below are from the "White House Special Files- Staff Member and Office Files" Collection, "President's Personal Files" File Category
192, 199: Box Name, Memoranda From the President, 1969-1974: RN Memos re 1968 to Memos- December 1969, Box No. 1, Memos- October 1969
193, 195, 197: Box name, President's Speech File, 1969-1974: October 7, 1969, Cahill to Holton to November 3, 1969, Vietnam Speech [2 of 5], Box No. 52, Vietnam Speech November 3, 1969, [1 of 5]
203: Box Name, President's Speech File, 1969-1974, [3 to 5] to December 15, 1969, Vietnam Statement, Box No. 3, November 3, 1969 Vietnam Speech [5 of 5] [RN Notes]

Ronald Reagan Presidential Library:
All below are from: Collection Name: White Staff Member and Office Files, Office Name: Speechwriting, White House Office of, File Category: Speechwriting, White House Office of: Research Office, 1981-1989, Series: Series I: Speeches, 1981-1989.
209: Box Name: [No Date] President's Trip to Normandy (8-11) to 6/14/1984 Taping: ACTV (American Coalition for Traditional Values) Voter Registration, Box Number: 162, Name of Folder: President's Trip to Normandy (8)
215: Box Name: [No Date] President's Trip to Normandy (8-11) to 6/14/1984 Taping: ACTV (American Coalition for Traditional Values) Voter Registration, Box Number: 162, Name of Folder: President's Trip To Normandy (10)

216: Box Name: 6/4/1984 Address: Irish Parliament- Dublin (7) to [No Date] President's Trip to Normandy (1-7), Box Number: 161, Name of Folder: President's Trip to Normandy (1)
220, 221: Box Name: 1/26/1986 State of the Union Address, 1986 (10)- 1/30/1986 Address: Conservative Political Action Conference Dinner (4), Box Number: 249, Name of Folder: Death of Space Shuttle Challenger Crew, 1/28/1986 [3 of 3]
231: Box Name: 6/5/1987 Satellite Worldnet Address (6)- 6/13/1987 World Address: Trade (2), Box Number: 325, Name of Folder: Brandenburg Gate/Berlin, 6/12/1987, Peter/Teresa [1 of 3]

Two below are from: Collection Name: White Staff Member and Office Files, Office Name: No Office Listed, File Category: Presidential Handwriting File, Series: Series III: Presidential Speeches.
212: Box Name: 6/1/1984-8/27-1984, Box Number: 16, Name of Folder: Folder 291- 6/6/1984 cont. -6/12/1984)
224: Box Name: 11/25/85- 2/25/1986, Box Number: 22, Name of Folder: Folder 420 (1/25/1986-1/28/1986)

214: Office Name: White House Office of Records Management (WHORM) Subject File, Primary Subject Category: SP- Speeches, Secondary Subject Category (Box Name): SP 889 [215045]- SP 891 [215060], Box Number: 222, File Case Number (Folder Name): (SP 891) 215027 [3 of 3]

Three below from: Collection Name: White Staff Member and Office Files, Office Name: Speechwriting, White House Office of, File Category: Robinson, Peter M.: Files, 1983- 1988.
228: Series: Series I: Speech Drafts, 1983- 1988, Box Name: Clean Water Bill Veto, February 19, 1987 to Pope John Paul II, September 10, 1987, Box Number: 9, Name of Folder: Subject File: Notes on Berlin from Pre-Advance
229: Series: Series IV: Chronological Files, 1984, 1987, Box Name: Series III: Reference Files, Vice Presidential Speeches to Series V: Personal Files, Time, Box Number: 19, Name of Folder: Chron Files: 9/29/1986-5/5/1987 (Binder- Marked Peter #1, Cont.) [3 of 4]
237: Series: Series I: Speech Drafts, 1983- 1988, Box Name: Clean Water Bill Veto, February 19, 1987 to Pope John Paul II, September 10, 1987, Box Number: 9, Name of Folder: Remarks, Brandenburg Gate West Berlin, Germany- June 12, 1987 [2 of 3]

236: Collection Name: White Staff Member and Office Files, Office Name: Speechwriting, White House Office of, File Category: Speechwriting, White House Office of: Speech Drafts, 1981-1989, Series: Series I: Speech Drafts, 1981-1989, Box Name: Berlin/Brandenburg Address 6/12/1987 (13) to Address to the Nation: Summit/Economy 6/15/1987 (4), Box Number: 335A, Name of Folder: Berlin/Brandenburg Address 6/12/1987 (13)

George H. W. Bush Presidential Library:
242/243: OA/ID 13655; White House Office of Speechwriting; Speech File Backup Files; Chron File, 1989-1993.
245: Photograph No. P00001-09; "Bush Presidential Inauguration," Jan. 20, 1989.
247: OA/ID 13474; White House Office of Speechwriting; Speech File Draft Files; Chron File, 1989-1993.

NASA:
166, 223

National Archives:
129: Messages of the President (SEN 77A-H1); 77th Congress, Records of the US Senate, Record Group 46, National Archives Building, Washington, DC.

The New York Public Library:
13: Reproduced from *Washington's Farewell Address*, ed. by Victor Hugo Paltsits, New York: The New York Public Library and Arno Press, 1971, p. 161, courtesy of the Manuscripts and Archives Division, New York Public Library, Astor, Lenox and Tilden Foundation
16: The George Washington Collection, The New York State Library, reproduced from Paltsits, Victor Hugo, ed. *Washington's Farewell Address*, New York: The New York Public Library and Arno Press, 1935,
17: Reproduced from *Washington's Farewell Address*, ed. by Victor Hugo Paltsits, New York: The New York Public Library and Arno Press, 1971, p. 105, courtesy of the Manuscripts and Archives Division, New York Public Library, Astor, Lenox and Tilden Foundation
18: Reproduced from *Washington's Farewell Address*, ed. by Victor Hugo Paltsits, New York: New York Public Library and Arno Press, 1971, p. 109, courtesy of the Manuscripts and Archives Division, New York Public Library, Astor, Lenox and Tilden Foundation
21: Reproduced from *Washington's Farewell Address*, ed. by Victor Hugo Paltsits, New York: The New York Public Library and Arno Press, 1971, p. 117, courtesy of the Manuscripts and Archives Division, New York Public Library, Astor, Lenox and Tilden Foundation